Stay, Watch, Pray

Stay, Watch, Pray

The Bible's Guidance in Prayer
and the Prayers of the Bible
—An Introduction

Frank Bahr

RESOURCE *Publications* · Eugene, Oregon

STAY, WATCH, PRAY
The Bible's Guidance in Prayer and the Prayers of the Bible—An Introduction

Copyright © 2022 Frank Bahr. All rights reserved. Except for brief quotations in critical publications or reviews, no part of this book may be reproduced in any manner without prior written permission from the publisher. Write: Permissions, Wipf and Stock Publishers, 199 W. 8th Ave., Suite 3, Eugene, OR 97401.

Resource Publications
An Imprint of Wipf and Stock Publishers
199 W. 8th Ave., Suite 3
Eugene, OR 97401

www.wipfandstock.com

PAPERBACK ISBN: 978-1-6667-9407-6
HARDCOVER ISBN: 978-1-6667-9408-3
EBOOK ISBN: 978-1-6667-9409-0

VERSION NUMBER 051722

The New Revised Standard Version Bible, © 1989 the Division of Christian Education of the National Council of the Churches of Christ in the United States of America. Used by permission. All rights reserved. (= NRSV)

The Holy Bible, King James Version. Cambridge Edition: 1769; King James Bible Online, 2021. www.kingjamesbibleonline.org.(= KJV).

New Testament, Greek: Nestle, Eberhard, Erwin Nestle, Barbara Aland, Kurt Aland, Iōan. D. Karavidopoulos, Carlo Maria Martini, Bruce M. Metzger, and Holger Strutwolf. 2012. Novum Testamentum Graece.

Hebrew Bible: Biblia Hebraica Stuttgartensia, ed. Karl Elliger and Wilhelm Rudolph, 5th edition by Adrian Schenker, © 1977 und 1997 Deutsche Bibelgesellschaft, Stuttgart (= BHS).

Septuaginta Rahlfs, Alfred; Bibelanstalt, Privilegierte Württembergische (1935). Septuaginta : id est, Vetus Testamentum graece iuxta LXX interpretes (in German). Stuttgart : Privilegierte wurttembergische Bibelanstalt. 2nd revised edition January 21st 2020. (= LXX)

Contents

Abbreviations | vii
Introduction | ix

PART 1: JESUS TEACHES US TO PRAY | 1
I. Two Parables of Jesus about Prayer (Luke 18) | 3
II. Prayer to Our Father | 13

PART 2: THE TRIUNE GOD AND PRAYER | 73
I. In the Name of Jesus Christ | 75
II. Prayer to God the Father | 111
III. Prayer in the Holy Spirit | 154

PART 3: THE PRAXIS OF THE PRAYING COMMUNITY | 175
I. Postures and Gestures of the Body | 177
II. Places for Prayer | 187
III. Times of Prayer | 198
IV. Forms of Prayer | 208
V. Prayer, Thanks and Praise (1 Timothy 2:1–8) | 221
VI. Prayer with Charity and Fasting | 226

PART 4: A CALL TO COMMON PRAYER | 253

Bibliography | 263

Abbreviations

EKK	Evangelisch-Katholischer Kommentar zum Neue Testament
LCL	Loeb Classical Library
NPNF	*The Nicene and Post-Nicene Fathers*, Series 1. Edited by Philip Schaff. 1886–1889. 14 vols.
PL	Patrologia Latina, edited by J.-P. Migne. 217 vols. Paris, 1844–1864.
SE	*Studia Evangelica I* (= TUGAL 73 [1959])
TRE	*Theologische Realenzyklopädie.* Edited by Gerhard Müller. 36 vols. Berlin: de Gruyter, 1977–2004.
TUGAL	Texte und Untersuchungen zur Geschichte der altchristlichen Literatur
WA	Luther, Martin. *D. Martin Luthers Werke: Kritische Gesamtausgabe.* 73 vols. Weimar: H. Böhlau, 1883–2009.

Introduction

PRAYING WITH CONFIDENCE

JESUS SAYS IN MATTHEW 6: *"your Father knows what you need before you ask him."* Actually, *all* passages in the Bible about prayer presuppose that God's people will pray with confidence. Despite temptations and doubts and despite all uncertainties in our daily lives, we are not only allowed but encouraged to pray confidently. It is in prayer that the psalmist recites God's promise: *"When they call to me, I will answer them; I will be with them in trouble, I will rescue them and honor them"* (Psalm 91:15).

In this way, the psalmist reminds himself of God's promise to answer prayer. In the book of the prophet Isaiah, God's promise is found in chapter 65, verse 24: *"And it shall come to pass, that before they call, I will answer; and while they are yet speaking, I will hear."* The prophet proclaims that God not only knows our needs but knows them better than we do. The psalmist expects God never to be absent, wherever his faithful pray (Psalm 139). Hence, in more philosophical terms, Christians base their confidence in prayer on their beliefs about God's omniscienc, omnipresence, and His being eternal.

Some traditional morning and evening prayers begin with verse 7 of Psalm 27: *"Hear, O Lord, when I cry aloud, be gracious to me and answer me."* This verse is not prayed because God's attention needs to be drawn to the prayers of his people, but rather because, by praying it, Christians remind themselves of a God who keeps his promise to listen. Another psalm professes (Psalm 121): *"He who keeps Israel will neither slumber nor sleep."*

While we are called to trust always and everywhere in God's all-knowing and all-powerful mercy, we don't always experience the fulfillment of our wishes. For that reason, we need to find ways to accept God's decisions when, where, and in what ways he takes care of our prayers. Any answer to the problem of seemingly unanswered prayer, however, will be appropriate and helpful only if it is not just some kind stratagem to dodge criticism. Christians are encouraged to pray confidently, but having confidence when confronted with everyday experience requires reflection and learning.

LORD, TEACH US TO PRAY!

The disciples of the Lord Jesus Christ asked their master (Luke 11): "*¹Lord, teach us to pray.*" For Jesus' first disciples, prayer was obviously not an ordinary thing to do. They knew that they were in need of instruction about prayer. For them, prayer would not just flow from the heart but needed to be taught and learned.

Nowadays our situation appears to be very different. In an adult Sunday school class, the astonished question was asked: How can it be that someone does not know how to pray? Christians today do pray, and most of the time they do not see any problem; prayer seems to be a part of their life, like eating and drinking.

Our mindset seems very different from the attitude of Jesus' first disciples, who wanted to be instructed about prayer. Is it possible that we know more about prayer than the apostles of the Lord did? Do we no longer need to be taught about prayer? If this were true, why should we even talk about it? Many people pray happily and are unperturbed by theological problems; shouldn't we leave it at that? Wouldn't it be irresponsible to question their prayer life?

Then again, there are practical questions that demand clarification. Our petitions are often centered on our wishes and personal experiences, and our prayers should indeed be genuine and sincere. But shouldn't we also consider what God wants to be asked for?

In our supposedly spontaneous prayers, do we ever pray for the holiness of God's name or for God's kingdom? We want to pray sincerely with our whole heart, then again there are people who are in need of our prayer, whether or not we personally know them or even like them. Will we ever spontaneously (Luke 6:28) pray for those who abuse us? How does prayer relate to social responsibility and the readiness to give up personal wishes (cf. Matthew 6 about fasting, prayer, and charity)?

We certainly would not call just any wish a prayer. But is it enough to add the word *God* to turn a wish into a prayer? How should Christians address God? In daily life, we speak in different ways to our spouse or parents, to friends or colleagues, staff or customers, clients or policemen, superiors or subordinates; hence our conversation might be obliging or brusque, casual or formal, polite or chummy. The manner in which we speak to God certainly depends on our beliefs about God. How is our prayer life related to our understanding of who God is?

In our Bible study class, someone said that prayer is *"communication."* But what does this mean, since prayer is not a conversation between equals; rather we speak to him who doesn't need to be informed about our needs (Matthew 6:8) because he is omniscient, whose love needs not to be acquired because he *is* love (1 John 4:8), whose powers do not need to be summoned because he is almighty already. Prayer expects God to take action, but how does that relate to our own actions, our love, work, and effort?

Guided by Jesus' teaching, Christians pray to God, the Father. In what way are Christian prayers shaped by the proclamation of God's qualities and deeds, by the rich imagery of the Bible? Christians pray *"in the name of Jesus,"* but what difference does it make for the content of their prayers? What does it mean for prayer that God's Son became flesh, suffered, died, and has been raised from the dead? How does the Holy Spirit lead in prayer? What does it mean for Christian prayer that the God of the Bible is the *Triune* God? For these practical reasons, we need to talk about *"God and Prayer."*

Many people still use written prayers taken from the Bible, from tradition, or from the prayer books of their particular denomination. Others prefer to speak from their hearts, rejecting traditional forms and prescribed content. Still, supposedly free prayers often repeat certain favorite phrases over and over again, which does not necessarily mean that they are not also heartfelt expressions. We need to explore the question: How are the prayers of the Bible, such as those found in the psalms, the canticles of the Gospels, and the prayers in the Old and New Testaments, relevant for Christian prayer?

When listening to prayers actually said on TV, in public meetings, or onstage (cf. Matthew 6:5), one wonders: Is the language appropriate for the content and addressee? Are the showcased casual postures and gestures, the style of the space, the hours, really appropriate for the words? Then again, most people don't like pretentious, la-di-da manners, either. Therefore we have to ask: Do form, language, location, time, and body language matter, or are they insignificant formalities?

Finally, what does it mean that the apostle of the Lord cautions us (Romans 8:26): *"for we do not know how to pray as we ought (. . .)"*? In this book, these questions will be explored.

PART 1

Jesus Teaches Us to Pray

Jesus both teaches prayer (Luke 11:1) and presents himself as a role model (Luke 6:12; 9:28; 22:40) for the praying community. He teaches *what* to pray, namely the "Our Father" (Matt 6), and he teaches us *how* to pray (Luke 18).

I.

Two Parables of Jesus about Prayer (Luke 18)

IN CHAPTER 18, SAINT LUKE[1] juxtaposes two parables of Jesus: the parable of 'The Widow and the Unjust Judge' and the parable of the 'Pharisee and the Tax Collector.' Saint Luke introduces the first parable (Luke 18:1) this way: "Then Jesus told them a parable about their need to pray always and not to lose heart." Hence this first parable teaches about faithful, persistent prayer.

The goal of the second parable is summed up in the tax collector's invocation: "Lord have mercy" (Luke 18:13). Hence this second parable teaches about humble prayer.

So in these two parables in Luke's Gospel, Jesus teaches that a person's correct attitude to prayer involves persistence and humility. The theological connection between the parables is indicated in the term *righteousness* (Luke 18:2; 18:14), just as it is in Matthew's account of Jesus teaching the Lord's Prayer (Matt 6, see below 1.II.).

1. THE CONTEXT IN THE GOSPEL OF SAINT LUKE

Saint Luke emphasizes the piety of Jesus, beginning with his parents (Luke 2:4–51). Jesus' praying is especially important in the Gospel of Luke. A comparison of the parallel pericopes of the synoptic Gospels shows that

---

1. Most of the exegetical information I collected from the commentary by Fitzmyer, *The Gospel according to Luke*. For the first parable cf. pages 1175–82 and for the second parable pages 1182–88.

in several places Saint Luke adds notes about Jesus' praying: Luke 3:21 (cf. Matt 3:13–17; Mark 1:9–11); 9:18 (cf. Matt 16:13–20; Mark 8:27), and 9:28 (cf. Matt 17:1–8; Mark 9:1–8). Hence it is safe to say that Saint Luke's account of Jesus' counsel in Luke 18—i.e., to pray persistently and humbly—is closely connected with Saint Luke's distinctive witness to the life of Jesus Christ.

Saint Luke describes Jesus as one would a saint, which is quite obvious in his version of the passion story, where Jesus appears as a martyr, saying (Luke 24:26): "Was it not necessary that the Messiah should suffer these things and then enter into his glory?" This sentence is similar to what Saint Luke says about the martyrs of the church: "There they strengthened the souls of the disciples and encouraged them to continue in the faith, saying, 'It is through many persecutions that we must enter the kingdom of God.'" (Acts 14:22). Saint Luke presents Jesus as a role model for Christians, for their piety and their conduct in persecution. Reading the parable of the poor widow and the unjust judge, which speaks about the righteousness of God and about prayer, we may keep in mind the suffering and death of Jesus and the martyrdom of his disciples. In view of the suffering of Christ and his followers—persecuted by unjust judges!—persistence in prayer is all the more necessary.

In the same chapter of the Gospel according to Luke where we read Jesus' parables about persistent and humble prayer, we also read about his announcement of his suffering (Luke 18[2]); but the disciples "[34]understood nothing about all these things; in fact, what he said was hidden from them, and they did not grasp what was said."

The disciples will begin to understand only after Jesus' death and resurrection (Luke 24): "[25] Then he said to them, 'Oh, how foolish you are, and how slow of heart to believe all that the prophets have declared! [26] Was it not necessary that the Messiah should suffer these things and then enter into his glory?' [27] Then beginning with Moses and all the prophets, he interpreted to them the things about himself in all the scriptures."

Jesus' instructions about prayer and the announcement of his passion in Luke 18 interpret each other: A life of prayer still means to bear the cross and our awareness that God's plans and justice are not obvious in this life. Neither luck nor misfortune allows us to make assumptions about God's plans. For this reason, we need to keep invoking God—persistently, like the widow in defiance of temporary outcomes; and humbly, like the tax collector, in defiance of sin and shame. In Luke's Gospel, Jesus warns us against judging by what seems to be obvious and against judging by immediate

---

2. Without parallels in Matthew and Mark.

personal experience: Neither the fate of the Galilean pilgrims who were killed by Pilate, nor the fate of those who were killed by the collapsing tower of Siloam, allows us to regard the victims as sinners (cf. Luke 13:1–9). Good fortune is, accordingly, not the confirmation of God's grace or a 'successful prayer.' Christian prayer cannot be just an immediate reaction to the mere appearance of God's righteousness fulfilling or denying our wishes, as the first parable teaches; and Christian prayer can certainly not be based on our own presumed righteousness, as the second parable teaches. Persistent prayer is necessary precisely because God's justice remains hidden in the shadow of the cross. Neither parable in Luke 18 allows us to rely on what appears to be divine poetic justice or on an individual's presumed righteousness (Luke 18:9–13).

Only the conclusion of the first parable explains what the justice of God is (Luke 18): "⁷ And will not God grant justice to his chosen ones who cry to him day and night? Will he delay long in helping them?"

In the context of the parable about the delayed answer of the unjust judge, this statement is obviously an encouragement to keep praying against the appearance of God's injustice. The righteousness of humanity is revealed at the end of this double parable (Luke 18): "¹⁴ ... for all who exalt themselves will be humbled, but all who humble themselves will be exalted."

Only persistent and humble prayer, foremost in praying the words God himself has given us, will keep us in the faith—faith in God's justice and mercy, faith that will be challenged by the everyday experience of injustice, faith that can be easily deceived by the experience of what appears to be justice, as reward or punishment for our deeds.

2. THE POOR WIDOW (LUKE 18:2–8)

Saint Luke's short introduction to Jesus' first parable says: "Then Jesus told them a parable about their need to pray always and not to lose heart." We read about the disciples' *need* to pray. The literal meaning of the Greek word translated as *they need to* or *they must* (δεῖν) is *to bind*. This word is used metaphorically for legal and moral obligations; in Rom 7:2 and 1 Cor 7:27, for example, it describes marriage. In the Gospel of Saint Luke, the word has a special connection with Jesus' passion (Luke 9): "²² The Son of Man *must* undergo great suffering..." (also in 13:33; 17:25; 22:37; 24:7). The word accordingly proclaims the certainty of the disciples' suffering in the last days (12:12; 21:9): "... do not be terrified; for these things *must* take place first." Therefore the wording of Saint Luke's introduction (Luke 18:1) to Jesus' parable places prayer in the context of obligation and perseverance in suffering.

It is true that in Saint Luke's Gospel, Jesus Christ is often proclaimed as *Lord*. (Luke 2:11), a title that also calls us to trust in his leadership in prayer. But this king is crowned with thorns (cf. Luke 23:38). Hence his disciples are obligated both to pray and to bear the cross of Christ. Only in this way will we have confidence in God's justice, a confidence that neither our own heart can provide, nor our immediate experience of what is perceived as answered prayer.

Saint Luke hands down Jesus' parable, along with advice not to *lose heart*. The meaning of the Greek word is not to behave remissly, not to neglect what needs to be done. The meaning of *losing heart* is here *lack of discipleship,* and it is the opposite of "that faith" that the Son of Man wants to find on Earth when he comes again in glory (Luke 18:8). Jesus' counsel aims at persistent prayer. The parable indeed tells us that persistence and repetition changes the mind of the "unjust judge."

This teaching about the efficacy of persistent prayer does not contradict Jesus' teaching in Matthew's Gospel (Matt 6, see below 1.II. and III.) that God knows our needs beforehand, because his omnipotence and omniscience and providence include our own plans and prayers, needs and deeds. God's plans need not be changed, but his plans include that we ask him, and ask him persistently (see below 2.III.3.7.). God always knows about our needs and knows them better than we do—and He cares. But He wants us to pray for what we need, and with persistent prayer we actively participate in God's providence. Therefore the widow is the role model of prayer.

In the Bible, widows are often depicted as women with few legal rights and without access to legal protections (cf. Exod 22:22-24; Deut 10:18; 24:17; Malachi 3:5; Ruth 1:20-21; Isa 54:4; Ps 68:5), because without a husband they had no legal representative. In the Gospel according to Luke, Jesus warns (Luke 20:27): "Beware of the Jewish leaders who devour the widows' houses."

In the time of the Old Testament, widowhood was often associated with dishonor. Whoever has attentively read the Gospel of Luke from the beginning will remember another widow: the prophetess Anna, the daughter of Phanuel, who never left the temple but worshipped night and day with fasting and prayer (Luke 2:36, see 3.VI.2.i). Saint Luke's account of her story marks a change to the role widows will play in the church. She who, due to harmful tradition, was socially marginalized could win in the church a special place of honor by her faithfulness, because she "continues in supplications and prayers night and day." Saint Luke presents the widow Saint Anna in the temple as an ideal of a life in prayer. Later, the early church would pay special attention to its responsibility for widows (cf. Acts 6 and Jas 1:27). What's more, widows held a special place of honor in the church

(1 Tim 5:3): "Honor widows who are really widows." And in the book of Acts (9:38–10:1) we find the phrase: "the saints and widows." Saint Luke's introduction to Jesus' parable about the widow in Luke 18 says that the disciples need to pray *always*, meaning like the widow presented in this parable as a role model.

The judge is characterized as *unjust*. The phrase "who neither feared God nor had respect for people" does not have the positive meaning of *unbiased* or *objective*, but on the contrary explains what is meant in describing the judge as *unjust*.

Since the story is called a parable,[3] it's better not to assume too quickly that the character of the judge is an allegory for God. But because the Lord says, "Listen to what the unjust judge says," it is useful to dwell for a moment on this literary character. He personifies our experience of injustice in this life, along with the reality of seemingly unanswered prayers. The lamentation Psalms do much the same, giving words to human pain and grief, along with complaints and even rebellion against God. The opportunity to say the words of these prayers brings relief to the praying and pleading people of God. It would be a false piety to bypass or suppress prayers of lamentation. The characterization of the judge as *unjust* spares the praying person both from dishonestly suppressing anger and lamentation against God and from despairingly passing judgment on her- or himself. The Bible permits, even encourages, lamentation, which is a great gift. The final revelation of God's justice is yet to come; only at the end of this passage (Luke 18:2–8), in addition to the parable itself, does Jesus speak about God's justice. Only then does it become clear that the character of the unjust judge is necessary to allow the argument to move from lesser to greater: "if *even* the unjust judge . . . how much *more* will God . . . ." God's justice may become clear to the faithful only at the end of a life of prayer.

In the parable, the judge's motivation to give in is not justice, nor his commitment to God, nor his commitment to the community, but the behavior of the woman. He muses whether she might even be capable of assaulting him. Saint Luke uses this word *assault* perhaps a little humorously; the word in the original Greek is borrowed from the language of boxing, meaning: *to give a black eye*. In the Greek world, the word has also a metaphorical meaning, but even the literal meaning is possible here. If one assumes that the

---

3. Parables and allegories are very different types of texts. In an allegory, all or most objects and characters in the narrative have meanings that lie outside the narrative itself. The characters of an allegory are usually personifications of concepts, ideas or qualities. The narrative speaks about how these abstractions interact. The parable, in contrast, has usually only one major point of comparison to something outside the narrative, called by scholars *tertium comparationis*.

unjust judge is an allegory for God, though it seems strange, one will probably still shy away from applying this feature of the parable, the idea that the woman might assault the judge, to God himself. It is, however, in the core of the Christian way to speak about God allowing himself to be beaten by man in order to bless man (cf. Gen 32:23, the story of Jacob wrestling with God); the Son of God is allowed to be killed by humans in order to save humanity. So it makes perfect sense that this word has a connotation of violence. The works and prayers of God's faithful, even their insolent demands, are part of the Creator's providence, whose justice will be revealed eventually. God wants us to pray faithfully and urgently, and employs our prayer for his works of providence. The judge will finally grant justice. The idea of wearing God out by persistent prayer is indeed accepted as part of God's plan.

As noted earlier, the frame of the parable (verses 6–7) gives the explanation that this story is an argument from lesser to greater: If even the unjust judge grants justice, how much more will God? Only here, at the end of our pericope, God appears as the just judge. The point of the parable is patience, obedience and persistence in prayer.

Verses 7–8 apply allegorical explanations to the parable: We are called to pray *day and night*. Continuous worship *day and night* is mentioned in Luke's second book: Acts 26:7. The word in Acts translated as *continually* (Acts 26:7) may also have the meaning *fervently*, but in Luke 18 it is clearly explained by the words *day and night*. Accordingly, Saint Luke's use of this word encourages continuous, faithful, persistent prayer. The same author tells us that during the imprisonment of Saint Peter (Acts 12:5), prayer was continually offered by the church.

The end of the world comes into view when Jesus speaks about the coming of the Son of Man: "When the Son of Man comes, will he find [that] faith on earth?" The text speaks not about faith in general, but *that faith* (τὴν πίστιν), referring to the faith depicted in the parable: faith that motivates the faithful to persistent prayer.[4] Such faith will not be found unless the disciples have learned the "need to pray always."[5] Our parable presents the widow as the role model of the *chosen ones* who *cry day and night*. The widow Anna in Luke 2:37, who prays in the temple day and night, is accordingly the role model for a Christian life of prayer.

---

4. Many translations omit the article, even though there is no textual variant. Without the article, this sentence, *"Will he find faith on earth,"* gains a completely different meaning, especially when isolated from its context. (The omission is perhaps due to the influence of the Latin versions, since there are no articles in the Latin language.)

5. Cf. the story of the faith of the centurion in Capernaum about whom Jesus said (Luke 7:9): *"I tell you, not even in Israel have I found such faith."*

3. TAX COLLECTOR AND PHARISEE (LUKE 9–14)

Saint Luke connects this pericope about the tax collector and the Pharisee with the preceding parable through the phrase, "He also told this parable." Both stories speak about prayer and righteousness. Again, a disdained person is found worthy to be a role model for Jesus' followers.[6] The preceding story called followers to faithful, persistent prayer; this story is a warning not to take pride in a pious life. Saint Luke juxtaposes the parables so that the stories are meant to be read as complementary teachings.

Saint Luke introduces and thus interprets the story (verse 9): "He also told this parable to some who trusted in themselves that they were righteous and regarded others with contempt." The evangelist tells us nothing about Jesus' audience; but because during the previous speech Jesus' disciples had been present, and because Saint Luke explicitly connects both stories, he undoubtedly presupposes that Jesus' disciples are among those *who trusted in themselves*. Therefore Saint Luke does not simply identify those *who trusted in themselves* with the Pharisees, but speaks about Jesus' disciples. Consequently, this criticism isn't aimed at the Jews of Jesus' time but at members of the Christian Church, of all times and all places.

The scene of the parable proper is the sanctuary (τὸ ἱερόν). The temple is known as a place for prayer (cf. Luke 1:9; 19:46; Acts 3:1; 22:17). Such an incident could occur at any time; but since the Pharisee of the parable mentions his observance of the daily prayers, it is quite possible and even likely that the traditional hours of prayer, perhaps the third hour of the day (9 a.m.) or the ninth hour (3 p.m., the hour for the Mincha–Prayer; cf. Acts 3), form the background of the story. Since both the Pharisee and the tax collector are in the temple at the same hour, this kind of observance is obviously not the issue.

The introduction contrasts *those who rely on themselves* with those *regarded with contempt*. The two characters in the parable are:

---

6. This story is the conclusion of the *"travel account"* unique in the Gospel of Luke (Luke 9:51–19:27).

Pharisee	tax collector
standing by himself	standing far off
thanks God for his state of righteousness	asks God for mercy
returned home without justification	returned home justified

The proverb concluding the story presents an analogue contrast:

all who exalt themselves will be humbled	all who humble themselves will be exalted.

In this comparison, the tax collector is presented as the role model. In the Gospels, Pharisees consistently appear as persons very concerned with their own purity and pride. Praying, fasting, and tithing (5:33; 11:42) is their characteristic behavior. In the Gospels, their primary role is to question Jesus' faithfulness to the law, and thus they are Jesus' antagonists. The portrayal of the Pharisee in our parable is consistent with this general picture. It is true that in the eyes of his contemporaries he is neither a tax collector nor a sinner; he is, however, depicted as a presumptuous man who disdains others.

It is important to note that the Pharisee's actual behavior, i.e., his praying, fasting and tithing, is not the target of the parable's criticism. The call to persistent prayer in the preceding parable is not forgone. The custom of tithing is based on Lev 27:30–33 and Num 18:21–32; tithing of grain, wine, oil, the firstborn of the herd and the flock is prescribed in Deut 14:22–23. In Old Testament times, fasting was an expression of mourning (2 Sam 12:21), of penance (1 Kgs 21:27; Ezra 10:6), and of supplication (Neh 1:4; Dan 9:3).[7] Fasting is certainly a custom among Christians (Acts 13 and 14). The Pharisee of the parable claims to live honorably before God, and for all we know he is right. We are never told what particular sin the Pharisee might have committed, if any; and the Pharisee actually fasts and tithes more than is expected of him. There's no criticism here of the customs observed by the Pharisee, nor his actual behavior. The goal of the parable is not to unveil any shortcomings or actual sins of the Pharisee, nor to abolish the practice of praying, fasting and tithing.

It is rather the content of the Pharisee's prayer that fails to justify him. The Pharisee says no prayer of petition but of thanks: he thanks God for

---

7. The passage about the Pharisee and the tax collector is the earliest evidence to the custom of Jews fasting twice a week. Jewish fasting on Mondays and Thursdays is attested to by a source from the time before AD 450: b.Ta'an12a. The Christian book Didache (dated by modern scholars to the first century) instructs Christians to fast on the fourth day (Wednesday) and on the day before the Sabbath (Friday): Didache 8:1.

being saved from a corrupt life. The Pharisee's prayer actually begins like a Psalm of Thanksgiving ("God, I thank you that . . ."), but, contrary to the biblical Psalms of thanksgiving, the Pharisee does not speak about any qualities and actions of God but rather about his own. Thus he has replaced the biblical prayer of thanksgiving to God with an expression of his own pride. While standing in the temple, the Pharisee physically separates himself from others; he maintains the honor of his own piety at the expense of others, and specifically at the expense of the tax collector. Thus the Pharisee damages the unity of God's people and gives preference to his own righteousness. At this point, we must again remind ourselves: Saint Luke's record of Jesus' parable doesn't take aim only at Jesus' contemporaries, but also at members of the church. Christians are always tempted to Pharisaic behavior.

Tax collectors were Jews who worked for the Roman government, and were therefore despised by Jews who opposed the Greek-Roman civilization. Tax collectors are often associated with "sinners" (Luke 5:30; 7:24; 15:1; cf. 19:2–7). But in contrast to the Pharisees, tax collectors time and again are those who accept the gospel.

In our parable the tax collector, like the Pharisee, isolates himself, but for a very different reason. *Far off* means of course within the sanctuary, meaning the Court of Israel as opposed to the court outside the temple, the part of the temple compound gentiles were permitted to enter. This means the tax collector still belongs to the people of God. But he separates himself because he does not attempt to seize a respectable place. He averts his eyes, a sign of humility, and he beats his breasts, a gesture of contrition, compunction and remorse (cf. Luke 23:48). Saint Luke tactfully avoids telling us what specific sins the tax collector had to confess.[8] The prayer of the tax collector is: "God, be merciful to me, a sinner!" Jesus' statement in verse 14a concludes the parable: "I tell you, this man went down to his home justified rather than the other." Through this verse, the story is closely connected with what are known as the parables of mercy in chapter 15, about the sheep and the coin lost and found, about the prodigal son lost and found, dead and alive again. These great stories about God's mercy are told when Pharisees complain about Jesus' practice of welcoming sinners and eating with them (Luke 15:2).

It might be puzzling that in the parable the prayer of the tax collector seems to be a means to achieve justification. But the assumption that one could *earn* justification by the merit of prayer would turn the meaning of the parable upside down. Jesus does not discuss abstractly the *merit of prayer* or

---

8. In Luke 7:37, the Evangelist shows the same sense of tact when he does not even mention what *actual sin* the sinful woman might have committed.

the *power of prayer*, or something of that nature, but simply contrasts the actual content of the prayers: The Pharisee gives thanks in his own words, not speaking about God's saving deeds but about his own pious status; the tax collector prays in the spirit of Ps 51: "³ For I know my transgressions, and my sin is ever before me." Thus, by praying and confessing guided by the word of God, we do not *earn* justification but rather hope both confidently and humbly for God's mercy.

The parable is summarized by Jesus' statement in verse 14b: "for all who exalt themselves will be humbled, but all who humble themselves will be exalted." This verse looks like a wisdom-saying,[9] the kind of sayings based on faith that we find, for example, in the proverbs of Solomon or the deuterocanonical book Ecclesiasticus (Jesus Sirach). In the context of Saint Luke's account, this saying concludes the parable. This form of a proverb suggests that the verse (verse 14b) is meant as universal truth, and thus makes it clear again that the parable is addressed not only to Jesus' contemporaries, but to all Christians and actually to all the world. It is true the parable suggests that a disciple should identify with the tax collector rather than with the Pharisee. Still, the parable reminds us that we all have to face our inner Pharisee. In Phil 3:4–6 (cf. also Gal 1:14 and 2:15) Saint Paul—speaking as a Christian—remembers his boastful past as a Pharisee when he was "confident in the flesh." True Christian prayer follows the lead of the tax collector, saying, "God be merciful to me a sinner."

Both parables, about the widow and the tax collector, are addressed to the Christian Church. We are called to persistent and humble prayer. As both parables focus on the actual content of prayer, it should be obvious that the prayers of the Bible will be of special importance. We are called to pray faithfully and yet without pride. Those who pray persistently and yet humbly, in prayers based on the word of God, trusting in God's mercy, will not disdain others. Participation in common prayer will keep us within the community of the faithful, who keep praying with the words of the prayers of the Bible.

---

9. The prophet Ezekiel (33:13) had already warned: "*Though I say to the righteous that they shall surely live, yet if they trust in their righteousness and commit iniquity, none of their righteous deeds shall be remembered; but in the iniquity that they have committed they shall die.*"

II.

Prayer to Our Father

OUR FATHER IS IN SECRET

IN THE GOSPEL ACCORDING to Matthew, Jesus teaches *about* prayer, and teaches *the* prayer, the "Our Father," basing this teaching about prayer on the doctrine of God, specifically on the doctrine of God's omniscience (Matt 6): "⁸your Father knows what you need before you ask him." Jesus teaches about the practical consequences.[1]

a. On the Mountain (the broader context)

The Lord's Prayer and its introduction are found in the context of Jesus' Sermon on the Mount. When his fame spread, Jesus and his listeners withdrew from the crowd and "went up the mountain." In this passage, the mountain is a place of revelation, as we find in two other prominent places in Matthew's Gospel.

According to Matt 28, the disciples worship the risen Christ on a mountain, where Jesus reveals himself as the one to whom "all power is given in heaven and on earth." It's on the mountain that Jesus' divine authority is revealed. According to Matt 17, Jesus' transfiguration takes place on the mountain, and here as well, Jesus' divinity is revealed, in the meeting with Moses and Elijah. The law was given to Moses on Mount "Sinai,"

---

1. Most of the exegetical information I collected from the commentary by Luz, *Matthäus* I (chap. 1–7).

according to Exod 19; according to Deut 5, the name of this mountain is "Horeb," and Mount Horeb is (1 Kgs 19) the place of the revelation to the prophet Elijah. Hence, the mountain is the place of the revelation of the law and the prophets. The stories of Moses and Elijah on the mountain tell us about humans listening to God and speaking to God. Jesus is the one on the mountain (Matt 17:5) to whom the disciples shall listen, and on the mountain he teaches (Matt 6) about the way God wants to be invoked.

The mountain is a place of revelation, but it's a revelation delivered in secret: We read about God who is (Exod 19) in a "thunderstorm" and then (1 Kgs 19:12) in "silence," who (Exod 19:9,16) reveals himself but in a cloud, who allows Moses (Exod 33:23) to see him, but only his back. The stories of the Old Testament show that God both reveals himself and remains in secret. The Gospel narrative of Jesus reveals God's glory, but Jesus dies on the cross and (Matt 27) "[45] darkness came over the whole land." The Holy Scriptures testify to God, who reveals himself and yet wants to remain hidden to the obdurate.

Prayer begins with searching for him who shows himself in a cloud and with listening to him who is (1 Kgs 19:12) heard in the sound of silence. Elijah prayed and received nothing more than (1 Kgs 19) some dry bread and water from a brook, but these gifts turned out to be enough to save him and consequently his people. We pray to him who has made himself known to us, and who still wants to be sought. (Jas 5) "[16] The fervent prayer of a righteous person" will not turn into triumphant boasting, but be done out of public view, in a chamber.

In Matthew's Gospel, the mystery of God's revelation in secret reaches its climax when Jesus prays on the cross (Matt 27:46 = Ps 22:1), "my God why hast thou forsaken me," and the earth quakes and darkness falls. Exactly then, the Roman soldier prayerfully confesses the Son of God (Matt 27:54) and Jesus dies.

b. *The Immediate Context*

According to Matthew, the context of Jesus' teaching about prayer is the Sermon on the Mount (Matt 5–7), which, according to Matt 5:2b, is meant to *teach* and is therefore perhaps not to be understood as a sermon of exhortation and consolation, but as revealed wisdom, as counsel and guidance. Within the Sermon on the Mount, the immediate context is a series of teachings about the Christian life as a life in retreat, a life of fasting, prayer, and giving alms (cf. 3.VI.). This threefold instruction has its heading in Matt 6:1: "Beware of practicing your piety before others in order to be seen by them."

The topic of righteousness is introduced in Matt 5:20 and is continued here with Jesus' counsel for the Christian life. This context already determines the meaning of prayer: It's not so much an expression of one's heart but something to be taught and to be learned, a matter of living according to righteousness revealed on the mountain, like the law and the prophets (see below Part 3.VI.).

The advice is to keep prayer short. The keyword *hypocrite* connects this piece of scripture with Matt 23 (KJV): "[14] Woe unto you, scribes and Pharisees, hypocrites! For ye devour widows' houses, and for a pretense make long prayers: therefore ye shall receive the greater damnation."[2] Retreat, truthfulness, and righteousness are the motivation for prayer in Matt 6:1–18. In a sense, the ethics of prayer are based on the doctrine of God: We have to bear in mind that God "is in secret" and our own actions are supposed to be done without boasting. We pray in our chamber and God answers our prayer in secret, meaning not by appearances, but hidden from the eyes of the world, without obvious manifestations of his power. Christian prayer prays to him whose power is not obvious to all, but in this time and world remains in secret. Hence Christian prayer requires trust and patience and the readiness to bear the cross.

c. Form

The verses 2–4, about alms; 5–6, about prayer; and 16–18, about fasting, form three stanzas, each with a positive and a negative part. Each stanza starts with a description of the situation. Each stanza has a prohibition (Matt 6): "[2] do not blow a trumpet before you," "[5] do not be like the hypocrites," "[16] do not look gloomy like the hypocrites." Each stanza announces the goal and the divine promise (Matt 6:4 = 6:6 = 6:18): "And your Father who sees in secret will repay you." Each warning includes a comparison with hypocrites. All three stanzas present the same oppositions: *public* versus *in secret*; *men* versus *Father*; *present reward* versus *future reward*. The word *Father* is found only in the positive sentences, never in the negative ones.

This beautiful design of the text corresponds with the design of God's plans, as Jesus says: "your Father knows what you need before you ask him." The beauty of this piece of literature discloses itself in faithful meditation and stands in stark contrast to an understanding of prayer that's about cause and effect, as well as the criticized abuse of prayer as a means of showing off impressively for God or human observers.

---

2. Some early manuscripts do not have this verse, therefore the NRSV omits it.

d. The historic background

Jesus says (Matt 6): "⁵ And whenever you pray, do not be like the hypocrites; for they love to stand and pray in the synagogues and at the street corners, so that they may be seen by others."

For the Jewish community of Jesus' era, certain times for prayer were mandatory; for example, morning prayer needed to be done by noon. The situation to which Jesus alludes was perhaps the audible prayer of an individual in the temple or in a synagogue or the usual prayers in public. Whether it was actually customary to pray on the streets cannot be confirmed by other sources. Standing for prayer and speaking in a low voice, however, was known to be customary (cf. Luke 18:10–13). The sensitivity to showing off described in this passage perhaps refers to the prophet Isaiah (Isa 26:20): "Come, my people, enter your chambers, and shut your doors behind you; hide yourselves for a little while until the wrath is past." In a situation when God's judgment is about to come upon his people, when God is calling to repentance, proud self-presentation to God or to other human beings makes no sense.

The meaning of the word translated as *vain repetitions* (King James Bible) or *empty phrases* (NRSV) is not quite clear. Many translations depend on the religious ideas and polemics of their era. The translation of the King James Bible, *vain repetitions,* obviously reflects the Protestant polemics of the Reformation era but does not really translate the word. The original Greek word is related to a word that means *stutterer.* Hence, the original Greek phrase was already a slur, so that the mentioned translations are indeed somewhat appropriate. However, just because this word is a slur does not mean this phrase, in itself, tells us what exactly is being ridiculed. Hence, in the history of biblical exposition, this word has become a wildcard for all kinds of things someone wanted to critique. Some said the meaning was *piling up epithets* of God, but this interpretation has no basis in the text. A common interpretation is that the text is rejecting merely external piety and the regular praying or chanting of the psalms or other form-prayers; but the problem of external versus internal religion isn't discussed in this text or context. It is important to note that in his teaching on the mount, Jesus does not speak just about *vain repetitions* in general but about "vain repetitions like the gentiles." Whoever Jesus was referring to, and whatever they did, it is certain that the Jews—including Jesus—did pray the Psalms, and the gentiles did not. The gentiles certainly did not pray the Lord's Prayer or other prayers of the church yet to be initiated by Jesus. The same Evangelist who recorded the Sermon on the Mount testifies to Jesus praying a Psalm on the cross (Matt 27:46 = Ps 22:1). The idea that Jesus would have refused to pray the word of God is absurd.

It is still possible to find an explanation for this polemic against *vain repetitions* in the context. The broader context contrasts the practice of piety in public with a practice of piety in secret. The immediate context of the phrase *vain repetitions* is the warning against praying *to be seen by men*; i.e., against showing off, presenting yourself with spectacular words aimed at impressing others. This is the opposite of faith in the God who is *in secret* and who *knows what you need before you ask him*. Neither God nor human observers will be impressed by the presumed ingenuity of human words.

To the problem of abusing prayer to show off, whether for God and for other people, Jesus gives a twofold answer: First, he advises: "go into your room and shut the door and pray to your Father who is in secret; and your Father who sees in secret will reward you." The other response is that he teaches the Lord's Prayer, which is, first, short, and second, a liturgical text that doesn't allow for any narcissistic self-promotion. Jesus' twofold response makes sense if the meaning of *vain repetitions* is *showing off*. If we choose a different interpretation of *vain repetitions*, it's hard to see how Jesus' counsel—i.e., the closet and the Lord's Prayer—could be an answer to the problem.

Those who recognize the vanity and self-love of our own talk, which we may presume to be original, spontaneous, and ingenious, will also recognize the emptiness and repetitiveness of our self-made words. When we no longer want to impress either God or other people, nor want to monitor our own state of piety, we begin to open our ears and hearts and begin to really listen to the words Christ is praying, the Lord's Prayer, the Psalms, and so on. *Listening* to God's word then turns into *praying* God's word.

e. *God's Son leads in prayer to the heavenly Father*

Jesus teaches *about* prayer and he teaches *the* prayer. For Christians, Jesus is not just a great teacher of the past; he is the Son of God today. He is *God with us*, a title Matthew's Gospel gives Jesus (Isa 7:14; Matt 1:23), in Hebrew *Immanuel*. Therefore Jesus, the Son of God (cf. Matt 14:33; 16:16; 27:54), leads us in prayer to his Father today. Without engaging in a lot of complicated Christological questions, we can certainly say: Together with him, and guided by him, who is (Matt 1:16) the son of Mary and (16:16) the son of God, we now pray to "our Father in Heaven."

Especially in the Gospel according to Matthew, Jesus is the ruler of the universe; to him "all power is given in heaven and on earth" (cf. Matt 28:18).

In the storm the disciples invoke him, "Lord save" (cf. Matt 8:27), addressing him by a title of God's majesty and thereby acknowledging him as God who is in power already; and they realize that "even the winds and the sea obey him!" Praying Jesus' words, we pray together with Jesus who is both a human being like us and the Son of God, ruler of heaven and earth. Hence, praying his words is not an experiment that every now and then works or fails. It is not an attempt to convince another person to do what he would otherwise not do. Instead, the Lord's Prayer is the words of him who knows and almightily does what his words say, because he is the ruler of the universe in person. Praying God's word means to recite the words of the creator. Hence, prayer is not so much an attempt to change God's will as to follow God's will. Therefore this prayer allows us to have absolute confidence.

Jesus starts with the address "Our Father" because he, and only he, can allow us to address *his* Father as *Our Father in Heaven*. Jesus Christ is *God with us* today; he stands on our side whenever we address God the Father. Listening to him who has come *from* the Father, we have the right words to speak *to* the Father.

So prayer isn't a supplement to fill the gap between our wishes and disappointments, between our ambitions and abilities, between our experience and our understanding, or between our responsibility and our slowness of heart. Rather, prayer is the answer to God's words and deeds, the answer to him who knows our needs—and knows them better than we do or ever will. With the words of this prayer we give to God's deeds the answer he himself has taught us to give. In humility we give this answer in the form of petitions, with the words of him who rules over heaven and earth, whose will is being done even if we do not pray. But through our prayer we learn to trust that (Ps 135) "⁶ Whatever the LORD pleases he does, in heaven and on earth, in the seas and all deeps." Thus praying God's words, we participate in God's kingship.

Guided by the Son of God, i.e., his creative word, we pray as a portion of God's creation and his community. The fact that the Lord's Prayer starts with *our* Father does not contradict Jesus' advice to pray in secret; but exactly because our prayers take place in the community of the church and of creation, it cannot serve the purpose of showing off or manipulating our fellow Christians, nor manipulating anything else God has made, nor magically manipulating God for our own purposes. It is precisely because Christians are part of a community that their prayers need to refrain from self-promotion in public. Self-centredness and prayer are mutually exclusive, but through prayer we are part of the community in Christ.

Given Jesus' twofold advice—i.e., to go into one's closet and to pray the liturgical prayer, the Lord's Prayer—it is perhaps a helpful custom in some liturgical churches that for prayer the leader does not face the congregation but, together with the congregation, faces the altar, thus leading the assembly in prayer to God and not standing in front of the congregation as if addressing them. Using a strict form for the prayers can help pastors and others refrain from promoting themselves (cf. 3.IV). The prayers of the Bible, especially the Lord's Prayer, the Psalms and the biblical canticles, should always have priority. Personal prayers should be done hidden from the public.

f. Jesus teaches the Prayer

Jesus' disciples want to learn about prayer (Luke 11:1), and Jesus teaches: "When you pray say . . . ." Jesus did not say *pray with this method,* nor *pray with this attitude;* he did not say, *pray what your heart tells you,* nor did he say *pray something like this.* He simply says: "Pray"[3] and gives them the petitions of the Lord's Prayer. Nothing in the Bible suggests that this prayer would be just a non-binding example. Whatever kind of answer the disciples expected back then, or whatever question we want to be answered today, Jesus' actual answer tells us that it is the specific content of what we are to pray that sets Christian prayer apart.

It has been said the Lord's Prayer would be a simple, modest, intimate prayer of Jesus the carpenter. However, monumental topics of biblical theology are engaged in the Lord's Prayer: The holiness of God's name, God's kingdom, God's will, the topic of guilt and forgiveness, the bread from heaven, temptation and our salvation from evil. True, the Lord's Prayer is short, but it is certainly not a prayer of simplicity. Only an impoverished understanding of the address *Father* could suggest this (cf. I.3 and II.3).

The petitions of Jesus, the one mediator between God and humanity (cf. 1 Tim 2), are the appropriate mediation. We are certainly allowed to pray as our concrete situation and needs require, and yet the Lord's Prayer is the norm and rule for all our praying. It marks the difference between our merely human wishes and prayer in the name of Jesus. Through this prayer, our communion with God is renewed. Prayer is the human response to God who is already present in Christ, and still in prayer we hope for God to come.

---

3. According to Matthew's Gospel, Jesus says: *"Pray then in this way (οὕτως)."* The meaning of the Greek word (οὕτως) is *so, thus, in this way.* I do not see how this word could justify the assumption that the Lord's Prayer would be just an example, and that we would not be bound to pray its actual petitions.

The Lord's Prayer became a part of the Eucharistic meal very early in the history of the church. Of course the Lord's Prayer was part of the prayers of the hours, of midweek services without Eucharist, and of private prayers. Only since the 1700s did the Lord's Prayer became more and more the conclusion of the 'prayers,' and in consequence the Lord's Prayer lost its significance as a prayer in its own right. Some orders of prayer services place the Lord's Prayer before the prayers of intercession, so that the faithful are reminded first of what the Lord wants us to pray. In a sense, the traditional common order of the prayers in church corresponds with the order of the petitions of the Lord's Prayer: First, the prayer for God's holiness, for the church (kingdom) and God's will, and only then for particular human needs.

THE ADDRESS: "OUR FATHER"

Saint Mark calls Jesus the "Son of God" (Mark 1:1), and according to all four Gospels, Jesus prays to God, his "Father." Jesus calls his disciples *brothers* (John 20:17)—Christ, however, is never called *our brother* in the Bible—and thus he leads us, the beloved children of God, in prayer to the Father.

The word *Father* is of course taken from the life of the family; the children of God are called to the trust and confidence only God can inspire. However, when we speak to God, our Father, we are always tempted to project our good or not so good experiences and ideas about parenthood onto the image of God the Father. This is certainly true for our individual experiences with fathers. But it is also true on a broader scale, for the experiences and ideals of various societies, past and present, and their predominant concept of fatherhood. These preconceptions influence the understanding of Christians who want to pray to the *Father*. When, for example, in a tribal society the head of a whole tribe is called *father*, the term suggests responsibility for a larger community over many generations. But a father who claims to defend his nuclear family by tax evasion, avoiding military service and refusing responsibility for society and creation is in a sense the exact opposite of what a *tribal* father is supposed to be.

The prayer to the *Father* tends to endorse and stabilize the predominant concept of fatherhood in any society, whatever that concept might be. The ideal of the 'normal' small family of the late twentieth century and early twenty-first century—father, mother, two or three children, one house, two cars, one dog, which was probably for most people never the reality, even in Western countries—does not necessarily provide the appropriate image of what the biblical term *Father* means. Due to widespread experiences with absent or abusive fathers, the address to God as *Father* is disturbing for many people, and may prevent them from praying. This makes it all the more important to learn about the biblical meaning of the term, which in turn can correct problematic concepts of fatherhood (Matt 11): "[27b] no one knows the Son except the Father, and no one knows the Father except the Son [i.e., Jesus Christ] and anyone to whom the Son chooses to reveal him." This biblical principle can liberate us from harmful traditions of fatherhood.

• a. "Father" among the First Christians

In New Testament times, the word *Father* was used by both children and young adults in family life. But in antiquity *Father* was also used as a respectful greeting for older men. In the Bible, the word *father* is used for the forefather of a nation (cf. "father Abraham" in Josh 24:3, cf. John 8:53). In Rom 4, Saint Paul explains that Abraham is the father not only of the Jewish nation but "the father of many nations." Therefore the prayer to the *Father* may open our eyes to the large community of all times and all places.

According to Gal 4:6 and Rom 8:15, the Christian Church invokes God as "Abba, Father." The fact that the early, Greek-speaking church retained this Aramaic word shows that it was important for Christians. The invocation *Father* indicates that the worshipper is a child of God; therefore the permission to address God as *Father* implies the promise of salvation.

• b. The Pauline Letters

Saint Paul, in the salutations of his letters, says "grace" regularly "from the Father" (Rom 1:7; 1 Cor 1:3; 2 Cor 1:2; Gal 1:3 etc.). God becomes *our* Father when in Holy Baptism our old self dies and we receive the new life (Rom 6): "[4] Therefore we have been buried with him by baptism into death, so that, just as Christ was raised from the dead by the glory of the Father, so we too might walk in newness of life." We are made God's children by adoption (υἱοθεσία, Rom 8): "[14] For all who are led by the Spirit of God are children of God. [15] For ... you have received a spirit of adoption. When we cry, 'Abba! Father!' [16] it is that very Spirit bearing witness with our spirit that we are children of God, [17] and if children, then heirs, heirs of God and joint heirs with Christ." In Gal 4:4–7 we find the same concept of adoption: With adoption as God's children we receive the gift of the Son's Spirit crying, "Abba! Father!" Adoption is here contrasted with slavery, and the consequence of our adoption is that we, in contrast to slaves, are heirs. From the standpoint of this adoption, Saint Paul professes (1 Cor 8) "[6]yet for us there is one God, the Father, from whom are all things and for whom we exist, and one Lord, Jesus Christ, through whom are all things and through whom we exist." Moreover Saint Paul professes (2 Cor 6) "[18]and I will be your father, and you shall be my sons and daughters, says the Lord Almighty." Hence, according to this passages the word *Father* reminds us of three fundamental concepts: monotheism, God the creator, and God's almightiness. Saint Paul, refuting the idols, professes God; and the Father is the one to whom at the end Christ "hands over the kingdom" (1 Cor 15:24).

This understanding of God as the Father has consequences for prayer: Praying to the one Father, Christians renounce all competing loyalties to false gods and powers. Praying to the Father, Christians trust that the creator has made and still sustains them together with all creation, and they trust that God unfailingly does his will. Knowing God the Father as the one, as the almighty one, as the creator and king, Saint Paul expects that (Phil 2) "[10] at the name of Jesus every knee should bend, in heaven and on earth and under the earth, [11] and every tongue should confess that Jesus Christ is Lord, to the glory of God the Father" (cf. Chapter 2.I.3). To summarize it: Prayer to God the *Father* invokes the *one*, the almighty one, the majestic one, the one who adopts his faithful as children and heirs.

The letter to the Ephesians emphasizes the oneness of God; therefore God is the Father of all and through all and in all (Eph 4:4–6). The author gives advice for prayer (Eph 5): "[18] be filled with the Spirit, [19] as you sing Psalms and hymns and spiritual songs among yourselves, singing and making melody to the Lord in your hearts, [20] giving thanks to God the Father at all times and for everything in the name of our Lord Jesus Christ. [21] Be subject to one another out of reverence for Christ." The word in the original Greek text for *thanksgiving* is here the verbal form of the word *Eucharist*. A moral consequence is drawn from the prayer to the Father: The reverence for Christ, in whose name Christians pray to the Father, leads them to reverence for one another. The letter to the Ephesians provides us with an actual prayer to the Father (Eph 3:12–21): "[13] I pray ... I bow my knees before the Father,[15] from whom every family in heaven and on earth takes its name." The word translated here as *family* (πατριά transcribed: *patria* cf. Pater = father) means a *lineage* going back to some progenitor, so that its meaning is also *race* or *tribe*, a *group of families*—all those who in a community lay claim to a common origin. We may especially think of Israel, whose twelve tribes descended from the twelve sons of Jacob. In a broader sense, the word means *nation* or *people*. Hence God, the Father, is here addressed mainly as the one from whom we have our common origin and who guarantees unity. The prayer in Eph 3 continues with: "[16] I pray that, according to the riches of his glory, he may grant that you may be strengthened in your inner being with power through his Spirit, ¹⁷ and that Christ may dwell in your hearts through faith, as you are being rooted and grounded in love. ¹⁸ I pray that you may have the power to comprehend, with all the saints, what is the breadth and length and height and depth, ¹⁹ and to know the love of Christ that surpasses knowledge, so that you may be filled with all the fullness of God. ²⁰ Now to him who by the power at work within us is able to accomplish abundantly far more than all we can ask or imagine, ²¹ to him be glory in the church and in Christ Jesus to all generations, forever and ever. Amen."

In the letter to the Colossians, again thanksgiving—Eucharist—is addressed to the Father (Col 1:11–20). The concept of the cosmic Christ reinterprets the concept of the *Father:* The Father is here the *invisible God,* and God is the Father of Jesus Christ, who is the *image (εἰκών) of the invisible God,* and *the firstborn of all creation,* in whom God is pleased to reconcile all things, whether on earth or in heaven. As Jesus is here called the firstborn of all creation, we shall call upon God the Father in a sense as Jesus' younger sisters and brothers. We invoke God the Father knowing that he is the Father of all creation, revealed in the image of the Son. We find a similar concept of Jesus, the image of God, in Rom 8: God is the Father of "²⁹ those whom he foreknew he also predestined to be conformed to the image of his Son, in order that he might be the firstborn within a large family[4]."

- ### c. The Letters of Saint Peter

In the Letters of Saint Peter, God, the Father, is the "majestic glory" who calls Jesus Christ his "beloved Son" (2 Pet 1:16–17), and therefore the letter gives advice about prayer (1 Pet 1:16–17): "If you invoke as Father the one who judges all people impartially according to their deeds, live in reverent fear during the time of your exile." Hence the meaning of the invocation *father* is here: the *majestic glory* and *impartial judge* who must be feared and revered.

- ### d. The synoptic Gospels

In the Gospels of Matthew, Mark, and Luke, the prayer to the *Father* is connected with various topics. The encouragement to address God as *Father* is based on the teachings about both creation and salvation.

---

4. The word is actually *brothers,* ἀδελφοί.

The *Father* is (Matt 23:9) the one God and (Matt 5:45) the loving creator "who makes his sun rise on the evil and on the good, and sends rain on the righteous and on the unrighteous." The Father is the one (Matt 18:10) before whom the angels intercede on behalf of the little ones; who (Matt 6:26) feeds the birds in the air; (Matt 10:29) who takes care of the sparrows—and (Matt 18:14) it is not the will of the Father in heaven that one of these little ones should be lost.

The Father is (Matt 16:17) the author of supernatural revelation. The Father is (Matt 11:27) revealed by the Son, and the heavenly Father is (Matt 10:32) acknowledged when Christ is acknowledged. This is the reason Jesus invokes his Father (Matt 11:25): "I thank you, Father, Lord of heaven and earth. . . ."

The Father alone (Matt 24:36) knows about the second coming and (Matt 20:23; cf. also Matt 15:13) prepares a place at his side for his people. In the Glory of the Father (Matt 16:27), the Son of Man will come to judge.

Similar to Saint Paul's concept of *adoption* we find in the Gospels (Matt 25:34) the word *Father* connected with the inheritance of the kingdom.

- ### e. *The Johannine writings*

In the Gospel and the Letters of John, we find the concept of God the Father in prominent places. The prologue of the Gospel of John tells about (John 1:1) the eternal birth of God's creating Word, which would (John 1:14) become flesh in Jesus Christ, the only Son of the Father, and (John 1): "[12] all who received him, who believed in his name, he gave power to become children of God." Jesus is the son of God who is close to his father's heart (John 1:18; KJV: *bosom*). Through the keyword *Father*, the prologue of the Gospel of John is linked with the resurrection story, where Jesus says (John 20): "[17b]go to my brothers and say to them, 'I am ascending to my Father and your Father, to my God and your God.'" Hence, the *Father* is the one from whom the Son comes and to whom he returns.

In the First Letter of John, the concept of God the Father indeed seems to have consequences for the concept of the family (1 John 2): "[12] I am writing to you, little children, because your sins are forgiven on account of his name. [13] I am writing to you, fathers, because you know him who is from the beginning. I am writing to you, young people, because you have conquered the evil one. [14] I write to you, children, because you know the Father. I write to you, fathers, because you know him who is from the beginning. I write to you, young people, because you are strong and the word of God abides in you, and you have overcome the evil one." Here in 1 John 2, Christians bear the name of Christ, and thus their sins are forgiven. The various addressees in this portion of the letter—little children, young adults, children, and fathers—are indeed different age groups. The human fathers are addressed as those who know the Son who was from the beginning (cf. John 1:1), hence the authority of fathers is qualified by the reference to the eternal Son of God. The young people are strong through the divine Word, i.e., the Son Jesus Christ, indwelling in them. Fathers and children alike are made children of God through the eternal word of the heavenly Father, the Son of God.

The letter continues: "^{15} Do not love the world or the things in the world. The love of the Father is not in those who love the world; ^{16} for all that is in the world—the desire of the flesh, the desire of the eyes, the pride in riches—comes not from the Father but from the world. ^{17} And the world and its desire are passing away, but those who do the will of God live forever." The 1st Letter of John contrasts the Father's love working within us with the desire of the flesh and with the pride in riches. We are tempted to confound our love for the giver with our craving for his gifts. But by addressing God as Father, the children of God know that they ultimately depend on the eternal creator who makes and rules all temporal things. Hence the address *our Father* is a statement of thanks to God and thus freedom from the world.

In the subsequent discussion, the author gives a warning against those who deny Christ, the Son of God. The meaning of the word *Christ*—in Hebrew *Messiah*—is: the anointed one, i.e. the anointed king (2 Sam 7). 1 John calls his addressees *anointed by the Holy One*, using the same root of the word *anoint:* He is the Christ; we are Christians, i.e., those who belong to Christ. The idea is that we participate in the majesty of Jesus Christ, who is the Son of God and the anointed King. Therefore, being allowed to invoke God the Father, we are honored to be brothers and sisters of the Christ, anointed by God.

The attitude of God's children is *confidence* (1 John 2:28: παρρησία) a specifically Christian word, whose meaning is simplicity, childlike trust, joyous reliance, humble courage, the certitude of being loved (cf. Eph 3:12; Heb 3:6; 4:16; 10:19; 1 John 2:28; 3:21; 5:14).

The following portion of the letter, 1 John 2:29–3:24, connects the idea of our being children of God with the love between brothers and sisters (John 3): "^{1} See what love the Father has given us, that we should be called children of God; and that is what we are." In contrast to Cain, who murdered his brother, the children of God are encouraged (1 John 3): "^{18} Little children, let us love, not in word or speech, but in truth and action."

According to the salutation of the Book of Revelation, Jesus Christ is witness to the Father "who is and who was and who is to come." God is praised as the Father who made us a kingdom and priests (cf: Rev 1:4–6).

- ## *f. Ethical Consequences*

The invocation of God as *Father* has some obvious ethical implications. Through adoption we are made children of God, and this gift involves an obligation to live accordingly; God's Son says (Matt 12): "⁵⁰For whoever does the will of my Father in heaven is my brother and sister and mother" (cf. also Matt 7:21). Life as the adopted children of God is a life of trust in the Father, of obedience to his majesty and of the desire to see our Father honored (Matt 5): "¹⁶ In the same way, let your light shine before others, so that they may see your good works and give glory to your Father in heaven."

Christians are people who are adopted to be children of the heavenly Father, and consequently they are brothers and sisters. The early Christian writer Cyprian (AD 200–258) says (Tr. Vii. 4)[5]: "We say not 'My Father,' but 'Our Father,' for the teacher of peace and master of unity would not have men pray singly and severally, since when any prays, he is not to pray for himself only. Our prayer is general and for all, and when we pray, we pray not for one person, but for us all, because we all are one. So also He willed that one should pray for all, according as Himself in one did bear us all." The mutual forgiveness of the children of God reflects the forgiving love of the heavenly Father (cf. Matt 18). We do not pray to *my* Father—which would be possible only for Jesus—but to *our* Father. Therefore praying to God the Father places us in the family of God. Jesus teaches (Matt 18:19): "¹⁹ Again, truly I tell you, if two of you agree on earth about anything you ask, it will be done for you by my Father in heaven." Brotherly charity compels us to pray together with and for others. The mutual forgiveness of the children of God reflects the forgiving love of the heavenly Father (cf. Matt 18).

The permission to pray to the *Father* is an encouragement to prayer. Being taught and allowed to address God as our *Father*, we have the assurance that God will hear our prayer just as a loving father listens to his children (Matt 7): "¹¹ If you then, who are evil, know how to give good gifts to your children, how much more will your Father in heaven give good things to those who ask him." This teaching of Jesus reminds us at the same time of what a human father on earth is supposed to be.

The prayer to the *Father* is also the solid biblical ground for spiritual exercises. The goal of our sanctification is (Matt 5): "⁴⁸ Be perfect, therefore, as your heavenly Father is perfect." This line in the Sermon on the Mount is immediately followed by Jesus' instructions about alms, prayer and fasting (Matt 6), or—in more general terms—about responsibility for our fellow human beings, prayer and self-discipline. According to church tradition,

---

5. Found in *Catena Aurea*, 1225–74.

the exercises of prayer, fasting, and alms form a discipline observed especially in the season of Lent.[6] Jesus, the son of God, practices and teaches this threefold discipline, and instructs that we should practice our piety in secret, and that our Father, who is in secret and sees in secret, will reward us. God's foremost quality to imitate is his mercy (Luke 6): "[36] Be merciful, just as your Father is merciful" (cf. also Eph 4:32). God, the Father, himself is the ideal to aspire to.

On earth, the perfect image of the Father in heaven is Jesus, who leads our way of perfection. Saint Paul encourages us to follow him (Phil 2): "[5]Let the same mind be in you that was in Christ Jesus" (see part 2.I.3.). We have been created in the image and likeness of God (Gen 2:26) and are now part of a fallen world; we are redeemed and now, as disciples of Jesus, we strive for perfection. This is possible only through the guidance of the Holy Spirit (Gal 5:15), by perpetual repentance and conversion. For at the end of the ages, Jesus promises (Matt 13): "[43] Then the righteous will shine like the sun in the kingdom of their Father." In the chapter about Jesus' prayer in Gethsemane (Matt 26:39; 26:42; 26:53) we will see how Jesus prays to his Father (see part 2.I.2).

THE FIRST PETITION: HALLOWED BE THY NAME

The Lord teaches his disciples to pray, and he teaches them what they are supposed to pray for—the content of Christian prayer. The question of "Why do people pray?" will be discussed in more detail in chapter 2.III.1.

The Lord teaches *what* to pray. The Lord's Prayer consists of seven petitions. The first three petitions (*you*-petitions) are about God, followed by four petitions (*we*-petitions) about our own needs.[7] With the Lord's Prayer, we first pray for God's name to be hallowed, for God's kingdom to come, and for God's will to be done. These first three petitions of the Lord's Prayer are prayed for God's sake and only indirectly for our own good. With the following four petitions for our own needs we profess God's generous love. Praying that the name of the Father shall be hallowed, we refer to God's unchangeable qualities.

---

6. See Part 3, VI of this book.

7. This structure reminds of the ten commandments, which were written (Exod 24:12 and 34:1) on two tablets. Church tradition, guided by Jesus' twofold commandment to love God and our neighbor (Matt 22:37-40), has divided the ten commandments into two parts, so that the first tablet speaks about God and the second about our neighbors.

a. God's Name

In the Old Testament, the proper name of God is Yhwh (in Hebrew letters יהוה); the vowels are unknown. Our English translations usually read LORD[8] when the Hebrew Bible reads the four letters of the *name*.

In the Old Testament, a name is not just a random label but often tells something about the bearer of the name. The meaning of Bethel (Beth-El), for example, is *house of God*. The meaning of Abraham is *a father of many*; Jacob is *the deceiver*; Israel is *a fighter of God*—actually against God (cf. Gen 32)! In the Old Testament we already find an interpretation of God's name (Exod 3): "¹⁴ God said to Moses, "I am who I am." He said further, "Thus you shall say to the Israelites, 'I am has sent me to you.'" Most scholars agree that the name indeed derives from some form of the verb for *to be* (היה). The Greek version of the Old Testament has translated the name as "the being (ἐγώ εἰμι ὁ ὤν)." Modern scholars agree that this translation is philologically and historically not convincing. However, only the Greek version of the Old Testament was used by the Christians in the time of the New Testament; and the New Testament adopts exactly this terminology (Rev 1:4): "John to the seven churches that are in Asia: Grace to you and peace from him who is [literally: the being = ὁ ὤν] and who was and who is to come, and from the seven spirits who are before his throne." So it is in Rev 1:8; 4:8; 11:17; 16:5. This name of God, *the being*, is perhaps the background of the seven *I am* words in the Gospel of John.[9]

God has made known his name in special historic revelations to Moses (Gen 3) and to the people of Israel in the thunderstorm on Mount Sinai (Exod 20:2-7; Deut 5:6-11). According to Gen 4, however, the name of the Lord had already been invoked in prehistory: "²⁶ To Seth also a son was born, and he named him Enosh. At that time people began to invoke the name of the LORD." Since the meaning of the word Enosh is just *man*, this ancient tradition perhaps supposes that the invocation of the Lord's holy name belongs to the essence of humanity, which was, however, declining until the days of Noah.

---

8. To avoid the misuse of the *name*, pious Jews, instead of pronouncing the *name*, read instead *Adonai*, which means *My Lord*. The marks for the vowels, provided later on to aid in reading the Hebrew text, are actually meant for the word *Adonai*, not for the four letters of the *name*. Consistent with this practice, the Greek version of the Old Testament, the Septuagint = LXX, always reads *Lord*. In some modern translations, the representation of the *name* (LORD =יהוה) is printed in capitals (LORD) in order to distinguish it from the from the usual noun.

9. The Book of Revelation uses the nominative of *the being* without proper declension (*Rev* 1:4 ἀπὸ ὁ ὤν), thus showing that it was perceived as a proper name.

b. God's Name is Holy

The ten commandments say (Exod 20): "⁷ You shall not make wrongful use of the name of the LORD your God, for the LORD will not acquit anyone who misuses his name." God's name is unchangeably holy in itself, but our use of the name is not; for this reason we need to be taught to pray for the holiness of God's name.

The meaning of *holy* is: set apart, pure, immaculate, clean. God's name is holy already, is always holy by nature, and not only because we try to hallow the name, always falling short of God's glory. This *is* actually the very meaning of God's holiness: God does not depend on anything, and he does not serve anyone's purpose or relevance, but He *is* the ultimate purpose. God's holy name is the greatest treasure in heaven and on earth and the most precious good. God's name is holy already. In teaching us this petition, Jesus wants us to realize and to acknowledge that God's name is holy. We pray that the name may be regarded as holy and sublime amongst us, as the greatest treasure on earth (cf. Luther, Large Catechism).

God is holy *in* himself, but God is holy not just *for* himself; he is holiness for us. Speaking about the Holy God, we speak about him who creates and sustains, saves and sanctifies, because he is love and he loves. In Moses' song (Deut 32) the praise of God's name (verse 3) is at the same time the nurturing word for his people; Moses says: "² May my teaching drop like the rain, my speech condense like the dew; like gentle rain on grass, like showers on new growth. ³ For (כי אקרא) I will proclaim the name of the LORD; ascribe greatness to our God!" Therefore she or he who invokes the holy name of the Lord says a word that at the same time helps and consoles, like dew on arid land.

Each person who is aware of his or her need of God prays for the help of a great God who is the source of all help and consolation. God has given us the Psalms, and together with this guidance to invoke him, we have also received God's promise that we will be heard, so that we can say (Ps 45): "¹⁷ I will cause your name to be celebrated in all generations; therefore the peoples will praise you forever and ever."

c. God's Presence in His Name

The *name of God* (שם) is the core of God's revelation (Exod 3 and 20; Deut 5). In the Bible, similar to God's *glory* (כבוד, cf. Isa 6:3; Ezek 8:4; 9:3; 11:22), the *name* is God's merciful presence on earth, especially in the sanctuary, meaning the presence on earth of him who is in heaven. Because the *name* is the heavenly God's presence on earth, the name offers God's accessibility in prayer. King Solomon, when dedicating the temple in Jerusalem, prays (1 Kgs 8): "[28] Regard your servant's prayer and his plea, O LORD my God, heeding the cry and the prayer that your servant prays to you today; [29] that your eyes may be open night and day toward this house, *the place of which you said, 'My name shall be there*,'[10] that you may heed the prayer that your servant prays toward this place."

For Christians, the presence of God is of course Jesus Christ, whose name is above all names (Phil 2:9).

d. God's Holy Name in the Prayers of the Bible

The Bible describes many ways to hallow God's holy name. The most obvious is the splendor of worship (Psalm 29): "[2] Ascribe to the LORD the glory of his name; worship the LORD in holy splendor." Ps 96 speaks of the "beauty of holiness" (Psalm 96:9 KJV). The praise of God's glory involves the soul and the inmost self in worship (Ps 103): "[2] Bless the LORD, O my soul, and all that is within me, bless his holy name." A glorious worship service will necessarily have its effect on everyday life (Ps 96): "[2] Sing to the LORD, bless his name; tell of his salvation from day to day."

Praying for the holiness of God's name, we acknowledge God's oneness and uniqueness (Ps 83): "[18] Let them know that you alone, whose name is the LORD, are the Most High over all the earth." We acknowledge God's majesty (Ps 8): "[1] O LORD, our Sovereign, how majestic is your name in all the earth! You have set your glory above the heavens.... [9] O LORD, our Sovereign, how majestic is your name in all the earth!" God's holiness is exclusive, i.e., his name alone is to be hallowed (Rev 15): "[4] Lord, who will not fear and glorify your name? For you alone are holy. All nations will come and worship before you, for your judgments have been revealed." Therefore the holiness of God's name inspires our humility (Ps 115): "[1] Not to us, O LORD, not to us, but to your name give glory, for the sake of your steadfast love and your faithfulness." The holiness of God's name fills the faithful with rejoicing (Ps 97:12) and gladness (Ps 33:21).

Acknowledging God's majesty, we sing praises to the Most High with our mouths (Ps 92:1; Ps 146), give thanks and glorify his name with our hearts (Ps 86:12), and bring offerings with our body (Ps 96). *We* exalt God's name because *he* has exalted his name (Ps 138): "[1] I give you thanks, O LORD, with my whole heart; before the gods I sing your praise; [2] I bow down toward your holy temple and give thanks to your name for your steadfast

---

10. המקום אשר אמרת יהיה שמי שם.

love and your faithfulness; for you have exalted your name and your word above everything."

We hallow God's name by commemorating his great deeds (Luke 1): "[49] for the Mighty One has done great things for me, and holy is his name." God did not only do a few sporadic acts of mercy at particular times for a few individuals. We invoke the name of him who is the Lord of the covenant which he has made with his people (Ps 111): "[9] He sent redemption to his people; he has commanded his covenant forever. Holy and awesome is his name." This God who is mighty to help, who is the faithful God of the covenant, is the creator of heaven and earth (Ps 124): "[8] Our help is in the name of the LORD, who made heaven and earth." Again and again, the Psalms connect God's holy name with the eternity of God's majesty and his faithfulness (Ps 102): "[12] But you, O LORD, are enthroned forever; your name endures to all generations." Accordingly, God's people want to be faithful in praising God's name (Ps 145): "[2] Every day I will bless you, and praise your name forever and ever." So it is in Ps 135: "[13] Your name, O LORD, endures forever, your renown, O LORD, throughout all ages;" and Ps 45 says: "[17] I will cause your name to be celebrated in all generations; therefore the peoples will praise you forever and ever." God's name is eternal and his glory is omnipresent. Hence the faithful pray (Ps 72): "[19] Blessed be his glorious name forever; may his glory fill the whole earth. Amen and Amen." (Ps 48): "[10] Your name, O God, like your praise, reaches to the ends of the earth. Your right hand is filled with victory." (cf. Also Ps 113).

The holiness of God's name also means that God's name is famous. God has revealed himself to his people (Ps 76): "[1] In Judah God is known, his name is great in Israel." Still, when praying *hallowed be thy name* we pray that his revelation is brought to all. The prophet encourages the congregation of the faithful (Isa 12): "[4] And you will say in that day: Give thanks to the LORD, call on his name; make known his deeds among the nations; proclaim that his name is exalted."

The faithful pray for themselves (Ps 79): "[9] Help us, O God of our salvation, for the glory of your name; deliver us, and forgive our sins, for your name's sake." But in appealing to God's holy name, the faithful also make intercession on behalf of all people in need (Ps 74): "[21] Do not let the downtrodden be put to shame; let the poor and needy praise your name."

It is God's honor to be a helper and redeemer. For this reason we acknowledge God's majesty, his power, and his will to sustain when we invoke his name and cry for help (Ps 116): "[4] Then I called on the name of the LORD: 'O LORD, I pray, save my life!'" We hallow God's name by praying for his help. The holiness of God's name is a blessing for those to whom God's name is proclaimed (Ps 20): "[1] The LORD answer you in the day of trouble! The name of the God of Jacob protect you!" cf. also Ps 118: "²⁶ Blessed is the one who comes in the name of the LORD. We bless you from the house of the LORD."

e. God's Holy Name and our Human Nature

No matter how we theologically understand that God is both just and merciful, both holy and loving—which is a whole other discussion—our reverence for God's holy name must correlate with our trust in God's love: We shall both fear and love God. God's power has created and sustains the whole world, and he loves the undeserving sinners. Therefore the heavenly Father is not just our daddy, and Jesus is not just our buddy. God deserves awe, respect, and veneration.

By revealing his name, God makes himself accessible to prayer. It is also true that the name of God, which we hallow in our prayers, is of frightening splendor—sublime, above everyday life, detached from the ordinary. In the book of Revelation we read about Jesus coming as the horseman on the white horse (Rev 19): "¹² His eyes are like a flame of fire, and on his head are many diadems; and he has a name inscribed that no one knows but himself. ¹³ He is clothed in a robe dipped in blood, and his name is called The Word of God."[11] We approach him whose name is grand and glorious, frightening and formidable more than we can imagine, whom we must never confuse with matters of this world.

Alas, since the fall of humanity we do not have, by nature, an attitude that would lead us to hallow God's name. We don't know much in our times about holiness or sanctity. Some pompousness might be experienced once in a while. But nearly everything has been desecrated. Breaking taboos is no longer an exciting challenge for artists and thinkers. In everyday life we rarely feel recognition and appreciation for outstanding persons, let alone awe and admiration. The great qualities or merits of exceptional men and women are perceived with suspicion, and the media are quick to doubt, if not to ridicule, grandeur. Marvels of nature or works of art are no longer valued for their own sake, but are appraised for their usefulness, their price on the market, even just for their material value. When in 2013 a Henry Moore sculpture was stolen by metal thieves, a newspaper headlined the story: "Jail for pair who stole £500,000 sculpture and sold it to scrap dealer

---

11. Cf. John 1. In Rev 19 the rider on the white horse is certainly Jesus Christ, king of kings, Lord of lords. This horseman is probably not identical with the apocalyptic horseman in Rev 6, who is perhaps a representation of the antichrist; however, there is controversy about this.

for ... £ 46." One wonders if jail and journalists are able to teach appreciation for the arts. Admiration is no longer an accepted attitude in our society; awe, adoration, and submission to the divine even less.

To learn respect for persons, arts, and nature once again, we need to build up culture. To learn the awe of God, we need the teaching of Christ. Hallowing God's name is no longer what our corrupted nature does. For this reason, Jesus must teach his disciples to pray: *hallowed be thy name.*

It remains true that human beings have a desire to respect and to admire; children, especially, want to believe in their parents and teachers. We need someone to look up to. The inherent reason is that we are created by God and for God. Human nature has an innate longing for the awe of God's infinite mystery. This is the reason we pray, *hallowed be thy name.* Awe is the origin and goal of human existence. Kneeling in awe and adoration to God makes a healthy and thriving life possible. A healthy life is a life that can praise. We need to know awe and adoration to have a healthy life, to be a complete and whole person.

But the paradox is that hallowing God's name is not about us. On the contrary, adoring God, hallowing God's name, means to dedicate ourselves to God alone. It means to forget about ourselves. To pray *hallowed be ...* means to pray for what God desires. It is when we pray oblivious to our own selves that this prayer, paradoxically, heals our souls. For this reason the savior reminds us what our sinful heart had forgotten: *Hallowed be thy name.*

It is impossible to fully understand God's qualities. When Jesus advised his disciples to pray for the Father's name to be hallowed, he taught them to maintain an attitude of expectation for more grandeur to be revealed. We turn to God, who exceeds all our understanding.

There would be a revolution in church and in society if we realized what this prayer means. It would be a revolution if we thought first of God's desires and only then of our own wants. Our desire for God can be fulfilled only if we forget about all desires and stand in awe before God's majesty.

f. God's name is to be hallowed

How do we hallow God's name? First, we need the right understanding and teaching about God; second, we need a life that honors God's name. In short: sound doctrine and holy life.

- *Doctrine*

The *name* is the core of God's revelation. To "hallow" God's name means to acknowledge that the one holy God reveals himself among humankind. Praying *hallowed be thy name* means: *We acknowledge that God has made himself known among us.* We ask God that he may stand up for his name, his justice and mercy.

When we want God's name to be hallowed, we want the truth to be told about God. Perhaps it's helpful to draw an analogy from human relationships: We want people to speak well about our spouse, parents or children. We want our loved ones to be praised and applauded; we want them to be recognized for what they really are. Children want to be proud of their parents, want to tell their schoolmates how great their parents are; they want to take pride in the abilities and deeds of their parents. Accordingly, we hallow God's name when we know and teach the truth about God. We pray that God's name will be hallowed in all the world.

Lots of inappropriate ideas are out there about God. Many people think of God as if he was just a nice guy, our daddy, and Jesus some buddy, and so they ignore God's power and majesty. Others speak about God as if he was a tyrant who demands obedience without mercy, so they ignore God's love. Still others think about God as if he was ever changing and adjusting to our wants and wishes, so they ignore God's eternity. Many more wrong ideas can easily be found. But hallowing God's name means to have a sound understanding; to believe, teach and profess a God who has revealed himself in Jesus Christ.

Therefore we hallow God's name by speaking about his qualities and deeds. We need to tell the truth about God. We need to speak about God's infinite power to sustain, about his eternity and faithfulness, his knowledge about everything and his willingness to help, about his love, about his righteousness, about his presence in Jesus Christ and his merciful support in the Holy Spirit. Praying *hallowed be . . .*, we pray that all the world will know and acknowledge, praise and proclaim who he is and what he does.

- *Daily Life*

In the laws of the Old Testament, the commandments are often concluded with the phrase (Lev 18): "I am the LORD your God." The word *LORD* of course represents the *Name*. This phrase proclaims the majesty of the lawgiver. It is beyond the scope of this book to engage the question of to what extent the Old Testament law is relevant for Christians. But it is still true that, with the prayer for the holiness of God's name, we pledge our loyalty to God, the creator and king, judge and savior.

The church father Cyprian, bishop of Carthage († 258), writes: "For this we daily make petition, since we need a daily sanctification, in order that we who sin day by day, may cleanse afresh our offences by a continual sanctification."[12] We pray that God may be glorified in our life. We pray that God may make us live in such a way that through us his name will be glorified. With this prayer we also pledge to shape our whole life, our thoughts, words and deeds in accordance with God's Holy Name. We ask that God's Holy Name may not be blasphemed because of us, but glorified and praised—and this not only in the celebration of our worship, when we kneel before God's majesty, in praising, praying and preaching. We ask that God's Holy Name may be hallowed by our daily life: by love for our neighbors, by working for others, by standing up for peace and justice, so that God's Name will be known on earth (Matt 5): "[16] let your light shine before others, so that they may see your good works and give glory to your Father in heaven."

Christians want to live for the glory of God. This is the main motivation for their lives, that their lives should hallow God's name. To live a Christian life does not just mean that we try to avoid sin, try to obey some commandments—and consequently judge others who fail to do so. That would be quite boring teaching. No, Christians pray that God's name will be hallowed through their lives, that they will live to honor God, to make their everyday life a praise to God. Christians do not seek their own glory but want to magnify the Lord (Ps 115): "[1] Not unto us, O LORD, not unto us, But to Your name give glory, Because of Your mercy, Because of Your truth." Martin Luther writes in his Large Catechism: "For since in this prayer we call God our Father, it is our duty always to deport and demean ourselves as godly children, that He may not receive shame, but honor and praise from us."

It also needs to be emphasized that the human race is made in God's image (Gen 1:26). Therefore God does not want to be glorified at the expense of human dignity. Rather, God is honored by our respect for our fellow humans, God's image.

---

12. Cyprian, *Treatise 4*, 183.

THE SECOND PETITION: THY KINGDOM COME

Introduction

Matthew summarizes Jesus' teaching (Matt 4) this way: "¹⁷ From that time Jesus began to proclaim, 'Repent, for the kingdom of heaven has come near'."[13] This summary is repeated in Matt 4:23 and 9:35. When Jesus sent out his disciples he told them (Matt 10): "As you go, proclaim the good news, 'The kingdom of heaven has come near'." When the church prays *your kingdom come,* its members answer Jesus' call. In the Gospels, we read often of Jesus' teaching about the kingdom: the term occurs more than forty times alone in the Gospel of Matthew. Because Jesus speaks about the *coming* of the kingdom, the term doesn't mean so much a territory as simply *God's rule.* It is also certain that the kingdom is not some kind of moral or political new world to be built by humanity. This petition is a prayer to God, and the word *come* suggests that an act of God's sovereignty is expected.

In the Gospel of Matthew, the Lord's Prayer is part of the Sermon on the Mount, which begins with the beatitudes in Matt 5. To understand the *kingdom* in the Lord's Prayer, it's helpful to look closely at that term as it appears in the beatitudes. In the shorter version, in the Gospel according to Luke (6:20–22), the *kingdom* is promised to the *poor.* The Greek word used here for *poor* is the strongest possible word, and it means the economically and socially destitute. An illustration for the beatitude is perhaps the parable of the rich man and poor Lazarus, which in the Gospel of Luke follows the announcement of the kingdom (Luke 16:16). Hence the prayer for the kingdom to come kindles both hope and patience in the poor and warns the well-to-do that their superiority will end and that justice will be done eventually. Whenever we pray the Lord's Prayer, we are on the side of the poor.

In the Gospel of Matthew, Jesus says: "Blessed are the poor in spirit, for theirs is the kingdom of heaven." Because the meaning of *poor* is usually *materially poor,* the addition *in spirit* is somewhat unexpected. In the history of the church, this verse has been understood in various ways, mostly as *humility,* or as a *distant attitude towards wealth.* Next to this interpretation, the idea of voluntary poverty was of great importance in the course of

---

13. According to Matthew, this message continues the preaching of John the Baptist (3:2).

history;[14] the beatitude was important in the history of monasticism.[15] The prayer for the kingdom to come is therefore an exercise of humility shaping our attitude towards earthly possessions.

a. The "kingdom"

The term *kingdom of God* or the synonym *kingdom of heaven* is rare in the time before the New Testament. However, the phrase *kingdom of God* is likely a short form for *The Lord is King!* (cf. Ps 47). God's people profess, proclaim, and celebrate the Lord as *king*.

In the era before Israel's exile, Isa 6 speaks about a heavenly realm with a royal court of angelic beings (cf. Ps 103). God is both present in the temple (1 Kgs 8, Isa 6, cf. Gen 28) and celebrated as the king of creation; appropriate prayers are the enthronement Psalms: Pss 47, 93, and 95-99. According to Ps 99, God is enthroned in the heavenly court; he is strong, he gives law and justice in Israel, and he guarantees the world order. His name is worshipped by the priests on the holy mountain.

God is king by his saving deeds in history; appropriate prayers are found in Exod 15; Pss 44; 145; 146. The Lord is also the king of creation—the second part of Isaiah (40-55), written for God's people in exile, confesses and teaches about God as the almighty and eternal ruler of all the earth. It connects the concept of God as the almighty creator with that of God as the savior of his people: The Lord is the one and only God and king; he is now and always was ruling all things, but he is not yet acknowledged everywhere. The prophet mixes proclamation, prayer, and meditation in Isa 45:15-25, asserting that the saving deeds for Israel that God is about to carry out will gain universal acknowledgment soon.

According to Dan 7, God's kingdom is yet to be established; still, Daniel leaves no doubt that God remains in control of events on earth. In Jewish Apocalyptic writings, *the kingdom of God* is rarely mentioned. In turn, the

---

14. *Poor* could mean literally poor or metaphorically poor. *Spirit* could refer to the Holy Spirit or to the human spirit. The grammatical form (dative case), usually translated with the preposition *In*, can also have the meaning *by, with, through* (instrumental dative, more specifically: dative of agency), or the dative could have the meaning *in regard to* (dative of respect or specification). Hence, there are a variety of possibilities: If the dative is an instrumental dative, *poor* still means *materially poor*. Both the human spirit or the Holy Spirit could motivate voluntary poverty. If the dative is a dative of specification, the spirit is hardly the Holy Spirit. The addition, *in spirit* would then refer to the human spirit and, as a consequence, qualify the word *poor*. The meaning of *poor in spirit* is then *disheartened* and *desperate*, or, more as a virtue, *humble* and *simple*.

15. For example, in *The Conferences* by St. John Cassian († 298). Conference 10, = The second conference of abbot Isaac. on prayer., chapter 11.

writings of the apocalyptic literature typically present historical reviews of the successive kingdoms, but those are not found in the New Testament, including the Book of Revelation (!). So framing an interpretation of the *kingdom* within the framework of Apocalypticism seems incorrect.

Rabbinic Judaism expected a new "Son of David," a kingdom of peace, and reestablishment of the law (cf. The Kaddish and the Standing Prayer, also called the *Shmoneh Esreh,* The Eighteen Petitions).

Whether Jesus spoke of a future or present kingdom is a subject for hot discussion, but that becomes a less crucial question when we realize that in the New Testament, the ways of speaking about the kingdom take the form of a call to repentance and of prayer. On the surface, the wording of any petition seems to expect some event that has not happened yet and expects God's action soon, like giving us bread today. Still, prayer makes sense only when we believe that God is in power now and not in some vague near or distant future. The worshipper expects God to be in control *now* (cf. 2.III.3. Excursus *God and Time*). A devout person will not accept that God's name can be blasphemed for the time being until it will be hallowed someday; a believer cannot assume that God almighty is not yet doing his will; a sinner does not want to live with his/her guilt until it will be forgiven in some future time; a young Christian does not play around with temptations until they cease to be appealing; no God-fearing man or woman wants evil to have dominion for a while; and the hungry man needs bread *this day.* We recite the petitions of the Lord's Prayer—as we do any prayer—because God is the ruling King of creation; was, is now, and ever shall be. Any petition professes God's sovereignty. And prayer does not necessarily presuppose that God is not doing his will unless we pray for it.

The prayer for the kingdom is an answer to Jesus' teaching about the kingdom. The kingdom parables in Matt 13 employ a variety of metaphors. However, the images have some traits in common. In all parables the kingdom is given by God, not made by humans; it has always existed and is as yet in secret. These traits are obvious in the parables of growth. In the parable of the wheat and the tares, the kingdom grows right now. The wheat is, for the time being, inseparable from the weeds, and it grows without human assistance. The yeast is already there but is hidden in the flour, and the dough grows on its own. The mustard seed is already sprouting, even though very small, and again it is growing on its own. In the next parables, the parable of the treasure found in the field and the pearl discovered by the merchant, the kingdom presents itself as a surprise, revealing that it has always been available but hidden. The parable about the fishing net probably speaks about the final judgment. However the imagery shows again that the kingdom already exists and just needs to be caught; the good fish are hidden first in the deep water, then among the bad fish, and of course the fishers do not produce the fish but merely catch them. Hence the prayer for the kingdom to come hopes for the already existing kingdom to grow among us—or to be found or caught.

Throughout the ages it has been the experience of any meditating person to wait, watch, and pray, and then still to be surprised by what was always there. The prayer for the kingdom expresses the individual's hope of finding the kingdom but also hope for a greater good that surpasses the desires of any individual.

b. *The King's People*

In the time before Israel's exile, God in heaven had a human king on earth ruling his people. The dynasty of King David and his sons was meant to last forever (2 Sam 7). In the historic context of the Old Testament, several Psalms, like Pss 2, 20 and 110, pray about this king on earth. After the kingdoms of Israel and Judah ended in political and military disaster, the word *kingdom* summed up all the hopes of God's people for a new king to come. The coming kingdom was part of Jewish prayers, especially The Eighteen Petitions (see above), which prayed for God to come to judge and destroy the heretics. These latter petitions, however, are omitted in Jesus' prayer. Therefore, nationalism, segregation, and destruction are not part of the *Our Father*. The disciples are sent to *all peoples* (Matt 28) to baptize and to teach.

The kingdom of God is materializing when Jesus calls his disciples. He does not organize a secret society, a special interest group, a political party or a private religious club; his call aims at the conversion of all. The kingdom is being established by the conversion of individuals and their lifelong commitment. Jesus appointed and sent the twelve *apostles,* meaning *those who are sent* (Mark 3:13-14). They are the recipients of the original message of Easter (1 Cor 15:3-5). In Matt 19:28, this group of the twelve disciples is explicitly correlated with the twelve tribes of Israel. Hence the new kingdom is, in a sense, the new twelve-tribe nation, the people of God, but it is no longer established through the bloodline of the twelve patriarchs but by the message spread by the twelve messengers of Jesus. In Luke 12:32, they are called a flock; in Mark 3:34-35, a family. Both terms refer to imagery for God's people in the Old Testament.

Therefore, when praying for God's kingdom, we pray for a common good and for a community that surpasses our individual lives and the lives of our nuclear families. As Christians we have a heavenly citizenship (Phil 3:20: πολίτευμα), and we are members of a body (Rom 12:5; 1 Cor 12:12-31;

Eph 1:21–22; 3:6; 4:6–16; 5:23; Col 1:18). Through the Eucharist we participate in the body of Christ (1 Cor 10:16,17). We have a relationship with the king by praying for his kingdom; in other words, by participating in the community of the king's people. In praying for God's kingdom to come, we remind ourselves that we are part of a large community, ultimately of the world, which is loved by God (John 3:16). We pray that we may abide in the kingdom and daily grow into its community; and we pray as well that the kingdom may gain acceptance among other people and proceed with power throughout the world. We pray that many may be led into the kingdom by the Holy Spirit so that we all remain together, forever, in the one kingdom which has now begun, and that *of this kingdom there will be no end* (cf. Luke 1:33).

The kingdom begins to materialize when Jesus bestows His Holy Spirit through word and sacrament. So we pray that the heavenly Father may give his word to us and throughout the world. We pray that it will be received in faith, and that it will work in us so that through God's Word and the power of the Holy Spirit, God's kingdom may prevail among us.[16] In Saint Paul's statement that the kingdom of God is *justice and peace and joy in the Holy Spirit* (Rom 14:17), the words *justice* and *peace* speak about the righteousness before God and peace with God (see below) of individuals. These words also suggest an organized people.

The growth of God's kingdom is not identical with the progress of culture and a just society (as the Catholic catechism rightfully states, CCC 2820), but it is precisely because Christians are adopted as citizens of God's eternal kingdom that they are called to get involved in working for peace and justice in this world.

In a sense, the kingdom is Christ Himself. We are baptized into him (Gal 3:27; Rom 6:3); we are members of his body; we suffer together with him; we pray and work together with him. Jesus Christ is the resurrection and the life (John 11:25), and we will rise from death united with him (cf. Rom 6). Accordingly, Jesus Christ, the anointed king, may be called the kingdom of God.

c. *The People's King*

In the time of the Old Testament, God ruled in Israel through a king, a descendant of King David, called *Messiah*, which means the one anointed to be king. *Christ* is the Greek word for Messiah, the anointed one, the King.

---

16. Cf. Stjerna, *Large Catechism of Dr. Martin Luther*, about the second petition of the Lord's Prayer.

In the New Testament his disciples professed Jesus as *Son of David* and as Messiah (= *Christ*, Matt 16:16). Saint Paul, speaking about the risen Christ, teaches that he is at the right hand of God and intercedes for us (Rom 8:34), and because of him God answers our prayers.

In prayer we wait for him *who is, who was and who is to come* (Rev 1:8). In prayer we await his second coming, his *advent in glory* (cf. Mark 13; Luke 21:34–36), and we wait for the second coming by recalling his first coming: He who is to come is the same Jesus who was hailed at the gates of Jerusalem and nailed to the cross on Golgotha; he who is to come is the same Jesus whom we know as the one who heals the sick, feeds the hungry, welcomes outsiders. Waiting for the second coming, we pray for the visible coming of him who is king already and whose kingdom will never end (Luke 1:33).

With this faith of the New Testament, the faith in an eternal kingship, it is consistent that biblical prayers again and again invoke God's providential rule (Ps 10): "^{16} The LORD is king forever and ever." Through his word, God rules on earth (Ps 147:15). We pray for the coming of him who is already king. Therefore, the prayer for God's kingdom to come involves two things. First, we pray for the final revelation, when Jesus will come again visibly so that all will realize that he is the Lord of heaven and earth and has always been. Second, we pray that he comes to us in word and faith, so that we believe and trust in him to whom all power in heaven and on earth is given (Matt 28). Saint Augustine writes about the second petition of the Lord's Prayer (Serm. In Mont. ii, 6): "This is not so said as though God did not now reign on earth, or had not reigned over it always. 'Come,' must therefore be taken for 'be manifested to men.' For none shall then be ignorant of His kingdom, when His Only-Begotten, not in understanding only, but in visible shape shall come to judge the quick and dead. This day of judgment the Lord teaches shall then come, when the Gospel shall have been preached to all nations."[17]

In this present time, the kingdom comes near in Jesus, who here and now calls us to faith and watchfulness, who is present in word and sacrament, and in the communion the faithful have in prayer (Matt 18:20). The faithful who continue Jesus' work of feeding the hungry and healing the sick, of laboring and suffering for the justice for all, reveal a faint glimmer of the kingdom's splendor, yet to be fully revealed.

Just as the name of God is in itself holy without our hallowing it, so his kingdom comes by itself, without our work and even without our prayer.

---

17. *Catena Aurea*, Caput 6, Lectio 5: "'Adveniat' ergo accipiendum est ut 'manifestetur hominibus'."

Still we pray that it may come to us, meaning we pray so that we are among those who have already accepted His kingdom. Saint Augustine writes (Epist. 130, 11): "For the kingdom of God will come whether we desire it or not. But herein we kindle our desires towards that kingdom, that it may come to us, and that we may reign in it."[18]

d. *Justice and peace and joy in the Holy Spirit*

Saint Paul rarely speaks of the *kingdom of God*. His understanding of the term is not necessarily the same as in Matthew and Luke. Hence we have to expect different aspects of the *kingdom* when we refer to Saint Paul to understand this petition of the Lord's Prayer. Saint Paul writes (Rom 14:17): "The kingdom of God is not food and drink but righteousness and peace and joy in the Holy Spirit." Saint Paul's sentence sounds almost like a definition. If Saint Paul quotes here a statement that had previously been used in a different context, it was probably one advising against gluttony.

For Saint Paul, the meaning is more subtle; here, the kingdom of God being proclaimed doesn't refer to external things, but rather to an inner kingdom in our souls. This concept is consistent with contemporary Stoic philosophy. Epictetus distinguishes: "Some things are under our control, (τὰ μὲν ἐστιν ἐφ' ἡμῖν) while others are not under our control (τὰ δὲ οὐκ ἐφ' ἡμῖν). What is under our control are conception, choice, desire, aversion—in a word, everything that is our own doing. What is not under our control includes our body, our property, reputation, office—in a word, everything that is not our own doing."[19] For Saint Paul, the kingdom is a matter of inner attitudes, not of external circumstances.

This distinction determines Saint Paul's position towards the Jewish ritual law (Rom 14): "[14] nothing is [ritually] unclean in itself, but it is unclean for anyone who thinks it unclean," i.e., we make a distinction between clean and unclean food as a mental concept, but it isn't about the qualities of the things themselves. Saint Paul, the former Pharisee, was certainly aware of the consequences. Now, some believers would argue that therefore the distinction the Old Testament law makes between clean and unclean food is obsolete. – Saint Paul is addressing those people, and he basically agrees with them; but he also reproaches them for scandalizing those brothers and sisters who are still concerned about unclean food. By insisting on the truth that *nothing is unclean in itself* they offend their brothers whose truthfulness

---

18. *Catena Aurea*, Caput 6, Lectio 5: "*desiderium nostrum ad illud regnum excitamus, ut nobis veniat.*"

19. Epictetus, *Encheiridion I*.

is just as valid, because for them some things are unclean indeed—if they think they are unclean. Saint Paul teaches that insisting on the truth that *nothing is unclean in itself* violates the love among Christians. This presupposition underlies his statement about the kingdom in response to this practical dispute in the church (Rom 14): "[17] The kingdom of God is not food and drink but righteousness and peace and joy in the Holy Spirit." By invoking the *kingdom* in the context of this discussion, Saint Paul reminds his listeners of the central role of brotherly love and peace in the church to settle the dispute.

This means that when we pray for the kingdom, we are asking for justice and peace among our brothers and sisters in the church, and for shared joy. Those things that make the kingdom of God, as described in Rom 14, Saint Paul elsewhere calls *fruit of the Spirit* (Gal 5:22–23): "the fruit of the Spirit is love, joy, peace, patience, kindness, generosity, faithfulness, gentleness, and self-control. There is no law against such things."

In Romans, Saint Paul speaks about the righteousness granted by God. However, other parts of the New Testament indeed speak about corrective justice. This corrective justice is not necessarily what our sinful heart wants to suffer, even though we tend to demand punishment for other people. And yet we pray for the fulfillment of the human need and hope for justice. Saint John had a vision of the martyrs under the altar who pray (Rev 6:10): "[10] Sovereign Lord, holy and true, how long will it be before you judge and avenge our blood on the inhabitants of the earth?" We are perhaps scandalized by those words, which sound like a call for revenge. But before we judge these words, we must consider that we ourselves will be judged. When we pray for God's kingdom to come, we must be aware that we ourselves are perhaps the ones who hinder God's kingdom from coming, who withhold justice from the poor, who cause pain to God's creation, who through our lifestyle cause harm and suffering so that now other people long for justice. Whenever we pray the Psalms and come across words about justice, revenge, and enemies, we need to remember that we ourselves are perhaps the enemies of God's kingdom. Hence, justice is not necessarily what our corrupted nature covets, but it is what we need. Praying for God's kingdom to come, we pray against our sinful hearts' desire. Our prayer for the kingdom must lead us to repentance.

e. Service

Praying for the kingdom, we remind ourselves that we are called to be servants of the king. The kingdom is not human-made, but *comes,* and we are servants of the king. With the prayer for God's kingdom to come, we report for service. The hope for the final revelation of God's kingdom makes us go into this world to serve (Titus 2): "[11] For the grace of God has appeared, bringing salvation to all, [12] training us to renounce impiety and worldly passions, and in the present age to live lives that are self-controlled, upright, and godly, [13] while we wait for the blessed hope and the manifestation of the glory of our great God and Savior, Jesus Christ."

On Pentecost, God has poured out the Holy Spirit; hence we are already holy, and we are supposed to persevere in that holiness unto the end. This holiness, however, does not mean that we are already perfect; we still have to fight sin and death, and strive for perfection. The prayer for the kingdom is a prayer for the kingdom to come into each of us, a prayer that God may reign in our hearts.

The prayer for God's kingdom kindles in us the desire for the mortification of the flesh. In a society focused on consumerism and the immediate satisfaction of wants, the prayer for God's kingdom gains us freedom from avidity and fear. Saint Paul writes (Gal 5): "[16] Live by the Spirit, I say, and do not gratify the desires of the flesh." We pray that we may be purified from all selfishness and corruption, and serve God's kingdom.

Waiting and fighting, serving and suffering for God's kingdom, we trust that on this march God will provide for us the necessities of life, and provide them in abundance. Christ teaches (Matt 6): "[33] But strive first for the kingdom of God and his righteousness, and all these things will be given to you as well." God will provide all temporal necessities while we strive for what is eternal.

Servants of the king are called to follow him in striving and suffering. Therefore the prayer for the kingdom trains us in the endurance of the cross. The cross is the way in which God advances his kingdom. As we submit to God's righteousness and accept the cross, God makes us participants of his glory.

As we serve the kingdom, we pray not only for perishable goods for this life, but for an eternal treasure, one that surpasses all our thoughts and desires. We need the guidance of this prayer to remind us that what we will receive is beyond the wishes of our limited imagination. We need to be taught to pray for God's kingdom, so that we learn we will receive even beyond our capacity to desire.

Jesus, the Christ, is the king who is rich and mighty, and who is able and willing to grant great gifts. As he teaches us to pray, he wants us to ask confidently. As servants of this king we are allowed to approach him and ask that our needs be provided. We actually honor the king by trusting that he is able to grant great gifts and will grant more than we can desire or imagine.

In God's kingdom, we do not serve to gain profit; rather we serve and suffer for the kingdom, trusting that God will, in this time and world, provide all things necessary to ensure we are free to do our duty.

THE THIRD PETITION: THY WILL BE DONE

With the third petition of the Lord's Prayer, we pray that God's will be done, the will of the one God who cannot be hindered to do his will by anything he has created.

This prayer does not suggest that God is weak-willed or hesitant about his decisions and actions, so that he needs to be motivated. On the contrary; with this prayer we confirm our trust in the all-knowing and all-powerful God because (Ps 135) "⁶ Whatever the LORD pleases he does, in heaven and on earth."

In the Bible the phrase *God's will* does not suggest arbitrariness. The God and Father of our Lord Jesus Christ (Eph 1) "⁹ has made known to us the mystery of his will, according to his good pleasure that he set forth in Christ, as a plan (εἰς οἰκονομίαν) for the fullness of time, to gather up all things in him, things in heaven and things on earth." Hence God does not play dice with us, but works according to his plan, which is already realized in heaven, and he has made his plan known to us in Jesus Christ. Praying the third petition, *Thy will be done on earth as it is in heaven*, we acknowledge that here on earth God's plan and purpose will be fulfilled, which he has revealed in Jesus Christ. Jesus actually *is* the plan and purpose of God, is God's word and logic (λόγος, John 1). With this prayer we submit our will to God's will.

a. *The Will of Jesus' Father*

According to Heb 10:7, Jesus Christ came into this world praying with Ps 40: "⁷ See, God, I have come to do your will, O God." Heb 5 testifies about Jesus: "⁸ Although he was a Son, he learned obedience through what he suffered." Jesus alone lived in full accordance with his Father's will (John 8:29).

On the eve of his passion and death, Jesus submitted to the will of the Father in the garden of Gethsemane (Matt 26): "³⁹ he threw himself on the ground and prayed, 'My Father, if it is possible, let this cup pass from me; yet not what I want but what you want.'" (cf. Part 2.I.2.) Here, in the garden, Jesus called his disciples to stay with him and to pray with him. Jesus called his followers to deny themselves, to take up their cross (Matt 16:24) and to follow him. According to Heb 2:11, Jesus calls us brothers and sisters, and so we are called children of God together with him, the one Son of God.

With the prayer to the Father, *thy will be done,* the faithful follow Jesus Christ and are ready to do and to suffer together with him God's will. We who are united with Jesus Christ through the Holy Spirit must expect to face temptation and to see the world and our own flesh become enemies. Following Jesus Christ, we learn obedience to the Father, to be steadfast and to suffer with patience when we are attacked, and to let go whatever is taken from us. In all the misery inflicted on us and in all the hardship we take upon ourselves voluntarily, we follow Jesus Christ to serve God and our neighbors. Therefore we pray Jesus' prayer: *thy will be done.* Jesus, the revelation of the Father's will, is our king and Lord, and he is the model for the godly life.

b. "As in heaven so on earth"

The clause *as in heaven so on earth* probably refers to all the first three petitions. The Angels in heaven hallow God's name and do his will; the angels are (Ps 103) "[20] the mighty ones who [do] his bidding, obedient to his spoken word." God's kingdom is already perfect in heaven. Eventually God will be acknowledged as king in all the world when all creatures subject themselves to his will. Saint Augustine writes: "*Thy will be done as in heaven, so in earth.* That is, as by the Angels who are in Heaven Thy will is done so as that they have fruition of Thee, no error clouding their knowledge, no pain marring their blessedness; so may it be done by Thy Saints who are on earth, and who, as to their bodies, are made of earth. So that, 'Thy will be done' is rightly understood as, 'Thy commands be obeyed;' 'as in heaven, so in earth,' that is, as by Angels, so by men; not that they do what God would have them do, but they do because He would have them do it; that is, they do after His will."[20] It is both an obligation and a great consolation that there is a perfect world somewhere.

c. Doing God's will

With this prayer we dedicate our human will, our suffering, and our activity to God. The third petition of the Lord's Prayer for God's will to be done includes our own will and doing. God's will is always that we be God's active partners. This view is confirmed in Matthew's Gospel (Matt 7): "[21] Not

---

20. Serm. in Mont., 2, 6, in *Catena Aurea*.

everyone who says to me, 'Lord, Lord,' will enter the kingdom of heaven, but only the one who does the will of my Father in heaven;" and (Matt 12): "[50] For whoever does the will of my Father in heaven is my brother and sister and mother" (cf. as well Matt 18:14 and 21:28–33).

From all this, we can see that the third petition is the human response to the proclamation of God's will. God's will is summed up in the double commandment (Matt 22:36–40) to *love God and love your neighbor*. In his farewell speeches according to John, Jesus says (John 13): "[34] I give you a new commandment, that you love one another. Just as I have loved you, you also should love one another" (cf. Also 1 John 3 and 4; Luke 10:25–37). God's call to do his will and his providence employ our will, mind, soul, and body.

With this prayer, we dedicate our will to God's will and plans, trusting that God's will cannot be impeded. Cyprian (AD 200–258, Bishop of Carthage) writes: "We ask not that God may do His own will, but that we may be enabled to do what He wills should be done by us; and that it may be done in us we stand in need of that will, that is, of God's aid and protection; for no man is strong by his own strength, but is safe in the indulgence and pity of God."[21] However, this prayer is supposed to concentrate man's attention on God's plan and purpose, to make the faithful trust in God's unstoppable ability to accomplish his will. The question of in what way God and man cooperate tends to turn the focus toward the praying person, who is, however, supposed to focus on God. Like the first two petitions, this petition is carefully worded with an impersonal passive verb so that we, when praying, do not speak of our own will and doing. Praying this petition, we learn that human beings can do nothing good without God's will. This prayer turns our attention away from our own will, from what our own will can endure, conquer or accomplish, and turns all attention to God's will. The third petition of the Lord's Prayer emphasizes that God's will is to be done by his creatures on earth as it is already being done in heaven. Hence this petition sets our minds on the things above (cf. Col 3:2). Truth and beauty, God's glory and power are set before our eyes. The whole point of this petition is that we, in following Jesus Christ, dedicate our will to God's will.

We commonly err in believing that our own willfulness in its present condition, i.e. since and despite original sin, produces good for ourselves and for others, and that the fulfillment of our wishes will produce happiness—at least our own happiness, at least in this life. By this measure, everything we want and are able to do, and everything that yields profit or pleasure, should be allowed. If this were true, appeals to truth, love, and justice would then

---

21. *Catena Aurea*, 2, 6.

seem like a hindrance to our private or professional success and happiness, even as obstacles to technology and economy. Obviously, only people who have material resources and power are able to live out and to realize their will outside the standards of justice and love and the pursuit of truth. But is the will of sinners really a source of happiness in this life—not to speak of the life to come? The New Testament again and again speaks of the conflict between flesh and spirit (for example Rom 7:14; 8:1–13; Gal 5:17). In the garden of Gethsemane, Jesus taught his disciples to pray (Matt 26): "[41] Stay awake and pray that you may not come into temptation; the spirit indeed is willing, but the flesh is weak." So the prayer *thy will be done*" guides us to acknowledging that our flesh and its will need to be controlled by truth, love, and justice—that is, by God's will. The third petition of the Lord's Prayer guides us toward renouncing the wants of our flesh and to dedicate our thoughts, words, and deeds to God. We are to deny ourselves and to pray that we may live in agreement with God's will, so that it's not our own pride but God's name that is glorified, and that we promote not our personal gain but his kingdom.

With this prayer, we seek to bear hardship with patience and overcome whatever we must endure, lest we break away from Christ. We pray that we may persevere in the commission we have for our life on earth. For our flesh, in itself, is still rebellious, even though we have accepted and believe in the Word of God. The prayer that God's will be done reminds us of God's loving will and plans for us, and kindles in us the zeal for the promotion of God's glory.

d. God's will on earth

We pray about heaven and earth. With this petition we pray that God's will be done throughout the earth. But the prayer that God's will be done isn't aimed only at our own individual obedience. The passive clause—*be done*—sets no limits as to who *does*: God willing, all creatures shall do God's will. So we speak this prayer on behalf of the whole world. We pray not only *thy will be done* by me, but *thy will be done* throughout the earth, by all creatures great and small. We pray that truth, justice, and love may prevail, and virtue may grow into reality on earth as it is already reality in heaven.

We have just prayed for the kingdom of God to come; now we pray that his rule shall be accepted, obeyed, and celebrated. The term *kingdom* in the previous petition suggests an analogy: We not only desire a wise, just, brave and patient king (parliament, president, or prime minister), but we also desire that the people will honor and obey the laws of the lawmaker. We need both good government and law-abiding citizens.

Because the third petition asks for God's will to be done in all the earth, it is fitting to have this petition as part of our common prayers, especially in the Eucharistic prayer, prayed by the community of the faithful. The church is the community of people who intercede together, with one another and for one another, a fellowship of people who have committed themselves to do and to suffer God's will.

e. Consolation

We have a true consolation in the promise that God's will eventually will be done. God's will must eventually prevail and his plans will be accomplished, with or without our consent, with or without our cooperation—even if we never prayed. God allows opposing forces to be successful for a while. But eventually his will must succeed, however strong the opposing forces are. Those opposing forces will fail and will be subdued and will have to acknowledge God's power and justice. This is a true consolation and gives us the confidence that our prayer is not in vain.

THE FOURTH PETITION: GIVE US THIS DAY OUR DAILY BREAD

With the first three petitions of the Lord's Prayer, the "you-petitions," Christians pray about the holiness of God's name, God's kingdom, and the fulfillment of God's will. With the prayer for *daily bread*, the petitions for our own needs begin, the "we-petitions."

According to Saint Augustine, the first three petitions pray about eternal blessings, while the next four petitions pray about temporal blessings—though these are, however, necessary to obtain what is eternal.[22] Praying for bread, we pray, as the First Commandment implies, to invoke the one God in every need.

a. The symbolism of bread

Bread is a central symbol of the Christian faith. *Bread* in its simple, literal sense is the basic daily food of a worker. Hence it is a symbol of all that is necessary for our body and for our temporal life. This short word reminds

---

22. Augustine, *Augustine Catechism*.

us of all the things necessary to provide bread: fruitful earth, a sufficient but not excessive supply of water, sunshine, laborers to till the field, tools and machinery for the work on the field, mill and bakery, everything necessary to produce those tools, and so on. Whenever we have a loaf of bread on the table, we may think of the wonder of our interconnectedness with God's creation. *Bread* may stand for other things necessary for life in this world. We pray that God may give us food and drink, clothing and house, home and health for our body, faithful neighbors and good friends, etc.; and the broader things we need: domestic and neighborly peace and quiet for our daily business, good government to protect us from crime and enemies, honor and good reputation.[23] We pray that God may preserve us from calamities and threats to body and livelihood. Bread is indeed a powerful symbol, both of the gifts of creation and of human work. Bread, the earthly gift which we receive for the nourishment for our body, is baked by human hands and is still God's gift, God's wonderful creation.

But the symbolism of bread and wine goes even deeper: When crops are cut, grains are ground, and bread is broken; when grapes are trodden, juice fermented, and wine is poured, they bear in themselves the mystery of life, the mystery of sacrifice. This mystery of life, the mystery of sacrifice, is perfectly revealed by the cross of Christ. Nature's gifts testify that through him, the sacrificed Lord Jesus Christ, all things are created and have their existence, through him who dies on the cross and rises from the tomb.

Jesus himself employs the symbol of *bread* to describe himself as the supernatural food (John 6): "[51] I am the living bread that came down from heaven. Whoever eats of this bread will live forever; and the bread that I will give for the life of the world is my flesh."

b. "This day"

This petition prays about the basic needs of each day, but not about wants and wealth. With this petition for bread, we day by day pray for what we need each day. One might think of a day laborer who does not know if he will be employed the next day. Praying for the bread of this day, we remind ourselves that it is granted but cannot be taken as a matter of course.

In the context of the Bible, the Lord's Prayer is not a spontaneous expression of an individual in an extraordinary situation of distress; it is something the Lord taught us to do. It is not the circumstances of the world or an invention of our soul that call us to pray the Lord's Prayer, but the Lord's instruction. The prayer itself suggests that we should pray it on a regular

---

23. Cf. Martin Luther's explanation for the *bread* in Stjerna, *Large Catechism*.

basis, reminding ourselves of what the Lord wants us to pray for, this day and every day.

We pray for bread to our Father in heaven, reminding ourselves of his permanent, trustworthy, and reliable power as the creator. Therefore the Psalmist prays (Ps 104): "²⁷ These all look to you to give them their food in due season; ²⁸ when you give to them, they gather it up; when you open your hand, they are filled with good things."

Every day we pray for our bread to the Heavenly Father, reminding ourselves that we are his sons and daughters, because God has revealed himself as the father of his Son Jesus Christ, and thus as a loving and caring Father, who gives abundantly (Matt 16): "⁹ Do you still not perceive? Do you not remember the five loaves for the five thousand, and how many baskets you gathered?"

Because the Sermon on the Mount is a teaching *with authority* (Matt 7:29), i.e., a revelation of God's will, the fact that we're instructed to say the Lord's Prayer is also a reliable promise that God will listen. He wants us to ask for his grace and help, because he wants to grant grace and help. God's commandment to pray is his promise to hear our prayer, although we are sinners. This should encourage us all the more to pray, because God has promised to be listening as we pray. Through the prayer of the Psalm, we may remind ourselves of God's promise (Ps 50): "¹⁵ Call upon Me in the day of trouble: I will deliver thee."

God wants us to pray, to lament, and to ask for the necessities of life *this day*, not because He would not know what we need, nor because he isn't sure if he wants to give them, but so as to rekindle a desire in our hearts to receive what God wants to give. God wants us to pray for our needs this day and every day, so that we may recognize that we receive everything from His hand, and thus understand His fatherly love. The Latin church father Tertullianus (about AD 200) rightfully called the Lord's Prayer a summary of the whole gospel.[24]

c. Ethical Implications

The Lord's Prayer is embedded in the Teaching on the Mount and thus in the context of *exceeding righteousness* (Matt 5:20). More specifically, the Lord's Prayer is the central part of the exhortation to piety in three articles about *charity, prayer and fasting* (Matt 6:1–18). In the same context Jesus encourages us (Matt 6): "³³ But ... strive first for the kingdom of God and

---

24. Tertullian, *De oratione* [On prayer] 1: *"in oratione breviarium totius evangelii comprehendatur."*

his righteousness, and all these things will be given to you as well." Hence the prayer for our bread has ethical implications.

Bread for me

This prayer for bread reminds us that life is God's gift. We call it *our bread*, but we pray that it may be *given* to us, for it is God's to give.[25] We need to do responsible work for our livelihood, and yet, in praying for our bread, we are reminded that our life ultimately depends on God, who gives us the ability to work in the first place. That's why it's a good custom to say a table grace individually as well as in Christian families and communities every day.

This prayer guides us to acknowledge that we are bodily creatures. When he's teaching about prayer, Jesus isn't speaking to ghosts without bodily needs, but beings composed of spirit, soul and body, to men and women of flesh and blood. Therefore he speaks about the needs of our bodies. We need to pray and care for our bodily life, which is God's good gift.

This prayer is also an exercise of contentment (cf. Matt 6:25–26). Jesus teaches us to pray not for money or for the gratification of lust, but simply for bread. Hence, in praying for *bread* we ask for what is necessary for our life, but not for riches. With this prayer, a disciple of Christ asks for each day's supply without longing for excessive pleasures. Bread is not sought for its own sake but for the health of the body while we are in our pilgrimage on earth. The New Testament teaches (1 Tim 6): "[7] for we brought nothing into the world, so that we can take nothing out of it; [8] but if we have food and clothing, we will be content with these." This prayer for bread reminds us of Jesus' word in the temptation story according to Matt 4; here Jesus quotes from the Old Testament: "[4] One does not live by bread alone, but by every word that comes from the mouth of God" (cf. Deut 8:4).

This prayer is an exercise of trust. This prayer is not supposed to express and reinforce our cravings, but to make us trust in God's power and love every day. We pray for the bread *this day,* because there is no day without need. This petition does not hope for bread in a distant future, which would leave us with a hopeless present without God, but insists on trust for *this day.* This prayer for bread asks for the supplies for our commission here and now. Jesus adds *this day* so that we do not trouble ourselves with worries about the coming day (Matt 6:25–34). This phrase reminds us of the story of the bread given to God's people on their desert journey in Exod 16; the people of Israel were allowed to gather the bread from heaven for only one

---

25. Gregory the Great, Moralia, XXIV 7, according to Catena Aurea on the Gospel according to Matthew.

day. They were called to trust in God to give them their bread on the next day again. Therefore, while we know we are sinners, we pray for continuing trust in God's persevering support, so that we may not be separated from Christ but abide in his continuous grace and guidance.

Bread for us

This petition shows again that the Lord's Prayer is not just a prayer of individual believers: We pray for *our bread*. It reminds us of the needs of all who are included in this word *our*. We pray for the necessities of our own life, but only after we have prayed for God's kingdom; thus this prayer opens our awareness to the needs of all of God's people. There are many people who starve because they have no bread. The prayer for bread reminds us of the hungry all over the world and calls us both to pray for them and to take responsibility. In his speech about the second coming, Jesus points out that whatever we do to one of the "least of my brethren" (cf. Matt 25:31–46) we do to the king himself. Our individual lives as well as our lives as citizens give us plenty of opportunities to do the right thing in our personal, social, economic and political relationships. With this prayer for *our bread*, we pray to be filled with Christian love for our neighbors, a love that will incite us to share.

As we pray for the fulfillment of the needs of all people, we participate in God's unlimited generosity, as the Lord himself teaches (Matthew 5): "^{44} But I say to you, Love your enemies and pray for those who persecute you, ^{45} so that you may be sons of your Father who is in heaven; for he makes his sun rise on the evil and on the good, and sends rain on the just and on the unjust." Therefore, while we remain sinners, we may pray with confidence.

d. The Eucharistic Bread

It is possible to understand the prayer for the daily bread as a prayer for the Eucharistic bread. For many centuries, this prayer for bread was nearly exclusively understood as a prayer for the *supernatural bread*. Only since the time of the Reformation did the meaning of the word *bread* as nourishment for our temporal life begin to prevail, and this understanding was slowly accepted in the Roman Catholic church.

The reason *bread* was understood as the bread of the Eucharist is the word we usually translate as *daily*.[26] In the original Greek, it is a word com-

---

26. The Greek adjective ἐπιούσιος combines the prefix ἐπι– = *on, upon, in addition to,*

posed of a prefix with the meaning *on, upon, above, in addition to* and a word with the meaning: *being, substance.* Therefore the literal meaning would be in fact *beyond (material) substance.* Hence it is plausible that this word has been interpreted as the supersubstantial or supernatural Bread of Life. It is then indeed not too far-fetched to connect the *bread* in the Lord's Prayer with the *bread* taken and given by Jesus at the Last Supper in Matt 26:26.

When we go beyond the Gospel of Matthew, we find in John 6:26–58 Jesus' long speech about the "[51] bread that came down from heaven," another text that in the history of the church was frequently connected with the Eucharist. Referring to John 6, Jesus' speech about himself as the *true bread*, the early Christian writer Cyprian (about AD 250) writes: "For Christ is the bread of life, and this bread belongs not to all men, but to us. This bread we pray that it be given day by day, lest we who are in Christ, and who daily receive the Eucharist for food of salvation, should by the admission of any grievous crime, and our being therefore forbidden the heavenly bread, be separated from the body of Christ. Hence then we pray, that we who abide in Christ, may not draw back from His sanctification and His body."[27] Cyprian presupposes that Christians daily participate in Holy Communion and pray that they may be preserved from the kind of sins that would exclude them from the daily Eucharist.

THE FIFTH PETITION: FORGIVE US OUR TRESPASSES

We have prayed for our daily food to be nourished in this life; now we ask for forgiveness to be saved for eternal life; because we ask to live not only in this present and passing life but wish to live eternally. Being nourished by God, we pray that we may live for God.

---

and an adjective derived from the noun οὐσία = being, substance. This compound word is not found in any extant writing prior to the New Testament, so that we depend on the literal translation, which is indeed *above (natural) being*. An ancient Latin version (Vetus Latina) translates "quotidianus" = "daily," but the common Latin version, the Vulgata, reads, in Matthew, *supersubstantialis,* which is a literal translation and shaped the tradition of the Western church for centuries. The translation *daily* is philologically possible, but the usual adverbial phrase for *daily* is καθ' ἡμέραν, and therefore the question remains why only here the New Testament would use such an unusual word just to say *daily*. Besides, *daily* plus *this day* seem to be somewhat redundant.

27. *Catena Aurea*, vol.1, 6:11.

a. The Words

The wording in the Gospel according to Matthew is "forgive us our debts (τὰ ὀφειλήματα)." The meaning of the Greek word for *debt* is: *that which is owed*, or *that which is legally due*.

The prayer in the version according to Saint Luke reads: "forgive our sins (τὰς ἁμαρτίας)." The meaning of the Greek word for *sin* is originally *missing the target*. In Greek drama and philosophy[28] the word came to denote the protagonist's failure of intellect or moral judgment which causes the drama to unfold. In the Greek version of the Old Testament, the word is used to translate a variety of Hebrew terms in various contexts. In the New Testament, *sin* is both a force ruling over human beings and the guilt of human actions (Rom 5:12; Gal 3:22; Acts 2:38; 3:19; Heb 1:3; 2:17; John 9:41). The version of the Lord's Prayer commonly used in church reads *trespasses*, a translation that takes into account that there are two versions of the Lord's Prayer in the New Testament and refers to God's law and order being violated by humanity.

The Latin church father Saint Augustine, when explaining the Lord's Prayer,[29] maintains the literal meaning of *debts* in the Gospel according to Matthew; he actually speaks about forgiving monetary debts. Consistent with his concept of finding spiritual meaning in the historic or material sense of the words and images of the Bible, Augustine finds in the word *debts* (Matthew) the spiritual meaning *sins* (Luke).

b. Forgiveness for God's Sons and Daughters

The beginning of the prayer instructs us to call God *Father*; therefore this prayer is meant to be prayed by the sons and daughters of God, for the forgiveness of their own sins. This petition obviously presupposes that Christians, believing and baptized, continue to be in need of forgiveness. In this world and time, Christians are not without sin, and thus not yet people "having neither spot nor wrinkle" (cf. Eph 5:27). This is why Christians pray the seven penitential Psalms (Pss 6, 32, 38, 51, 102, 130, 143); only Christians receive the body and the blood of Christ "for the forgiveness of sins" (Matt 26:28); only Christians pray the Lord's Prayer with its petition for forgiveness.

In the early church, the Lord's Prayer was not given to the catechumens but was reserved for those already baptized, because in baptism we

---

28. Most important: *Poetics*, by Aristotle †322 BC.
29. Augustine, *Sermon on the Mount*, 2, 8.

are adopted as children of God and thus privileged to address God as *Our Father*. Early in history, the Lord's Prayer became a part of the Eucharist, both because it was understood as a table grace and because of the petitions for bread and forgiveness.

As Christians, we pray the prayer for forgiveness and thus we are reminded of our sins. "If we pretend we have no sin, we deceive ourselves and the truth is not in us" (cf. 1 John 1:8).

c. *Longing for Forgiveness*

Christians feel the burden of their sin and long for forgiveness. The more we are committed to work for God's glory, laud and honor, and the more we are advanced in our personal life as disciples of Christ, the more we become aware of our shortcomings and failures—in fact, of our unwillingness and rebellion against God. We are blessed if we become aware of our sins and are frightened of God's wrath, because then we ask God not to count our sins against us and to grant us again a joyful heart to confidentially pray and work.

Feeling the burden of our sin and longing for forgiveness, we need the encouragement of the Lord's Prayer to pray for forgiveness, because Christians know that the majesty and justice of God would not allow us to bother him with our own concerns. Under the law, sinners are not allowed to approach the God of righteousness. But by the commandment to pray for forgiveness, Jesus plainly gives us to understand that the all-powerful creator and just judge is also the loving Father who will not chase us away from his majesty, although we are sinners, but wants us to be again sons and daughters of God and contributing members of his holy people.

If we long to be daughters and sons of God, the teaching to pray for forgiveness is God's welcome for us. He does not bind us to our past sins but wants to receive us back into his loving arms. Jesus commands (Luke 11): "[9]Ask, and it will be given you; search, and you will find; knock, and the door will be opened for you."

The commandment to pray for forgiveness can be and should be understood as a beautiful encouragement: If we desire the forgiveness of our sins, we are invited to pray confidently. However, the Lord's Prayer teaches us as well to pray for things we perhaps do not desire but should. We still need to be taught to ask for forgiveness.

d. Encouragement

The fifth petition reminds us that, although we have a calling to hallow God's name, although we are workers for God's kingdom, although we have the commission to proclaim and to do God's will, we still go astray, transgress God's commandments, and do harm to our neighbors. The teaching to pray for forgiveness keeps us humble. It is healthy for us to be reminded that we are sinners and thus to be compelled to pray for forgiveness for our negligence and our rebellion against God.

In Jesus Christ, God has called us to be his holy people. God wants us to be proud of this call and purpose. He has honored us with the commission to hallow his name and to proclaim his kingdom, to suffer and to do God's will. We no longer believe that we are the measure of all things, but we adore God's greatness. Therefore we cannot but confess our lowliness. When we confess God's majesty we will inevitably confess to be sinners. Confession of sin simply follows from the awe of God. Understood in its context—previous petitions for God's holy name, kingdom and sacred will—this petition for forgiveness does not necessarily mean feeling bad about ourselves, denying our self-worth, or giving up our dignity. But by confessing our sin, we acknowledge God's greatness, justice, and majesty. We remain in God's *debt* because we fall short of our goal to appropriately honor God's name, proclaim his kingdom and do his will; we miss the target, we *sin,* because we misunderstand, neglect and/or rebel against God's holiness, kingdom, and will. We (Rom 3:23) "fall short of the glory of God." But with the confession of sin, we return to our status as God's people, called to glorify God.

Preachers sometimes assert that God "wants to lift you up," or something of that nature. But this assertion simply presumes our lowliness and unworthiness without allowing an opportunity to respond to the insinuation. What is meant to be an encouragement is then easily perceived as disdain—and perhaps rightfully so. This well-meant assurance is likely to provoke defensiveness and to meet resistance: Why would I need to be lifted up? By contrast, the call to *humble yourself to God* allows that our whole self, including our pride, actual accomplishments and rightful self-esteem, acknowledges God's infinite superiority. Hence it is exactly this call to humility, the call to confess our sins, that preserves our dignity as God's own people.

It is our honor to hallow God's name, to proclaim the kingdom and to suffer and do God's will. With the prayer for forgiveness, we return to our dignity of being God's people. In the context of the previous petitions, the call to humble ourselves is a call to acknowledge and praise God's greatness, which again is our ultimate dignity.

e. As we forgive those who trespass against us

The prayer for forgiveness is so important that it is the only petition Jesus explains (Matt 6): "[14] For if you forgive others their trespasses, your heavenly Father will also forgive you; [15] but if you do not forgive others, neither will your Father forgive your trespasses." Obviously human and divine activity do not happen in exclusive spheres, but rather work together in some way.

The subordinate sentence, *as we forgive those who trespass against us,* is both a condition and a consolatory exhortation (cf. Matt 18:23–35). When we receive God's forgiveness, we shall be confident everything is forgiven and pardoned before God in heaven; but we also shall forgive our neighbor. We daily sin against God, and He forgives everything, in his grace; accordingly, we must always forgive our neighbors who might do wrong to us.

There were previous Jewish parallels to this prayer, and the connection between human and divine forgiveness was not unheard of, but the idea that human behavior is a central part of a prayer is unparalleled. Jesus, when teaching us to pray, binds the petition for forgiveness to the condition that we must forgive those who are in debt to us. The same goodness we ask of God, we should grant our neighbors. The Bible gives stern warnings against a selfish trust in God without love and forgiveness for our neighbors. In 1 John 4, we read, "[20] Those who say, 'I love God,' and hate their brothers or sisters, are liars; for those who do not love a brother or sister whom they have seen, cannot love God whom they have not seen." Those who pray for forgiveness must know that the answer depends on their own willingness to forgive.

However, it cannot be that we may pray this prayer and ask for forgiveness only if we are certain that we have forgiven everyone in our hearts. If we understood this petition in that way, we would either be hypocrites who deny the hatred and contempt for our neighbors still lurking in our hearts, or we would fall into despair, because any mindful and sensitive heart would think that it can never be forgiven. Thus trapped between denial and despair, we should pray as Christ has taught us, and not as we feel. Praying Jesus' words, we may trust that his Father hears and answers this prayer, because the Father knows the words and the intention of his Son, and he will answer this prayer which Christ's wisdom has given us. Praying this prayer, we ask for God's forgiveness and we encourage ourselves to forgive.

Love for God cannot be separated from love for our neighbors, because God wants us to live together in his community. That's why the parable of the unforgiving servant (Matt 18:23) concludes Jesus' teaching about the community of the church in Matt 18. By asking our neighbors for pardon and by granting forgiveness, we turn enemies into friends and reestablish community.

Forgiveness for one another is the obvious response to God's forgiveness. But the parable of the unforgiving servant shows as well that the commandment to forgive *from our heart* remains a challenge. We need to keep asking God for faith in his forgiveness so that we find the strength to forgive others.

f. Forgiveness in church

This petition points us to the long biblical tradition of repentance, confession of sins and prayer. The penitential Psalms of the Bible and the litanies of the church's tradition may be prayed as an amplification of this petition of the Lord's prayer.

With this petition, we both confess our sins and profess God's mercy. God is certainly a forgiving God without our prayer; God's mercy has been obtained by the sacrifice of God's Son so that we have forgiveness of sins (Col 1:14; Eph 1:7). With this prayer we return to the Lord like the prodigal son to his father (Luke 15:11–32), or like the tax collector (Luke 18:13), like David (Ps 51) and Manasseh (2 Chr 33:19),[30] who were kings of God's people, or like Saint Peter and Saint Paul, who were teachers of the church. The worship service is an opportunity to remind ourselves of our reconciliation with the community of the faithful. Jesus teaches (Matt 5): "[23] So when you are offering your gift at the altar, if you remember that your brother or sister has something against you, [24] leave your gift there before the altar and go; first be reconciled to your brother or sister, and then come and offer your gift." It is a good custom in a worship service to share a sign of peace before we share the meal.

Traditional forms of worship connect the office of the keys (cf. Matt 16 and 18, John 20), the Lord's Prayer with its petition for forgiveness, and the body and blood of Christ "given and shed for the forgiveness of sins" (Matt 26).

---

30. Church tradition would also refer to the deuterocanonical book *The Prayer of the Manasseh*.

THE SIXTH PETITION: LEAD US NOT INTO TEMPTATION

The Lord has called us to participate in prayer and work for marvelous things: for the holiness of God's name, for God's kingdom and for the fulfillment of God's will. He adds a lesson of humility when he teaches us to pray: *and lead us not into temptation*. In the light of the grand things for which we pray, work, and suffer, we humbly confess that we are still sinners and commend ourselves to God's mercy and care.

a. *The nature of temptation*

What is the meaning of *temptation* (πειρασμός) in the Lord's Prayer? Some think that "temptation" would refer to the distress of the latter times. But if this were true, the wording would be: *the* temptation, with the definite article. Moreover, the word *temptation* has never been used in texts relating to the end times, neither in the New Testament nor in contemporary Jewish literature. Hence it is unlikely that this petition refers to the pangs of the end. Another possibility is that this petition is simply speaking about everyday temptations, about all kinds of distress or suffering, about temptations like excessive food, drink, sex, or sloth. This explanation, however, rests on an interpretation of the Lord's Prayer as being just a simple prayer like our spontaneous prayers in special circumstances. But nothing in the text supports this interpretation. The most appropriate way to understand the sixth petition of the Lord's Prayer is to read it in its context, both immediate and more broadly. Temptations arise during the work, fight and suffering of Jesus' followers for the holiness of God's name and for God's kingdom, their striving for God's will to be accepted and to be done. As for the wider context in the Gospel of Matthew, the Lord's Prayer is embedded in the "Teaching on the Mount,"[31] in the context of striving for exceeding righteousness (Matt 5:20). Through the Lord's Prayer, we ask to be preserved from those temptations that particularly befall the followers of Christ on their mission.

Praying this petition, *lead us not into temptation*, we give account of the status of our soul; we admit our weakness, lest we exalt ourselves. We need to ask: Are we ready for God's kingdom? Do we live a life appropriate for those who want to hallow God's name? Are we doing God's will? At the moment, perhaps we're doing God's work and loving our neighbors, but

---

31. Traditionally this passage in Matthew is called the *sermon on the mount*. However, Matthew does not call it a *sermon* but tells us that Jesus sits down and teaches his disciples.

temptation is always lurking around the corner. Having the great commission, we struggle not only with our shortcomings, but with the temptation to neglect and to actually do harm; we are still fighting the battle between flesh and spirit.

Christians will certainly be tested, as Saint Paul writes (1 Thess 2:4): "*God . . . tests our hearts*" (δοκιμάζειν, KJV translates: *trieth*). Some tests make our character grow in patience, perseverance and hope (cf. Rom 5). Whenever our natural strength and moral fortitude suffer defeat, we learn that our strength needs to grow, in order to win the day next time. These tests are challenges that every self-respecting woman or man desires to face, to have an opportunity to prove him- or herself.

But temptation is different from tests.[32] *Temptation* is far more serious, not a test of my strength but the loss of all strength (Ps 38:11) and the experience of feeling forsaken by God (Isa 54:7). Temptation in the biblical sense of the word leads to death (cf. Jes 1:14–15). Therefore Christians pray: *Lead us not into temptation*. We also need to distinguish temptation from *consenting* to temptation. We will certainly feel temptation all our lives. But as long as it is against our will, as long as we want to live in God's kingdom of love, as long as we want to remain in the beauty and order of God's creation and in the community of God's people, as long as we want to walk the pathway to heaven, temptation cannot do us any harm. But if we succumb to temptation and do not resist and do not pray against it, temptation kills us.

It is a serious question, whether it is God who leads into temptation. For many people, this thought perhaps sounds offensive, but we cannot dismiss this possibility in just a theoretical way. The Bible indeed tells stories about temptations by God: Abraham experienced temptation (Gen 22). David was tempted to order a census (2 Sam 24); according to the parallel version in 1 Chr 21 it was Satan. According to Exod 9:12, it is God who hardens the heart of Pharaoh. The prayer seeking not to be led into temptation presupposes that God is omnipotent, and Christians believe, teach and confess God's almightiness. But we are tempted to draw from this right understanding the wrong conclusion and hold God responsible for the origin of evil. This is why Saint James admonishes us (Jes 1): "[13] No one, when tempted, should say, 'I am being tempted by God;' for God cannot be tempted by evil and he himself tempts no one." The petition of the Lord's Prayer does not release us from responsibility. On the contrary, it reminds us of the daily battle against temptation. Neither God nor his works are guilty, when we submit to temptation, but only we ourselves. Some translations of

---

32. I learned this distinction from Bonhoeffer, *Temptation* [*Versuchung*], 1938.

the Bible and some prayer books[33] read: "Save us from the time of trial" or something like that. The reason for this paraphrase is that *temptation* has been interpreted as the pains of the last days of world (cf. above). The other reason for those paraphrases is that many Christians no longer accept the concept of God's almightiness, so that this petition is perceived as offensive. Moreover, those translations tempt to hold the *trials* responsible and to distract from our own guilt. The origin of temptation cannot be explained. In the temptation story of Gen 3, the serpent is called a creature of God, and perhaps one wants to discuss if it is an external creature or a creature in our soul. Still, the Bible does not give any rational explanation for the origin of its evil intent; it is just there. The very fact that we cannot explain the origin of evil is temptation: in temptation, God seems to hide his face and seems to leave us in the dark (Isa 54:8). In other words, the tempter tries to turn us away from God's revelation (Gen 3): "[1] Did God really tell you . . . ?" This is exactly why, in temptation, we need to turn to the almighty God and invoke him alone: *Do not lead us into temptation.*

b. Three sources of temptation

Following the witness of the Bible, church tradition (for example, Luther's Small Catechism) has distinguished three main sources of temptation: our flesh, the world, and what is called the devil.

Our Flesh

The first source of temptation is our own corrupted nature, our desires and weaknesses. The Bible calls it *flesh*. Our own fallen nature seduces us every day to inchastity, gluttony, avarice, laziness, anger, envy and pride, moreover to deceiving and defrauding our neighbors. We need to know that in the Bible our *flesh* is not necessarily the same as our *body*. Our whole being, to the degree that it is not in accordance with God's word, is flesh. We are creatures composed of both body and soul; both are created good by God, both are corrupted by sin, both will be restored in the resurrection to eternal life. It is an interesting fact that the serpent's question in paradise did not seduce Eve's body but her soul when asking her: "[1] Did God really tell you . . . ?" The battle between Spirit and flesh is not a battle of our *ratio* against our body. The human body is, after all, called by Saint Paul a "temple of the Holy

---

33. So does the Lutheran hymnal *Evangelical Lutheran Worship* and supplemental books.

Spirit" (1 Cor 6:19). But the Spirit of God and his word fight against the corruption of both body and soul and for the restoration of both.

Our flesh can be tempted by vanity, envy, gluttony, lust, anger, greed and sloth. The objects of anger or lust, God's creatures, are not evil; but temptation makes us forget God's order and intent. Likewise, our desires are not necessarily wrong, but we are tempted to yield to our desires in such a way that peace and life together, both in a human community and in creation, are damaged or destroyed. Temptation means that we forget God the creator; we are tempted to say: I have needs; what is wrong with the needs of my body? The tempter wants to talk us into a sense of entitlement, and we are tempted to ask: As I am so special, need I do what everyone does? Why should I not bend the rules for my higher purpose?

The flesh can be tempted by suffering. Suffering in general is, for example, sickness or poverty, which are consequences of the fall of man. God does not want our sickness, suffering and death, and we rightfully grumble against our suffering. But suffering can lead to grumbling against God. Job is the biblical paradigm of this temptation. Speaking to his friends, Job insisted on his innocence when they suspected some hidden guilt; however, the narrator of the book neither takes the side of Job's friends and nor criticizes Job's grumbling against his suffering when his experience and his sense of justice do not add up. But the end of the book tells us that Job stands in awe before God's greatness. At the end, Job acknowledges the unfathomable majesty of God and submits to God's eternal wisdom. It is the awe of God's greatness that eventually transcends Job's sense of justice. Job, when confronted with God's majesty, confesses to be a sinner, and God justifies him before his friends.

- **The World**

The other source of temptation is the *world*. Things around us seem to compel us to envy, avarice, lust, sloth, vanity, anger and gluttony. Life among our fellow citizens may cause us to defame, to defraud, to curse or even to use violence. Knowing that the *world* is a source of temptation, we must maintain that God's good creation is not responsible for any vice, but our own soul alone is guilty. It is true that Jesus gives a strong warning (Matt 18:6) not to cause anyone to stumble. But giving in to temptation is still the guilt of the one who commits sin. The word *world* must not be misunderstood in such a way that we despise God's beautiful creation or hold it responsible for our faults. But temptation takes the opportunity to abuse what is good and to turn it into something evil in us. There is nothing wrong with the beautifully maintained garden of my neighbor; my envy and laziness are very wrong.

We are not good people in a bad world, but on the contrary, we are tempted to violate the original peace and beauty (Gen 1:31) that God has given to his creation: We hate or covet God's creatures and thus fall out of the beauty and order which the creator has intended.

- ### The Devil

A third source of temptation is called by church tradition the *devil*. The literal meaning of this word in the original Greek of the New Testament is *slanderer* or *liar* (διάβολος). The main work of the devil is to spread distrust against God's word and to make false promises. He specifically tells Jesus about entitlement and power. He suggests Jesus would be entitled to the satisfaction of his body's desire; he suggests that Jesus, being the Son of God, would be entitled to protection from harm; and the devil promises power (Matt 4 and Luke 4). The devil steals God's word from our heart (cf. Luke 8:12, the kingdom-parable about the sower), causes us to betray our Lord (cf. John 13:2, Judas at the last supper), and flatters our pride (1 Tim 3:6).

We might call "devil" whatever tears us away from word and sacrament, or makes us forget faith, hope and love. But we must not give to the devil too much credit and not turn him into a second God. The first three chapters of the book of Job show that the devil cannot do anything without God's permission. Praying the sixth petition, we acknowledge that adverse powers cannot prevail against us unless God permits it. Therefore no hostile force needs to be feared, appeased or implored. All devotion and supplications ought to be addressed to the almighty God alone. For this reason, in temptation we invoke only God, saying: *Lead us not into temptation*.

c. Spiritual Temptations

Following the Bible, church tradition speaks of spiritual temptations (cf. Matt 12:31): false security (presumption), despair, and apostasy.

- ### False Security

A blessed assurance is granted to all penitent sinners (John 10:28), who receive God's grace by means of word and sacrament. Different from that is false security or presumption (cf. Rom 11:20; Matt 26:41). Saint Paul writes (1 Cor 10): "[12] So, if you think you are standing, watch out that you do not fall."

False security means that we take God's grace as a matter of course, deceive ourselves about God's wrath against sin and about his judgment, so that we feel entitled to grace without contrition and confession. Consequently, we stir up our desire to sin by expecting grace even before we commit sin. False security leads to laziness in prayer, slackness in work, complacency about studying and meditating on God's word, to neglecting the sacraments and to unfaithfulness to our faith-community. False security prevents us from striving for God's will, from confessing our sins and thus from receiving God's grace.

- *Despair*

Despair is the flip side of false security. Despair begins with doubts about God's grace granted through word and sacrament in church. Uncertainty about God's grace, which is revealed in his word, incites us to demand extraordinary experiences. In the story of Jesus' temptation (Matt 4), the devil demands a sign of proof that Jesus would be the Son of God. If we desire special personal experiences, we tempt God because we do not rely on God's word revealed and proclaimed to us. Demanding additional proof of God's mercy, we try to turn our own distrust into a shortcoming of God's revelation: Is it possible that the word of some pathetic minister or a morsel of bland bread could be my salvation? Doubts continue to destroy trust in the proclamation of forgiveness (Matt 16; John 20) and in the sacraments instituted by Jesus; destroy our trust in the prayers prayed by Jesus. Eventually we feel that we never really belonged to God, to his Church[34] or even to the community of his creation. We end up thinking: God will never forgive me, because my sin is too big. Not believing in God's proclaimed forgiveness, we eventually turn away from obeying God's order. Despair will then lead to self-destruction, even to suicide, like Saul or Judas.

- *Apostasy*

The last temptation is the appearance of Satan (Matt 4), advertising his big sale. He wants to make us knowingly and willingly deny God, and promises all happiness on earth.

---

34. Cf. Bonhoeffer, *Temptation* [*Versuchung*], 1938.

This temptation seems too obvious to be a real threat; however, apostasy can be the ultimate consequence of false security, when God's grace is taken as a matter of course, and when his commandment and judgment are no longer taken seriously. Then, learning and believing God's word, confessing and receiving forgiveness, praying, and celebrating the sacraments all seem to be expendable. Eventually God himself will simply be forgotten.

Apostasy can be also the consequence of despair when God's grace in word, prayer and sacrament is no longer taken seriously, when we crave desperately for some additional personal experience, and when law and judgment remain the only things we know about God. Then we are tempted to deny our disappointment, to ignore our fear and misery, and try to find relief in ignoring God's existence altogether. Both presumption and despair will eventually lead us to ignore or even renounce God.

Apostasy is the sin for which there is no repentance, because it is the denial of God's grace in Christ.

d. The Prayer to Overcome Temptation

(Matt 4): "¹Jesus was led up by the Spirit into the wilderness to be tempted (περισθῆναι) by the devil." The tempter, who had once prevailed against Adam (Gen 3), is now vanquished by Jesus Christ (Matt 4). Jesus Christ has come and overcome. He has come to lead us in prayer, and we fight our temptation by praying together with Jesus: *Lead us not into temptation.* Praying together with him, we call temptation what it is, and thus reject it.

From now on, in all temptations we are tempted as disciples of Jesus Christ, and Christ is tempted together with us (Heb 2): "[18] Because he himself was tested by what he suffered, he is able to help those who are being tested." (The word in the original Greek is actually *tempted* = περασθείς). All desires and fears of the flesh were in him, too. He, too, was condemned and far from God (Heb 4:15). We entrust our lives to Jesus, and he leads us in prayer, prays together with us and for us against temptation. For Christians, the practical answer to their temptations is to realize that they are followers of Jesus Christ and pray together with him: *lead us not into temptation.* Praying these words, we are joined to Jesus Christ and his prayer, and so we turn our back to the tempter. To participate in Jesus' temptation means to participate in his prayer and victory.

Jesus does not fight with special human or superhuman powers, but he vanquishes Satan by reciting a word from the Bible, a word that calls us to prayer (Matt 4): "[10] Worship the Lord your God, and serve only him."

Therefore we must not fight temptation by our own presumed strength,[35] but surrender ourselves to the leadership of Christ, and hold together with him the Word of God against the tempter, the word that calls us to invoke God: *Worship the Lord . . . only him.* We may turn to Jesus' use of the Holy Scriptures, and entrust ourselves to the prayer-book Jesus used: the Bible, specifically the penitential Psalms, Psalms of trust and of praise. Praying *lead us not into temptation,* we identify a temptation as a temptation and are joined to Jesus in refusing temptation.

In our temptations we need to know five things.[36] First, the devil tries to employ God's word to confuse us about Christ's way. He wants to discuss difficulties and ambiguities of God's word (cf. again Matt 4). Second, we should not discuss our sin with the devil. He wants to show us opportunities for sin and to distract us from God's revealed word. About our sin, we speak with God alone. For that reason, it is God we need to address: *lead us not into temptation.* Third, when we are tempted to despair of God's mercy, we must remember that Jesus has called sinners, not saints. Therefore we can turn to the prayers of sinners, especially the seven penitential Psalms of the Bible and the fifth petition of the Lord's Prayer, and also to the litanies of the Church. We want to join the grand community of sinners saved by Jesus Christ. Fourth, we are blessed when in temptation our sin is revealed. Because when we realize and acknowledge our sin, we have taken the first step toward healing. In temptation, our ingratitude and disobedience, our presumption or despair becomes obvious and thus can be healed. By unmasking our hidden sins in this way, the devil unwittingly does God's work. We may pray with a prayer of the Bible (Ps 69): "⁵ O God, you know my folly; the wrongs I have done are not hidden from you." Thus the healing process begins, and we should thank God for his judgment. Fifth, when we are tempted by suffering, we are granted to know that we are nailed to the very temptations of Jesus, who cried out on the cross. Temptation joins us to Jesus Christ, who was tempted and who conquered.

By praying together with Jesus, *lead us not into temptation,* we turn away from the tempter and turn to God. If we keep mulling over temptation, if we keep pondering its threats and promises, its costs and rewards, we will likely rekindle desires and fears, false hopes and despair, and so we are bound to fail. To overcome temptation, we need to immediately turn to Jesus and pray with him: *lead us not into temptation.*

---

35. Cf., again, Bonhoeffer, *Temptation* [*Versuchung*], 1938.
36. For the following thoughts cf., again, Bonhoeffer, *Temptation* [*Versuchung*], 1938.

Jesus, the Son, (cf. John 17:1) prays to his Father for us: "Holy Father, protect them in your name that you have given me, so that they may be one, as we are one" (John 17:11). We can be sure that Jesus' prayer is answered by the heavenly Father, because it is the prayer of his Son. His practical advice is (Matt 26): "[41] Watch and pray, that ye enter not into temptation." From the temptations of the flesh, Christians turn to the prayer of Christ to his Father. From the temptation of suffering, we turn to the suffering Christ; Christians are proud to suffer together with their Lord. They know their suffering is judgment on their sin, but they know as well that they suffer as sinners justified through Jesus Christ. We are joined to Christ and suffer God's judgment on sin together with Christ; and because Jesus accepted God's judgment, Christians are exempt from eternal judgment. Joined to Christ crucified, we accept God's temporal judgment and are saved from the judgment to come.

Jesus encourages us to keep watch (cf. Mark 13:9,23,33–37; 14:38; Luke 12:35–40; 1 Cor 16:13; 1 Thess 5:6; 1 Pet 5:8). *Keeping watch* is a key phrase in the New Testament, meant to describe a basic Christian attitude, also translated as *take heed*, *stay awake*, or *be watchful*. It means to abide with the teaching of Jesus: (Mark 13): "[23] But take heed; see, I have told you all things beforehand." It means also to abide in prayer as the Lord himself says (Matt 26): "[41] Watch and pray, lest you enter into temptation. The spirit indeed is willing, but the flesh is weak" (cf. 2.II.2.). The apostles' teaching in the early church continues Jesus' teaching (Col 4): "[2] Persevere in prayer, being watchful in it with thanksgiving." The word translated as *thanksgiving* is the Greek word for the Eucharist (εὐχαριστία).

THE SEVENTH PETITION: BUT DELIVER US FROM EVIL[37]

With the seventh petition—only found in the Gospel according to Matthew—we pray that we may be delivered and preserved from evil.

We pray for our salvation, that we may one day receive eternal life; therefore in the meantime we pray for the preservation of our temporal life from evil.

---

37. The Roman Catholic church adds the so-called *embolism* to the Lord's Prayer: "Deliver us, Lord, we beseech you, from every evil and grant us peace in our day, so that aided by your mercy we might be ever free from sin and protected from all anxiety, as we await the blessed hope and the coming of our Savior, Jesus Christ." In Latin: *Libera nos, quæsumus, Domine, ab omnibus malis, da propitius pacem in diebus nostris, ut, ope misericordiæ tuæ adiuti, et a peccato simus semper liberi, et ab omni perturbatione securi: expectantes beatam spem et adventum Salvatoris nostri Iesu Christi.*

God wants us to pray for the salvation of our souls, but also for all things that affect our body. It would actually not be especially pious if we tried to ignore the needs of our body, which is created by God, is the temple of the Holy Spirit (1 Cor 6:19), and will be raised from death to eternal life. Hence both body and soul, both temporal and eternal life are in view when we pray this petition to be delivered from evil.

The seventh petition is the prayer of disciples who are called to hallow God's name and who are committed to His kingdom and will, and who therefore experience the power of evil that wants to hinder them; in this battle, Jesus' disciples have the certain hope that this prayer will be answered.

a. *The Deception of Evil*

In praying *deliver us from evil,* we acknowledge the reality of evil and ask for deliverance from its power. *Evil* in the original Greek text can be understood as both neuter or male, therefore it might speak of anonymous powers and circumstances or *the evil one.* Many similar texts in the time of the New Testament, however, speak about evil things rather than about the evil one, which suggests that this word in the Lord's Prayer also refers to evil things, not a person: everyday experiences such as disease, distress, a bad neighborhood, our own evil desires and deeds, and the consequences of our actions interfere with our discipleship.

However, it might still be helpful to personify those things that attempt to prevent our prayers from being answered, when we pray for God's honor and the holiness of his name, for God's kingdom and will, for our daily bread, a clean conscience, etc. Personifying evil as the *evil one* gives us, first, the opportunity to directly and personally renounce evil, so that we seek and expect help nowhere but from God. Second, by renouncing the evil one, we confess that God does not like the evil that befalls us[38]; he does not like our poverty, pain and shame, our death, or any of the calamities from which we ourselves and all the creatures on earth suffer.

One of the words for the *evil one* is the word *devil,* which derives from the Greek word *diabolos,* the meaning of which is *liar.* We should not believe the falsehood of the devil, when he claims he has the power to fulfill promises or to carry out threats.

It is indeed dangerous to grant the evil one a status that would come close to that of a second, equally powerful although evil God. If the evil one, sometimes called Satan, is believed to be able to give goods or to cause damage, if he is believed to be able to withhold or to grant powers, the temptation

---

38. Cf., again Bonhoeffer, *Versuchung 1938.*

will arise to make deals with the devil. If Christians give too much credit to the potential of Satan, they may unwittingly be responsible for the spread of occultism and satanism. We may believe that there *is* a devil, but we do not believe *in* the devil. About all evil that befalls us, about all our sins, we need to speak to God alone. To the evil one, we may only say (Matt 4): "¹⁰ Away with you, satan! For it is written, 'Worship the Lord your God, and serve only him.'" Hence we should be very cautious of speaking about satan.

All our calamities do not originate in God's gracious will but are consequences of sin and the deceiver. Therefore we need not stoically submit to those evils but may rightfully rebel against our fate. The devil wants to drive us into despair and even suicide; therefore we should also know that the devil is not only a liar but also a murderer, actually, "A murderer from the beginning, . . . a liar and the father of lies"; *Satan is* "the deceiver of the whole world." (John 8:44; Rev 12:9). By renouncing the evil one, we return to God, who alone holds power.

b. *The Truth of God*

We need to believe that Satan has no power unless God permits him to do evil (cf. Job 1–3). Ultimately we depend on God alone and must never negotiate with the devil. The petition *deliver us from evil* is another confession of faith in the one God, almighty creator of heaven and earth. Against the enemy, we need to pray without ceasing to this one God. For unless God preserves us, we are not safe from the lies and deceptions of Satan. In renouncing evil, we believe that we are created by God and that we live as a portion of the world created by God, sustained by God, and loved by God (John 3:16).

The devil tries to make us forget God's name, hinders God's kingdom from coming, and wants to talk us out of doing God's will. In short, he wants to make us sin. Because all evil has its origin in sin, we need to believe firmly that God, for the sake of Christ's sacrifice, takes away our sin and pardons the faults of all penitent sinners, and therefore protects us and preserves us from harm: "If God is for us, who is against us?" (Rom 8:31). The wording of the petition *deliver us from evil* points us to the reality that deception and damage affect not only individual believers but the community of God's people and ultimately the whole human family. This prayer to the creator of all opens our eyes to the suffering of all people, and opens our awareness to the reality that all people are in peril of being deceived, misguided or seduced.

With Jesus' prayer to be delivered from evil, we turn to God's love for this world. In Jesus' own prayer that he offers as the high priest on behalf of his disciples, he prays (John 17): "¹⁵ I am not asking you to take them out of the world, but I ask you to protect them from the evil [one.]"³⁹

c. *Through Christ our Lord*

The evil one seems to prevail when Jesus dies on the cross. Evil destroys both culture and nature: betrayal (Matt 26:24), greed (Matt 26:15), cowardice (Matt 27:69ff) and the perversion of justice (Matt 27:26) destroy social life, and when the one whom the wind and the waves obey (Matt 8:27) dies on the cross, even the sun fails (Matt 27:45, cf. 24:29) and the earth quakes (Matt 27:52). All evil—the evil we suffer and the evil we do—is an attempted assault against the Lord himself.

Therefore, when we suffer from evil, we suffer together with Jesus. Even in our experience of feeling forsaken by God, we suffer together with Jesus crucified (Matt 27:46), who prayed (Ps 22): "My God, my God, why have you forsaken me." Because Jesus suffered from all we suffer, he is always on our side, so that we cannot be separated from the love of God (Rom 8): "³⁸ For I am convinced that neither death, nor life, nor angels, nor rulers, nor things present, nor things to come, nor powers, ³⁹ nor height, nor depth, nor anything else in all creation, will be able to separate us from the love of God in Christ Jesus our Lord."

Believing in Jesus Christ and praying with the words of God's Son, we, the daughters and sons of God, trust that this prayer is answered by the Father in heaven. In this last petition, all the distress of the world is brought to God, the heavenly Father of Christ, who has (Rev 1): "¹⁸ the keys of Death and of Hades."

When Jesus died the death he freely accepted, he won the victory over the "ruler of this world" (John 14:30), and the ruler of this world is "driven out" (John 12:31; Rev 12:10). Praying the Lord's Prayer, we are part of God's plan that he has revealed in Jesus Christ (Eph 1): "⁹ [God] has made known to us the mystery of his will, according to his good pleasure that he set forth in Christ, ¹⁰ as a plan for the fullness of time, to gather up all things in him, things in heaven and things on earth."

---

39. *The evil* or *the evil one*; here again, both translations are possible.

PART 2

The Triune God and Prayer

ONLY IF WE KNOW God is prayer possible and meaningful. Our ability and willingness to pray depend largely on our beliefs about God. Our practice of prayer is closely connected with our understanding of who God is, whether we are consciously aware of our concept of God or not.[40] However, reflections on the topic of *God and prayer* often start with personal experiences and sometimes philosophical considerations. To encourage simple and spontaneous prayers, various words are typically collected from the Bible, but these rarely refer to the person and deeds of Jesus Christ. Simple prayers are often addressed to the almighty God, who is viewed as a very powerful individual. His omnipotence is usually understood as the ability to intervene in the world and to enforce his will at his discretion, to break resistance, and to overcome limitations. His will is also the good will of a loving Father who is always approachable, ready to help, full of foresight, trustworthy, but susceptible to being influenced. Jesus is, accordingly, supposed to be someone who teaches this understanding of the almighty God. The Holy Spirit is believed to strengthen our childlike trust in prayer.

But with this simple concept, the address *Father* is reduced to a mere anthropomorphism, which more often than not mirrors the experiences praying people have had with their natural fathers, which may be good or not so good. Hence simple prayers to the almighty God often fail to show that the spirit driving those prayers is actually the Spirit of Jesus Christ. Simple prayers rarely show that it is Jesus Christ who leads us in prayer. This

---

40. Within theological scholarship, prayer is, if at all, usually considered in the framework of ethics or practical theological studies, rarely in the context of theology proper. An interesting exception is a work in three volumes, *Dogmatik des Christlichen Glaubens*, by the German theologian Gerhard Ebeling.

means that the content of many contemporary prayers is not shaped by the prayers Jesus prayed, eg. the Psalms, by Jesus' teaching, or by the example of his life, his suffering, death and resurrection. God is often addressed as the *almighty God* or as *dear God*. There can be no doubt that somehow the Christian God is addressed; but in regard to the content of the prayers it hardly seems to matter who the actual addressee is. But what is it that makes a prayer a Christian prayer? The Trinitarian framework of the Bible collapses in many contemporary prayers. It's presumed that God once in a while intervenes in nature's processes and humanity's affairs, which are, however, basically on their own. This kind of thinking contradicts the fundamental biblical concept of the continuous, creative power of God, who directs and perpetually governs the world (Ps 135): "⁶Whatever the LORD pleases he does, in heaven and on earth, in the seas and all deeps."

A variety of issues must be discussed in this context. The Bible teaches that God continues to govern the world and also that he has established routines and laws by which the world functions (Gen 8): "²²While the earth remaineth, seedtime and harvest, and cold and heat, and summer and winter, and day and night shall not cease." The Bible encourages prayer and leaves no doubt that God performs miracles. But are miracles meant to interrupt the good order? Christians believe that God answers prayer, but what does this mean in view of Jesus' suffering to the end? Furthermore, how can we speak about answered prayers and divine interventions for us and for our loved ones while a whole world remains in desperate need of help? How can we speak about God's answer to prayer in the light of the first three petitions of the Lord's Prayer?

Another issue is the relationship between work and prayer. Is there a conflict between effective prayer and responsible work, so that we pray when we are too lazy to work, or work because we are too faithless to pray? Or is prayer just a supplement when our own work is done or when our strength is spent and all options are exhausted? The classical monastic rule by Saint Benedict prescribes: *Pray and Work*. But the word *and* requires clarification.

I

In the Name of Jesus Christ

IN JESUS' TEACHING AND in most of the Apostles' teachings, prayers are addressed to the Father. Christians pray to the father *in the name of Jesus,* as many Christians still say. To have a solid basis for our prayers to the Father, we should start with the revelation through his Son, Jesus Christ, confessed by the Church as true God from true God.

The most basic way to understand prayer *in Jesus' name* is: We are disciples, meaning students of Christ, our teacher from God (John 3:2). We are disciples of Christ and his followers. The English word *disciple* derives from a Latin word *discipulus*, meaning *student* or *pupil*. The original Greek word has exactly the same meaning.

Jesus was by trade a carpenter (Mark 6:3), hence it makes sense to employ the imagery of master and apprentice to understand what disciples are supposed to do. We are apprentices of Jesus, we learn our trade, and we learn by watching our master, by listening to his advice, by imitating him and by practicing what we have learned. This is the way an apprentice learns his/her trade. As apprentices we strive to be assistant carpenters and journeymen, and we strive for mastership. As apprentices we strive for perfection in our trade, and we are to be sent out to continue the master's work. Disciples are people who continue the work and teaching of their master.

In our baptism we have been accepted as students and apprentices of Christ. We are disciples of Christ by grace alone. It was Christ's decision to accept us (John 15:16). Nobody is entitled to be a disciple. It is grace and a privilege to be accepted as a disciple. We cannot earn it, we cannot learn it, but once we are accepted as disciples of Jesus, we start learning and striving to fulfill the hopes an ambitious master has for his apprentices.

1. STAY HERE AND KEEP WATCH WITH ME (MATT 26)[1]

Jesus offers his prayer in Gethsemane when he is about to be arrested, to suffer and die for our salvation. Jesus prays when he sacrifices himself for us. In Gethsemane, Jesus teaches, encourages and leads his disciples in prayer.

The story of Jesus' praying in Gethsemane is closely intertwined with the whole story of Jesus reconciling believers with God. In Gethsemane, Jesus was accompanied by the same disciples who had been with him on the mount of the transfiguration, when Jesus' glory was revealed; now they see his humility. The Gethsemane story reminds us as well of Jesus' conversation with the mother of the sons of Zebedee (Matt 20:20–24), where the *cup* (cf. below) was already mentioned, indicating that the students would soon follow their master into death as martyrs. The wording of Jesus' prayer in Gethsemane reminds us of course of the Lord's Prayer.

The outline of the Gethsemane story is simple: During the Passover meal with his disciples, Jesus had instituted the Eucharist (Matt 26): "[30] When they had sung the hymn, they went out to the Mount of Olives." Jesus warned the disciples that they would betray him, and "[36] then Jesus went with them to a place called Gethsemane." There he picked three disciples: Peter and the two sons of Zebedee. Then Jesus separates again from this group of the three disciples. The story unfolds in three episodes (39–41 and 42–43 and 44–45a). Three times Jesus retreats for prayer; three times he encourages his disciples to "watch and to pray."

a. Jesus Leads in Prayer

This story in the Gospel tells of Jesus teaching his disciples and encouraging them to pray:

First, Jesus orders his disciples to pray, so he wants the disciples to live a life of prayer; hence prayer is an exercise.

Then the story of Gethsemane invites us to sympathize with the suffering and praying Lord, so that the story calls us to sympathize with all of his suffering creation; hence prayer is a work of love.

Finally Jesus, the suffering man, is with us in all our prayers, so in all the pain and fear we endure, Jesus is with us and prays together with us; hence in prayer we experience God's grace.

---

1. I took important exegetical information from Luz, *Matthäus*.

- *Exercise*

In the garden of Gethsemane, Jesus prayed and thus gave himself as an example for us. He calls his disciples to follow his role model of a life in prayer: "Stay with me and watch with me, watch and pray." Jesus' command *watch!* leaves prayer neither to coincidence nor to our whims and woes. Prayer must not be reduced to spontaneous responses to whatever happens to go on in our immediate environment or whatever happens to be on our mind in a given moment. But by giving his command to keep watch, Jesus wants us to stay and pray with him, meaning to pray faithfully, guided by the word of God; he wants us to pray in remembrance of his suffering; he wants us to take responsibility and pray in communion with all his suffering creatures everywhere.

The story of Jesus in Gethsemane is told with words taken from the Psalms of lament (Pss 41:6; 6:23; 42:5). Hence the Psalms of lament, the Lamentations of Jeremiah and many other biblical prayers may guide our prayer when we lament the situation of humanity before God and ask God that he may save us from suffering. By saying *watch and pray*, Jesus indicates that he wants us to be faithful in prayer; he wants us to be guided by biblical prayers, which are both human prayers and God's word. The content of the biblical prayers is at times hard to understand and reveals itself only with practice and over time, but it is richer and more meaningful than all expressions of our own poor souls.

In the story of Gethsemane, Jesus prays three times (verses 39–41 and 42–43 and 44–45a). He prays three times because Jesus' prayer is never a vain repetition. Repeating the words of the Bible intensifies prayer, strengthens us in our prayer, teaches us regular prayer. Complaints about repetitive prayer were neither for the disciples in Gethsemane an excuse to fall asleep, nor for us today an excuse to become lazy in our daily prayer. Jesus himself did repeat his prayer, and he wants the disciples to keep watch with him.

The words *watch and pray* may be taken in a very literal way, as an encouragement to a special spiritual exercise. Church tradition knows the exercise of night-watches, especially during the Triduum, the three days of Maundy Thursday, Good Friday until Easter morning. During those night-watches we may remind ourselves of Jesus' words: *watch and pray*. The term *watch* both teaches an attitude of awaiting God's mighty deeds and suggests the exercise of keeping watch.

- *Love*

The Gethsemane story presents the Son of God as a real human being suffering from the pain of his body and the fear of his soul. The story calls us to sympathize with Jesus and to love the suffering man. Hence we are called to love all that suffers from angst and pain.

In the midst of persecution and pain, Jesus, the man of sorrows, asks his disciples to stay and *keep watch* with him. He asks because the human heart all too easily forgets and perhaps wants to forget the suffering of Jesus, forgets the pain of our fellow creation.

As Christian faith believes in Jesus Christ, the suffering Lord, sympathy for all suffering creatures is central for this faith. Believing in Christ Crucified, we are compelled to keep watch, to look out for our fellow creation in pain. The two words of the phrase *watch and pray* have probably about the same meaning. It is, however, not an over-interpretation to say that the order to *watch* means as well *watch the news!* Keeping ourselves informed about the world in need should be part of our prayer life.

Watching the news of the world and keeping up our prayers for the world in need requires continuous effort. Jesus wants us to be faithful in prayer. Keeping up prayers for the world in need, whose stories might disturb us or—let us be honest— sometimes bore us, keeping up prayer requires discipline. Prayer together with the suffering Lord Jesus establishes community and calls for responsibility. Jesus in his agony longs for our prayer, and he asks us to join and to stay in the community of prayer and love.

- *Grace*

Jesus wants us to pray with him. He also prays with us in our own fear and pain. Jesus is a teacher who has gone through all human temptations and trials himself. The story of Gethsemane shows Jesus praying in a deeply grieved way. The Son of God has become a real human being and thus endured all fear and pain any human being experiences. The blunt words of the story about Jesus, about the angst of his soul and the pain of his body, show that he is really a human being amongst us, without any alleviation of his pain. Jesus fully experienced the pain and suffering of all fellow creatures.

The story of Gethsemane describes Jesus' sorrow with strong language (Matt 26): He "[37] began to be grieved and agitated." The phrase *until death* is taken from the prayers of the Old Testament and indicates where this story will end. In our own pain, choking fear, and rising despair, the prayers of the Bible, prayers Jesus himself prayed and continues to pray with us, allow us to talk to God in bold words. In all our prayers for release from pain, in all our anxiety, Jesus prays together with us. (Rom 8): "[34] It is Christ Jesus, who died, yes, who was raised, who is at the right hand of God, who indeed intercedes for us." Thus He is amongst his friends even in our darkest hours, even in the hour of death.

Jesus did not only suffer all that we have to suffer from the body bruised and life slain. He also knows our vanishing hope, directionless despair and rejected prayer petitions. God seems to be far when the henchmen are nigh. In pain and fear, the questions about God's helping power and the doubts about his loving will can be overwhelming. God seems to hide himself from us, and no speculation about God can give consolation; all wise and perhaps true answers will sound cynical. But Jesus does not speculate about God; he invokes God. He prays together with us, and thus he leads in prayer to God. In Heb 5, a testimony independent from the Gospels, we read: "[7] In the days of his flesh, Jesus offered up prayers and supplications, with loud cries and tears, to the one who was able to save him from death, and he was heard because of his reverent submission."

Jesus is here with us and prays together with us in our most serious and sorrowful praying. With the prayers of the Psalms, He gives us daring words to pray. In all our humble prayers, Jesus is with his disciples, sharing our pain and guiding us. Jesus shares our wrestling with God and leads us in prayer to the Father. Thus Jesus Christ is God's grace for us.

b. Prayer as Spiritual Combat

Within the story of our salvation—meaning the story of Jesus' passion, sacrificial death and resurrection—we hear Jesus' prayer and how he involves his disciples in his prayer. Jesus leads his disciples, leads *us*, into spiritual combat.

The Gospel tells how, on the eve of his death for our salvation, Jesus celebrated the last meal with his disciples and said the prayer of thanksgiving (Matt 26:27). *Thanksgiving* is the translation of the word *Eucharist*. *Thanksgiving* again is meant to be both a particular activity of Christians and a constant attitude. The disciples sang the praise hymn (Matt 26:30) and thus they were supposed to be thankful. Then they went into the garden of Gethsemane to pray. Thanksgiving, praise and prayer are combined in the narrative that leads through suffering and death.

In Gethsemane, Jesus prays three times (39–41and 42–43 and 44–45a). Jesus gives a direct order. He wants us to watch and pray with him. The repetition of Jesus' prayer in Gethsemane and the repeated encouragement for his disciples indicate that his order to watch and to pray is meant to be more than merely a spontaneous response to a given situation. Even when facing pain and death, Jesus demands the continuous and regular exercise of prayer, in defiance of our weakness and the menace we may face in this world. Jesus keeps praying in imminent danger, on the eve of his certain death.

Jesus teaches his disciples: *watch and pray*. He says: "[41] Stay awake and pray that you may not come into the time of trial; the spirit indeed is willing, but the flesh is weak." Jesus' words call us to spiritual combat, to fight the temptations of the flesh by keeping watch and praying.

- ### Sleep

Jesus calls his disciples to watch and to pray, but he finds them asleep, "for their eyes were heavy" (v.43). The literal meaning of the phrase is that they were physically exhausted. But the metaphoric meaning of *sleeping* is quite obvious. Sleep is the attitude of Christians who fail their Lord and his commandment to watch and to pray. The disciples were sluggish in their discipleship. Sleep damages and destroys community with Christ and the community amongst his own, who have committed to follow his command: *watch and pray!*

On this evening, Jesus has taken the same three disciples with him as he has done in the story of the transfiguration. There the disciples had seen Jesus' glory; here they see his sorrow. There with Jesus, and with Moses and Elijah, the men of heaven, the disciples wanted to build dwellings, to stay in that day of glory; here in the gory night, they fell asleep. Jesus addresses Peter with the command: *watch and pray!* (verses 40–41). But Peter the loudmouth falls asleep, just as the others do. The disciples, Jesus' closest friends, fall asleep, and this is a warning for us who are certainly not as strong and as close to the Lord as they were. Jesus still finds us falling asleep.

Jesus asks the question (Matt 26:45): "Are you still sleeping and taking your rest?" In the history of the Church, this verse has sometimes been read as an imperative, as if Jesus gave permission: *Now you may rest*. This is, however, an unlikely twist, because in the narrative Jesus' arrest follows immediately. Therefore the sentence is most likely a reproachful question: *Are you still sleeping and taking your rest?* We, in our prayer life, still must answer Jesus' question.

- **Temptation**

On the mountain, Jesus had taught his disciples to pray: *lead us not into temptation!* (Matt 6); in the garden again he encourages his disciples, us, to fight temptation through prayer.

The word in the original text indeed reads *temptation (πειρασμός)*. The word *temptation* does not necessarily refer to the distress of the end times or to a final defection from faith.[2] The temptation in the context of the Gethsemane story is the temptation of the disciples to fall asleep on their watch. Jesus speaks about the temptation of the disciples who are committed to follow Christ on the way of the passion but who are weak and exhausted. Disciples of Christ are tempted externally by persecution, but also by the seductions of a comfortable life. Ease and comfort, prosperity and security, but also the demanding world of business and the expectations of personal relationships can cause our spiritual life to fall asleep. Disciples can be tempted internally by boredom and listlessness or by false hopes and expectations. We might be misled to expect that spiritual life will serve our private happiness or business success. We forget that God is not a means to an end, but the start, the course and the finish of the race we call our life.

Jesus encourages his disciples (Matt 26), "⁴¹ Watch and pray, that ye enter not into temptation: the spirit indeed is willing, but the flesh is weak." The English word "that" is somewhat unclear; a more clear translation is "so that."[3] Being preserved from temptation is not just the content of the petition, but as the wording indeed suggests, prayer is in itself an effective means to fight temptation, because prayer led by Jesus joins us with our savior and with the community of the faithful.

The story of the disciples' temptation to fall asleep reminds of course also of the sixth petition of the prayer that Jesus had taught us, the Our Father: *lead us not into temptation.*

- *Spirit and Flesh*

Jesus encourages his disciples (Matt 26), "⁴¹ Watch and pray, that ye enter not into temptation: the spirit indeed is willing, but the flesh is weak." In this opposition of spirit and flesh, the spirit is of course just the human spirit, not the divine Spirit. This opposition of *spirit and flesh* should not be interpreted in terms of pagan philosophy, as if it meant *mind versus matter,*

---

2. See above: III. Jesus teaches the Prayer (Our Father). The sixth petition: Lead us not into Temptation.

3. In Greek ἵνα, not ὅτι.

or *mind versus body* or *the invisible versus the visible*, or the *inward versus the outward*, or something like that. Here the language of *flesh and spirit* means mere intent versus actuality, mere promise versus actual deed. The spirit is the strength of action, as opposed to the weakness of inaction. *Flesh* means to give in to the pressure or seduction of the world, or to give in to idleness caused by the discomfort or the desires of our heart. *Spirit* means to actually take time and effort to kneel down and say the prayers. Prayer is demanding and is to be done against the wants of the flesh. The disciples need to struggle with their weakness.

Watch and pray describes a fundamental attitude of piety. *Spirit and flesh* calls us to spiritual combat. Jesus' words *watch and pray* and *spirit and flesh* call us to be ready to suffer for Christ's sake (cf. Col 4:2f. and Acts 16:26).

c. *The Praying King and his People*

Jesus leads his disciples into the garden of Gethsemane. In the face of death, Jesus is the leader of his people: Jesus, David's Son, is the King. We have a hint of Christ's kingship at the beginning of the story: The name of the place, Gethsemane, means *oil press*. *Oil* is a strong symbol in the ancient world. With oil, the king of Israel is anointed with the Holy Spirit (1 Sam 10:1; 16:13). The word *Messiah* means *the anointed one*; the word *the Christ* is the Greek version of *Messiah*. Therefore the name Gethsemane, oil press, is a hint to Jesus' royal dignity within the story of his suffering and death.

Our king, Jesus, reconciles us with the heavenly Father (1 Tim 2): "[5] For there is one God; there is also one mediator between God and humankind, Christ Jesus . . . ." The suffering man in Gethsemane is the Christ, the Messiah, the king.

- ***Obedience***

Jesus prays in Gethsemane when he is going to suffer and to die. In the very situation when he is about to be arrested, to suffer pain and death, he is still his disciples' royal leader, who prays with his men and orders them to keep watch. Jesus is still the king overseeing the situation and he briefs his men (Matt 26): "[45] See, the hour is at hand, and the Son of Man is betrayed into the hands of sinners."

At the end of the story, when the time of prayer must come to its conclusion, when Jesus is going to be arrested, the Gospel shows Jesus as the one who is in control of the whole situation, commanding his men: "Get up!" Jesus himself leads his disciples (verses 45–46) to the next chapter of the unfolding story: For the third time he announces that the Son of Man would be handed over. The Gospel thus shows that Jesus knowingly and willingly goes into suffering. His hour has come, and the king leads his men on.

Matthew shows Jesus' humility as he implores God in his prayer. But in the very scene of his arrest, Jesus shows the authority of him who knows all things. Therefore we may follow his command and face the enemy. With Jesus we may face the painful challenge of this weakening life to meet the last enemy, death. *Get up!* says the Lord.

- **Encouragement**

Jesus commands his disciples: *Get up!* He and the disciples are ready to meet the enemy. Jesus' prayer of pleading and acceptance now leads to submission. He submits to being handed over to sinners: first to the Jewish authorities, then to the soldiers. Jesus prays both foreseeing and foretelling his fate, and thus remains the captain of his destiny.

Jesus, in giving his command *Get up!,* shows that he is not helplessly dragged by an anonymous fate or by an unknowable God. In his prayer, Jesus professes that his *Father* is the Lord of our life and death. In prayer, Jesus directs our nameless fears toward the heavenly Father, and therefore we ourselves are not dragged by an anonymous fate but guided by the will of the one God whom we know and trust. When we follow Jesus' command to *get up!* even in suffering and dying, we are no longer helpless victims, but followers of the Son of God, who prays for help and then knowingly and willingly accepts the way that God, the heavenly Father, has decreed.

Many churches in North America display a picture of Jesus praying in the garden. Those pictures comfortingly show Jesus praying for his own, sometimes with his disciples sleeping nearby. This image assures us that Jesus keeps praying for us even if we give in to our weakness. It is also an encouragement for us to keep watch with him. The image of Jesus praying in Gethsemane invites us to feel with Jesus, to meditate on his passion and to assimilate our life into his.

The name of the place, *oil press,* could also reflect the anointing for Jesus' burial (see Matt 26:12). Jesus, the anointed king, is anointed for his burial, to be raised to his eternal throne, where he prays for us and raises us to eternal life.

Praying with Jesus Christ in the midst of suffering, we are dignified to speak to the Father of our Lord Jesus. Praying with Jesus, we accept God's decree and are ennobled to follow Jesus' leading through death to life.

- **Unity**

We pray as the people of the King, the Christ, the Messiah, the Lord. Jesus leads us in prayer, and we are unified as his people, praying together the king's words to his heavenly Father.

We pray as members of the kingdom, of a community, and yet prayer requires privacy. In the beginning of the Gethsemane story, just as in the story of the transfiguration, Jesus retreats with his disciples to a secluded location to meet with God. There he separates from them again. Prayer requires privacy and is not meant to show off in public—not even, or especially not, among his own people. Time and again, we read in the Gospel that Jesus seeks secluded places for prayer, just as he had taught (Matt 6). Prayer seeks God and does not watch for the effects it might have on people. When people see our piety, our prayers will certainly have desirable side-effects in the world. But those effects will paradoxically come about only if we focus on God alone, without ulterior motives. Christians at prayer do not want to watch the effect of their piety and prayer on other people; neither will Christians monitor the effect of prayer on their own souls: "Oh how humble and pious have I been today!" But prayer needs to be offered sincerely to God alone, unspoiled by any hidden agenda.

These considerations do not contradict the fact that we pray in the community of God's people. In the story of Jesus praying in Gethsemane, we read five times the important word *with*, the word that connects Jesus with his disciples. Jesus' disciples are called to join the Lord at prayer. Jesus prays with us, and our prayer is truly prayer, when we pray *with* Jesus. Jesus, the king, establishes a people of prayer. When he is severely grieved about his imminent suffering and death, he seeks consolation in the community of his disciples when he says: *Watch with me and pray!* Thus we are still called to watch and pray together with our suffering Lord.

Prayer both establishes and is embedded in Christ's community. After all, the prayer Jesus taught himself begins with *our* Father. Jesus, the suffering king, is present among his people wherever there is sorrow and pain. There he prays to his heavenly Father, together with his suffering sisters and brothers all over the world, with the unemployed, with the sick and suffering, with the aging, with the prisoners, both the innocent and those lawfully sentenced, with all people full of fear. Jesus wants to be their king, and he leads them in prayer. We may stay with him, watch and pray. In Jesus' parable of the last judgment, the judge says (Matt 25): "[40] Truly I tell you, just as you did it to one of the least of these who are members of my family, you did it to me."

Prayer with Jesus is a prayer in community with all his suffering humanity. When we want to pray with the Son of God, we need to know his pain. So we should learn about the pain and suffering of his people everywhere in all the world and bring their suffering to God in prayer. *Stay with me, watch and pray*, Jesus calls us. When the king calls us to *watch*, he wants us to be informed about the pain of his kingdom. That's why Christians must watch the news. When Jesus says *pray*, he wants us to take sides. Jesus the King fights for and suffers with his people. Watching and praying with Jesus, we remember those who suffer in the whole hurting world. In prayer, we connect with all those whom Jesus suffers with, all of suffering humanity. Meditating on Jesus' suffering and dying, we may join his prayer that he offers for all.

d. Acceptance

Matt 26: "[39] And going a little farther, he threw himself on the ground and prayed, 'My Father, if it is possible, let this cup pass from me; yet not what I want but what you want.'" Jesus wants to avoid pain and death, just as any human being would—and should. Suffering in itself has no value. Jesus prays for his life, and thus Jesus allows, even commands us to pray that God may take pain and suffering from us. Christians will take care for their life and health in this world and will pray for it.

- *Facing God's majesty*

Jesus falls on his face to pray. The wording is similar to the Greek version of Gen 17:3; 1 Kgs 18:39; and Dan 8:17. In those stories, God both reveals his frightening majesty and at the same time makes promises that are both wonderful and hard to believe. Thus, Jesus in Gethsemane is confronted with both the terrifying *cup* and God's promise of life eternal.

With his arrest being imminent, his trial closing in and the cross looming, Jesus faces the living God who rules over life and death, who is judge, who gives the cup of wrath and who saves. Jesus is confronted with God, who wants to be invoked, who wants to be implored, who even wants to be lamented to.

Confronted with suffering and death, Jesus is confronted with God himself as he prays in the garden. By first praying for the cup of suffering to pass from him, just as any human being naturally wants to avoid suffering, Jesus guides us to pray for our life to be saved and pain to be spared. The Son of God, truly human, exceedingly sorrowful until death, humbly prays to God to be spared the suffering.

Jesus asks his disciples, asks us, to *pray and keep watch* with him. In the midst of our own personal, economic or political disasters, God is there! We are confronted with his overpowering majesty and at the same time are called to believe his promises. Jesus' gesture of prostration leads his disciples both to invoke God with all urgency and pious desire, and then to surrender to his decree.

- **Facing Reality**

The first time Jesus prays (verses 39–41), he says: "My Father, if it is possible, let this cup pass from me; yet not what I want but what you want." In this first of the three prayers, the main petition is to be spared the suffering. Christians are supposed to pray confidently; prayer is not meant to be a kind of experiment, putting God to the test. Nor are God and prayer substitutes for our efforts, or a last resort when all other means are exhausted; we pray amidst our planning, hoping, and working. Thus prayer requires unqualified trust in God.

Then again, prayer does not mean denial! Jesus had announced three times that the Son of Man would suffer and die. Hence Christians are supposed to face their situation with open eyes. Prayer must not be based on wishful thinking or on denying imminent realities. When we pray for those in need, when we pray at the bedside of a suffering and dying friend, when we ourselves are in any need, then our prayer should encourage hope but not denial. When death is imminent, it would be irresponsible to prevent the necessary preparations to meet one's maker. Prayer must not tie us to the mindset of denial, but on the contrary guide us on.

Therefore, when Jesus retreats for prayer a second time (verses 42–43), he says: "My Father, if this cannot pass unless I drink it, your will be done."

In this second prayer, the words are different from the first prayer. Now the main petition is the fulfillment of God's will: *Your will be done.* Now Jesus knows that the cup of his death cannot pass away from him but that he has to drink it. From the petition to be spared the pain, Jesus has proceeded to the prayer of acceptance and obedience. The wording is the same as in the *Our Father*. Jesus, the Lord, prays just as he had taught his disciples to pray; he now leads us all in prayer. Jesus' prayer in Gethsemane leads us from urgent pleas toward acceptance.

Readers of the Gospel of Matthew will also remember Matt 20:20–23, because this passage speaks about the same brothers, the sons of Zebedee. Here, Jesus asks the disciples: "can you drink from the cup that I drink?"—thus announcing that they will follow Jesus to martyrdom.

- *Facing God's love*

Praying to his heavenly Father, Jesus wrestles through to acceptance: "Yet not what I want, but what thou wilt," and "your will be done." He or she who prays will not give up prematurely, but keep on praying with confidence, and will overcome both denial and despair and, eventually, after long wrestling, come to acceptance. Addressing God as *Father* and praying *yet not what I want, but what thou wilt* and *thy will be done*, is what we do whenever we pray the Our Father.

Jesus wrestles through from rebellion against his fate to the acceptance of God's will. Thus, Jesus is our leader and guide when we pray in the midst of our own suffering. Jesus prays together with us to God, with faith and love for God. Jesus prays to his heavenly Father, who wants us to invoke him. When Jesus' basic wish just to live was denied, the Son of God shared our human struggle with God. God imposes sorrow and suffering, pain and eventually death, but Jesus is with us in our experience of petitions denied.

The story of Jesus praying in Gethsemane shows him as an obedient servant of God, praying and pleading and eventually accepting God's will. In Gethsemane, Jesus humbly surrenders to God's plans and obediently follows God's command, trusting in the Father's love. Jesus is on our side when we have to accept God's plans. There are, in fact, not many stories in the Bible that tell us about praying people whose wishes were fulfilled. But Jesus' wrestling with God is presented by Matthew as a powerful image for Christian prayer that trusts in God's love. Jesus indeed went through all the pain and despair we endure so that no prayer of ours will be without him praying together with us. Jesus still leads on. He urgently prays that the cup of suffering might pass from him and eventually accepts the decree of the loving Father. Thus Jesus is with us, Emmanuel, *God with us,* in human form.

e. *The cup*

Only a short time earlier, Jesus had instituted the Eucharist (Matt 26): "²⁷ Then he took a cup, and after giving thanks he gave it to them, saying,

'Drink from it, all of you; [28] for this is my blood of the covenant, which is poured out for many for the forgiveness of sins.'" Now Jesus prays in Gethsemane that he may be saved from suffering and death, saying: "[39] My Father, if it is possible, let this cup pass from me." The feast with his disciples had concluded with singing the hymn of praise (Matt 26:30). Now Jesus prays to his heavenly Father to take the bitter cup of suffering from him (Matt 26): "[39] My Father, if it is possible, let this cup pass from me; yet not what I want, but what you want."

Many scholars link the *cup* to words of the Old Testament prophets (Isa 51:17, Jer 25:15). There, the *cup* is an image of God's angry judgment against the sins of his own people. In the light of those Old Testament passages, taking the cup means to accept God's righteous judgment against sin.

The word *cup* reminds us of course of Jesus' conversation with the mother of the sons of Zebedee (Matt 20:20-24). Here, *cup* indicated that the disciples would follow Jesus' way of suffering and self-sacrifice as martyrs. The Gethsemane story actually reminds us of martyr stories.

Accepting the cup means to accept what is imposed by God, to accept striving and suffering together with Jesus and for the sake of Jesus. The line (Matt 26:38) "My soul is exceeding sorrowful" is used as the antiphone on Maundy Thursday, the celebration of Jesus' Last Supper.

Whenever we accept the cup, we accept God's judgment on sin (Matt 26:28), and we accept that we will follow Jesus' way of the cross (Matt 16:24) and are reconciled with God.

2. IN THE NAME OF JESUS (PHILIPPIANS 2:5-19)

Saint Paul's Letter to the Philippians summarizes the teaching of his letter with an encouragement to joy, mutual love and prayer. The Apostle writes (Phil 4): "[4]Rejoice in the Lord always; again I will say, Rejoice. [5] Let your gentleness be known to everyone. The Lord is near. [6] Do not worry about anything, but in everything by prayer and supplication with thanksgiving let your requests be made known to God. [7] And the peace of God, which surpasses all understanding, will guard your hearts and your minds in Christ Jesus." This conclusion of the letter, with its encouragement to pray, is not just some isolated addition to the main part of the letter but an ending based on what Saint Paul writes about Jesus Christ in the chapters before.

A meditative prayer focused on Jesus Christ, his humiliation and his triumph is found in the second chapter. This early Christian poem ends with the line (verse 10): "In the name of Jesus every knee shall bow," which is certainly an invitation to use this piece of scripture in common prayer.

Because we find in this passage strong words about Jesus Christ, it has been considered mainly to develop the church's teaching about Jesus Christ (Christology). There are, however, words in this text that suggest a different use of this poem: *confessing Jesus as Lord, glory to the Father* and *every knee shall bow*—these phrases indicate that the primary use for this text is the common prayer of the church. Therefore it makes sense that this piece of scripture is used, for example, by the Roman Catholic Church for the evening prayer on Sundays.

a. The Context in the Letter to the Philippians

Many scholars assume that the verses in Phil 2:5–11 are the lyrics of a hymn composed some time before Saint Paul wrote his letter and were summoned by the Apostle as a testimony already accepted and respected by his readers. Hence, this poem in Phil 2 is perhaps one of the oldest Christian hymns. It is still helpful to understand this marvelous poem in the present context of Saint Paul's letter.

After the customary greeting and a prayer of thanks for the congregation, the Apostle encourages the church (Phil 1): "²⁷ Only, live your life in a manner worthy of the gospel of Christ." The meaning of the Greek word that we translate as *live*[4] is more exactly to *live as a citizen*, to *have citizenship* or to *be a member of the community*. Therefore, from the beginning Saint Paul's encouragement places his readers in community. Their conduct and prayer are meant to be participation in something that surpasses their individuality. The other verbs of this encouragement are *to stand firm* and *to strive side by side*; the latter expression is in the original Greek only one word, a compound word (συν–αθλοῦντες) composed of a word that means *together*, and the verbal form of a word we know in English as *athlete*. Hence Saint Paul speaks indeed about spiritual exercise done in community: prayer is a kind of team sport. Saint Paul's encouragement continues (Phil 1): "²⁹ For he [God] has graciously granted you the privilege not only of believing in Christ, but of suffering for him as well." Next to striving and suffering, the topic of *unity* is emphasized with various words: (1:27): *striving together, one soul* and then (2:2): *be of the same mind* and *be of one mind*. This unity is in verse 3 contrasted with partisanship that defies humility. What it means to be *of the same mind* is explained in the next verse (Phil 2): "⁴ Let each of you look not to your own interests, but to the interests of others." Saint Paul encourages readiness to serve and to suffer, and he encourages unity. Both topics are intimately connected, because the same wording that Saint

---

4. πολιτεύμαι cf. πόλις = city.

Paul employs to encourage unity in the church, *be of the same mind,* he uses when he says (Phil 2): "⁵ Let the same mind be in you that was in Christ Jesus." All the members of the church should have the same mind, because they all should have the same mind that is in Jesus Christ, the humbly suffering and striving Lord[5].

This concept complements Saint Paul's idea of the church as *the body of Christ* (1 Cor 10:16; 12:12; 12:27, cf. Also Eph 3:6; 4:12; 5:23; Col 3:15). Unity with Christ means both unity of the church and unity with Christ's suffering and humble service for others. Saint Paul teaches an *imitation of Christ* realized through serving, through praying and suffering with one another and for one another. Therefore Saint Paul recites the following hymn to present Christ as a role model. He is our example for humility, and thus He is the Lord in whose name we pray to the Father.

The letter to the Philippians was written while Saint Paul was imprisoned (Phil 1:7,13,14,17), and he thanks the Philippians for their support (Phil 4:10–18), which means the situation of author and addressees is already a realization of what Saint Paul says in this passage of Phil 2 about community, meaning being of one mind with Christ and suffering with Christ.

b. The meditation on Christ itself

The poem of Phil 2 tells the story of Jesus Christ's way of giving up *the form of God* to become a human and a slave, and eventually to receive from God a name that is above all names. The purpose of this prayerful reflection on Jesus' way is the exhortation: "Have the same mind that was in Christ Jesus (Verse 5, KJV)." The basic meaning of the word translated as *have the same mind* (φρονέω) is *to be minded*.[6] This piece of scripture itself guides us to prayerfully consider Jesus' way and thus shapes our mind to become Christlike.

The text continues (Phil 2): "⁶ who, though he was in the form of God, did not regard equality with God as something to be exploited . . . ." The

---

5. The verb is φρονέω.

6. The word when being connected with other words can assume meanings like *to be high-minded, to be high-spirited, to be understanding, to be wise* or *to be prudent,* or *to have old fashioned notions, to be minded like.* Therefore the King James Bible is quite right to translate: *"Let the same mind be in you that was in Christ Jesus."* The following translations of the word in Phil 2 are good as well: *"Your attitude should be the same as that of Christ Jesus"* (NIV), *"Have among yourselves the same attitude that is also yours in Christ Jesus"* (NAB); a translation, however, like "consider Jesus Christ," does not quite translate the meaning of the word.

pronoun *who* in verse 6 refers to *Christ Jesus* in verse 5. Jesus Christ gives up the position of a sovereign lord. Different from human biographies, the hymn starts at a point long before the day of birth; it starts in eternity, in heaven. Scholars agree that this hymn draws on the imagery of the suffering servant in the book of Isaiah. But Jesus is viewed as a divine being. Just as the prologue in the Gospel of John proclaims Jesus' preexistence—that is, existence before his birth as a human being—Phil 2 describes the path of the divine being down from heaven to earth and back to heaven. The hymn does not explain what makes Jesus a special or even a divine human being, but he was in the *form of God*, which means: He was God.[7] The phrase *Christ Jesus was in the form of God* was perhaps meant to repudiate those who falsely claim divine dignity. Saint Paul rebukes *empty pride* just a few verses earlier. Seeley[8] has collected the criticism of both Jewish and Roman writers against Emperor Caligula, who with certain costumes tried to appear as a god.[9] Caligula was human and wanted to appear as a god; in contrast, Jesus was God and wanted to be human.

Phil 2 says about Jesus: He "⁶ did not regard equality with God as something to be exploited." The meaning of the word translated as *something to be exploited* is: *robbery* or *taken advantage of*. Saint Paul writes: "but emptied himself, taking the form of a slave, being born in human likeness and being found in human form." There are two basic meanings of the word that we translate with *to empty* (κενόω). The metaphysical meaning is simply *to empty*. The metaphorical meaning is *to be of no reputation* or *to be nothing*. These interpretations do not necessarily exclude each other.

Contrary to those who arrogate status, glory and power, Jesus had in fact all of this, but, truly being equal with God, he gave it up to come down to us, to be with his own, to serve his own, to pray with his own. Following Jesus therefore means that we know about our dignity as daughters and sons of God because we are *adopted* children of God (Gal 4, Rom 8); we are God's

---

7. Hotly discussed is the word that we translate as *shape* or *form*. The basic meaning of the Greek word *form* (μορφή) is indeed *shape*, something that is perceived by the visual sense. Most scholars view our verse in the context of the philosophy of Aristotle: Form is opposed to matter. Matter is that of which a thing is made. Form, in contrast, is the quality or shape of a thing that makes it belong to a particular class of things. The example given by Aristotle is a signet ring dipped in wax and making an imprint. The matter, wax or whatever material, is of no significance: what is important is the seal (cf. Aristotle, *Physics*, book 2, chap. 12). The form, according to Aristotle, makes a thing belong to a class of things. Therefore the phrase that Jesus was in the *form of God* means: He is God.

8. David Seeley: *Background*.

9. Cf. Josephus, *Antiquities of the Jews*, 18.257-309; Philo, *Embassy to Gaius*, 93-114; 110; *Caligula*, 22.3-4. Images of the emperor were spread throughout the empire.

own people (2 Cor 6:16), but we give up pride and privilege and, as part of God's suffering creation, we want to serve and to pray together with God's Son.

Jesus emptied himself of the *form of God* (verse 6a), of being *equal with God* (ἴσα Θεῷ, 6b),[10] and took on the *form of a slave*, being made in the likeness of a man. Jesus freely gave up his privileges in order to live among us to serve others, and we are called to have this same mindset: to live voluntarily in this world, to serve his creation and suffer as a portion of God's creation.

The way of Christ Jesus is not only that he became human, but that he was a servant; he died the cruel and humiliating death of a slave convicted of a crime. The suffering Jesus Christ is called *Lord*, in clear distinction from God the Father (cf. Phil 1:2). The goal of Jesus' descent from heaven, his way through humiliation back to the heavenly throne, is worship *in the name of Jesus* and the glorification of God the Father by confessing Jesus as Lord.[11] We are called to follow Jesus' rough way through humiliation, service and death, and to praise God the Father. We follow Jesus, the Lord; we follow his way, and we pray in his name.

Eventually, at the name of Jesus every knee shall bow. In the New Testament the phrase *in the name of* always means: *on behalf of, in representation of*.[12] In Jesus' farewell speeches in the Gospel of John, especially, the disciples are encouraged to pray *in Jesus' name* to God the Father (John 14:13,14; 15:16; 16:23,24,26). According to 1 Pet 4:16, Christians praise God *in his name*. According to Jas 5:14, the presbyters pray and anoint *in the name of the Lord*. In our hymn, Phil 2, worship is accordingly not a response to

10. The question may be asked: of what exactly did Jesus Christ empty himself? If one assumes he emptied himself of his deity, could he still be God? How can we take seriously that Jesus Christ was a suffering man, without diminishing his deity? How can we speak about Jesus Christ as the almighty, omnipresent, and omniscient God without diminishing the reality of his suffering and death? A discussion of this question is beyond the scope of this book. The traditional orthodox answer is that Jesus Christ emptied himself by adding to his divine essence his human nature.

11. The title *Lord* (κύριος) is here not the substitute for God's *name* YWHW. Saint Paul frequently calls Jesus *Lord* in clear distinction from God the Father, especially in the salutations of his letters; thus, it is in our letter (Phil 1:2), but also in various other contexts, for example Rom 1:4+7; 4:24; 5:1+11; 6:23; 7:25; 8:39. The concept that Jesus Christ is *Lord* with God the Father (Phil 1:1–3; 2:11) is found not only in Saint Paul's writings, but also in other contexts. Most famous is perhaps the request of the disciples (Luke 11): "¹Lord, teach us to pray!" Jesus is our lord and leader in our worship of the Father.

12. In the Bible, the phrase *in the name of* never indicates the addressee of worship. Most often the phrase *in the name of* is used to describe the activity of the apostles who speak and act on behalf of Jesus, both before Easter (Luke 9:48) and after (Acts 3:6). The phrase *in the name of Jesus / of the Lord / of Christ* is also used in the context of prayer to God (the Father).

Jesus and his way described in the hymn, but it is worship *in the name of Jesus*, meaning: We shall *"have the same mind that was in Jesus."* Jesus is the suffering Lord, leader and guide of our worship, and the confession to Jesus' leadership aims at the glorification of God the Father.

Phil 2:10b says: "every knee should bend, in heaven and on earth and under the earth." Who are those worshippers? The Old Testament suggests the worship of all parts of creation (Isa 45:23; Isa 6:3; Neh 9:6; including the dead as in Ps 22:30). In the poem of Phil 2, Jesus' exaltation corresponds with his being adored (verses 9–10). Jesus is already enthroned, and universal adoration in his name, the glorification of the heavenly Father, is beginning already.

c. Jesus, Universal King and Role Model

Saint Paul calls us to have the same mind that was in Jesus Christ. In order to understand what this meant for Saint Paul's readers, it is useful to consider the religious and cultural context of this poem. As for the background of the teachings about Jesus Christ in this poem of the Bible, a variety of concepts have been considered as a foil upon which our hymn can be understood: the suffering servant of Isaiah, the gnostic savior, the Old Testament wisdom-literature (cf. especially Prov 8), or Adam's fall and restoration, or—less likely—the Persian king in Isa 45.

A tradition that gives us a framework to understand the hymn in Phil 2:8–9 is the motive of the suffering righteous one[13] who has to choose the right lord even when threatened with torture and death. The deuterocanonical Books of the Maccabeans (2 Macc and 4 Macc) give us impressive examples, and along with the stories of Joseph in Egypt or Daniel might belong to a whole genre of literature about the suffering righteous that exists both in the Jewish and in the Hellenistic world. The depiction of Jesus Christ in the hymn of Phil 2 shows the pattern of the noble death as it is well known from the Hellenistic world: Jesus is a martyr. Thus Jesus becomes the supreme leader and ideal for the praying community. The Old Testament is hardly a sufficient framework to understand the idea of Jesus' divine origin and the expression *the form of God*. Saint Paul indeed teaches something new that surpasses the thought of the Old Testament.

It is important that the words about Jesus Christ, who *did not regard the form of God as something to be exploited*, correspond with the ideal of a ruler in antiquity. According to the Greek author Plutarch, King Alexander

---

13. Conf. Seeley, *Background*.

did not consider his conquests as loot[14] but rather sought to do good for his new subjects. Greed was a behavior exactly contrary to what one expects from a good ruler. The idea that Christ *emptied himself* corresponds, according to Seeley,[15] exactly with the idea that Caesar was supposed to dedicate himself selflessly to the world, that the ruler is supposed to devote himself to the state for the welfare of his subjects, as Roman writers such as Seneca or Cassius Dio demand. Cassius Dio actually compares the role of a ruler to that of a slave of the state, laboring for the benefit of others.[16] Elsewhere, Cassius Dio compares the ideal ruler with the sun, because the sun suffers slavery (δουλεία) for the sake of others. In fact, the sun is being consumed by its own fire for the good of the world. An Old Testament prophet compared the Messiah to the sun (Malachi 4): "² But for you who revere my name the sun of righteousness shall rise, with healing in its wings." Seeley reports several other authors with similar ideas. Hence, acceptance of the idea in our Pauline hymn that the king in human form humbly serves and suffers for his kingdom, and eventually ascends to heaven and from there rules forever, was well prepared in antiquity by common ideas about the ideal ruler. Jesus Christ is the ideal Lord who denies himself and selflessly lives and dies for the sake of his subjects. His sacrifice exceeds those of other rulers, because he gives up the divine form. We are called to consider prayerfully Jesus' way and to have our minds shaped by the mind of Jesus, the sovereign Lord who forgoes his glory to become a servant of all and thus to gain eternal glory.

The hymn in Phil 2 does not refer to specific historic events but reveals a cosmological horizon. Jesus is not just a political ruler among others but acquires power over everything in heaven, on earth and under the earth, and thus eventually becomes the one cosmic lord. Evil powers are not mentioned at all, not even in the context of Jesus' death. 1 Cor 2:8 is actually the only place in Saint Paul's writings that mentions evil rulers. Jesus Christ is God's anointed king above all.

Jesus Christ receives a name which is above every other name. Because Jesus Christ has become the universal king on earth, in heaven and under the earth, he is the king of all who pray to the heavenly Father: "in the name of Jesus every knee should bow. . . ." In the kingdom of David and Solomon, all of the kings' subjects worshipped the God of Israel; in Jesus' kingdom, all in heaven and on earth and under the earth shall bow their knees to the glory of God the Father.

---

14. ἅρπαγμα the same word as in Phil 2:6; Seeley has collected more examples. *The Background of the Philippians Hymn.*

15. For the following thoughts cf. again Seeley, *Background*.

16. Dio Chrysostom, 1,22–23.

d. Every Knee shall Bow

Following Jesus Christ, we are supposed to deny ourselves and pray selflessly. And indeed, at the bedside of a loved one, in the pale light of an ICU with the beeping of a life-support system and the smell of soiled linen, we will no longer focus on ourselves. Those situations easily free us from the preoccupation with our own heart and feelings and turn our focus on God and on our ill friend. Whoever has to face those challenges needs no instruction about the focus of prayer.

Life, however, doesn't consist of those exceptional times. Everyday work, excessive demands of work and social life, and also the burden of boredom can choke our soul. Moreover, prayer meetings in our time often focus on merely personal issues of family life, health, exams or job. The hymn in the letter to the Philippians widens our horizon beyond the life of individuals. In fact, the hymn places us in the context of the whole creation, of all times and places. This widened horizon, in turn, can provide a new perspective on each individual life. I will no longer view my life as isolated from the world, but I will understand my personal life better if I carry it in prayer to him who rules over all the world and suffers in the world, from the world and for the world.

Paul recites—or composes—this hymn and thus answers the question: What does it mean to live as a Christian; what is Christian living? The answer is, be minded as Jesus is, the Lord of all creation who suffers as a servant; life as a Christian means to stay with him in the unanimity of faith, service and prayer. As we live a Christian life in the world and as members of the Church, we find our own way in Jesus' way, in his prayer and obedience, and entrust our life to him who knows the horror of betrayal, torture and death, and is eventually installed by God as Lord over all. Thus we entrust to him what is going to happen to the world and to us. We can entrust our individual life to the Lord of all, because the Lord did not simply disguise his divine power, but with his divine reality he immersed himself in a real human experience, with all its finiteness and frailty, even death—and thus he prayed.

In view of all the horror in this world, we know that God is not just a nice guy; he does allow crime, wickedness and blindness to prevail—for a while. He does allow innocent people and harmless bystanders to be made victims. This raises questions, doubts and anger against God. But God's Son lived through all this, indeed became one of us, *Emmanuel, God-with-us*. He even reproachfully cried out, "My God why hast thou forsaken me." Jesus took off his glory, and this incarnation, this *becoming man*, ended in betrayal and humiliation, and Jesus maintained obedience and prayer up to the point of senselessness and death. Christ Jesus both became flesh and was humiliated; thus he is the consolation for all who suffer and strive, who doubt and rebel in this world. Jesus prays for us and with us (Heb 4): "[15] For we do not have a high priest who is unable to sympathize with our weaknesses, but we have one who in every respect has been tested as we are, yet without sin."

In our hymn of Phil 2, the meditation on Jesus Christ's way encourages us to suffer and pray together with Christ, in humble service with one another and for one another. Jesus is the leader for the Christian life in humility and selflessness, generosity and self-restraint, giving in and forgiving.

The call to prayerfully follow Jesus in humble service and thus to participate in his kingship is amplified by the ethical teachings of the Letter to the Philippians. In Phil 4:8ff, Saint Paul gives us a catalogue of ethical topics that are quite similar to the virtues of Greek philosophy, especially of the Stoic school. Humility is, however, a specific Christian virtue. The prayer of the hymn in Phil 2 could promote a culture of humble service, of doing more than required.

As we meditate on the way of Christ, praying in the name of Christ and thus glorifying God, the Father, we may open our heart to the neighbor, bear the burden of life together with all suffering fellow creatures, and trust in the Heavenly Father with obedience, knowing that this obedience is true freedom. Humble service and obedient suffering with Christ also bears the consolation of his presence among his praying people. Thus, with this prayer in the name of Jesus to his heavenly Father, we participate in Jesus' dignity, his divine origin and his Lordship over heaven and earth.

3. INTERCESSION OF THE BRANCHES IN THE VINE

Jesus gives us another image for the prayer of intercession in the Gospel of John: We pray as branches in the vine, meaning Jesus; we pray to the gardener, meaning to the Father in heaven (John 15:16).

a. "Whatever you wish:" Prayers of Intercession

Many things can be said about our prayers of intercession in church. The spiritual direction that, according to John, Jesus himself gives us is certainly of special significance.

Jesus encourages his disciples to pray (John 15): "⁷If you abide in me, and my words abide in you, ask for whatever you wish, and it will be done for you;" and a little later (John 15): "¹⁶ I appointed you to go and bear fruit, fruit that will last, so that the Father will give you whatever you ask him in my name."

Those verses are embedded in Jesus' farewell speeches (John 13-17). In the composition of the Gospel according to John, these speeches are given on the eve of Jesus' suffering and death. The setting in John's Gospel (John 13:1-5) is that Jesus and his disciples are at table for the Last Supper. Jesus washes his disciples' feet, which is a servant's work. Even though Saint John does not tell the whole story of Jesus' last meal with his disciples, the imagery of the set table with bread and wine is still present. Here, Jesus gives his disciples instructions for the time after his death and resurrection. The immediate context is Jesus' speech about the vine, its branches, and its fruit (John 15:1-17). The speech about the vine is perhaps meant to elaborate on the wine, in a corollary to Jesus' speech about the bread (John 6).

b. Bearing Fruit

Jesus speaks about God the vine grower, and the vine, meaning Jesus himself, and the branches in the vine, meaning his disciples. We are to abide in Jesus, the vine, so that we bear fruit. It is a beautiful imagery of growth, greening and grapes, an image for the life of the church: We are branches in the vine of God. Of course branches in a vine are supposed to bear fruit. No vine grower would plant a vine and take care of its branches if he did not expect fruit from the vine. God wants us to live as fruitful branches. We pray in this life here on earth because Jesus promises that the great gardener will provide.

We are supposed to bear fruit as individuals: We are carpenters or teachers, builders or pastors, engineers, artists or nurses. We have all kinds of trades that we use for the common good; thus we bear fruit. As a local church we need to know what the purpose and fruit of our life is: We are to baptize and to teach, to celebrate the Eucharist, to visit the sick, to provide forgiveness, to bless, to pray for all in need, to sing God's praise, to care for the needy, to contribute to the protection of creation and so on. We may also learn about and be challenged by particular needs in the neighborhood and in the world. The church has the purpose to bear fruit, and God has promised to provide whatever is necessary so that she can fulfill her task.

However, Jesus speaks about fruit, not about work. He does not urge us to work harder, to commit more strongly, to donate more. We should take a moment to contemplate Jesus' image of the vine: The sap of the vine, water and nourishment flow through the capillaries of the trunk, vines and twigs into the grapes. Sun and rain from heaven nourish and warm the plant and make the fruit ripen. All the branches need to do is to abide in the vine, to be nourished by the vine; and thus they will bear fruit.

c. Abiding

In John's Gospel, Jesus calls us to abide (John 14:15; 15:4,6,7,10); and *abiding* is, in the writings of John, the work of the Holy Spirit (1 John 3:24; 4:13). The Holy Spirit makes us, the branches, abide in Jesus Christ, the vine. Therefore it is the result of neither our work nor our merit. Abiding in the vine means that we participate in the nourishment that flows from the vine. It means that we continue to listen to the word of God, that we are nourished by the Lord's Supper and that we remain a part of the praying community. He or she who breaks away from listening to God's word, who separates from the communion of the table, from praying the Great Thanksgiving (= Eucharist), cuts himself or herself off from the vine. We are given that great and beautiful gift of Jesus' body and blood; this gift, like water flowing from the roots through the branches of the vine, wants to nourish and sustain us in this life and for eternal life.

The image of *abiding in the vine* certainly means as well abiding in prayer. The term *abiding* in Saint John is consistent with Saint Paul's encouragement to "Pray without ceasing," which means regularly and persistently, not just when we feel like it. Abiding in the vine, in Jesus Christ, means abiding in the community of the faithful, whose members pray for and with one another. The Father of Jesus Christ, the gardener of the vine, will care for the vine and thus will care for all individual branches who abide in the vine. Jesus continues to speak about this image by saying: "[16] I appointed you to go and bear fruit, fruit that will last, so that the Father will give you whatever you ask him in my name."

d. Jesus the Vine

Jesus, the vine, is both promise and standard for our prayer. We have a promise: *Whatever you ask in my name,* he says. It is a great, wonderful and reliable promise. The heavenly Father will give whatever we pray for in Jesus' name. There is hope and boldness, future and solid confidence in this word of Jesus: *Whatever you ask in my name.* From those verses we derive the custom of concluding our prayers with the formula: *in the name of Jesus we pray* (cf. next chapter). We have adopted this biblical phrase to remind ourselves that we may trust in God's promise given to us in Jesus Christ. In Jesus' name, we are bold to pray. Jesus is the vine who is loved by God, the vine grower. The vine-grower takes care of the whole vine and is mindful of the needs of each branch. When we pray in Jesus' name, we participate in the strength of the vine, are nourished by the vine, and as branches of the vine are cared for by the heavenly vine-grower.

The vine is also the standard for our prayers. *If you abide in me,* Jesus says, and *if my words abide in you.* When Jesus says *whatever you wish* ... he does not abolish all standards, but he speaks about prayers *in his name.* Whenever we say *in Jesus' name we pray,* we remind ourselves that not all our wishes and cravings are appropriate. But we want to ask God for what is consistent with referring to Jesus' name. Often we want to express our wishes, our desires and hopes. But when we start praying about them with Jesus in mind, we realize that what needs to change is not so much God's ways with us, but our own ways. If we are angry and perhaps wish something nasty to happen to our neighbor, in prayer we will soon realize that we cannot invoke Jesus' name for such a wish.

Prayer purifies not only sinful cravings but also our just natural desires. We desire beauty, wealth and glory, but in view of Jesus' life of poverty and suffering, of his compassion and service, we would hardly tell our Father in heaven that in the name of Jesus we want to be wealthy, famous and beautiful. When we pray *in Jesus' name,* we clarify, purify and cultivate our desires.

God, the vine grower, is aware of the needs of the branches in the vine. He will do what is good for the branches, which is not necessarily what they covet. Even cutting and pruning might be necessary. But we can be sure: God will listen and answer.

Whenever we have the experience that God does not answer our prayers in the way we had hoped, we may thank God that his answers are wiser than our requests. People who are experienced in prayer have learned that God answers prayer always, but often, by not fulfilling our wishes, he gives the most helpful answer.

e. Branches among Branches

Jesus says: "[16] I appointed you to go and bear fruit, fruit that will last, so that the Father will give you whatever you ask him in my name." Whatever is good for the whole vine—growing, ripening and bearing fruit—we may pray for to the vine grower.

In John's writings, Jesus speaks about both abiding in the vine and abiding in love (John 15:9–10; 1 John 4:16). This includes abiding in the prayers of intercession: abiding in prayer for one another, abiding in thanksgiving to God, abiding in our petitions for the needs of the church, the needs of our government and the needs of all who long for God's helping power. Praying as branches in the vine, we abide in love.

We do not pray for other people just when we feel like it, or because we happen to think of them, or because we especially like them. On the contrary, in prayer we remind ourselves of all people in need, including those whom we do not like. Our heart is actually not a very good guide for our intercessions. The standard for prayer is not our own sinful heart, but that of God, the loving Father, and the needs of those who hunger in any way. Jesus encourages us to pray even for our enemies (Matt 5:44), which means to pray against our hearts' desires. When we kneel for our evening prayer and do not express our feelings, but, knowing that we should pray for him whom we loathe and hate, still pray for him, we learn a lot about ourselves and about the loving gardener, who cares for the whole vine and all of its branches.

We do not pray because we are nice people doing a favor for others. On the contrary, when we stand or kneel, addressing the majesty of God almighty, creator of the universe, king and judge of all the world, we are not in a position to do God or other people a favor. Standing in the presence of God's majesty, we can only say: "We humbly beseech thee."

The real reason we pray for and on behalf of others is that we are all branches in the same vine. We can live and bear fruit only when the whole vine is healthy. Therefore we pray for one another.

f. The Gardener

We pray as branches of the vine planted in the earth, created by God the Father in heaven. God is the vine grower, the gardener who has planted his garden so that he can take delight in it and harvest fruit from it. All the trees clap their hands to glorify his name (Isa 55:11).

We are the Church, branches of the vine, Jesus. With this vine we are planted in God's garden and sing with all creation. In the Bible we find prayers of all creation (Ps 96): "[1] O sing to the LORD a new song; sing to the LORD, all the earth . . .[12] then shall all the trees of the forest sing for joy." Ps 148 is a beautiful prayer that connects us with the praises that all creation is already singing. As we listen to God's word, especially the Psalms, the prayers of the Holy Bible, we may bring our own prayers. With earth and sky, with sea and dry land, with all the nations, we continue to praise God.

Praising God, the Lord of the vineyard, is what we do in church. Praising God is what we are created for: to pray for God's love and to praise God's name. We do this, of course, in our daily life. The deep meaning of Christian life is that in all we think, say and do, we praise God. This is what we do in worship explicitly, in our hymns, our liturgy, our confession of faith, with our church music and arts. It is the goal and thus the rule of all we do in church, that God be honored.

We sing God's praises together with all creation (Ps 98): "[4]Make a joyful noise to the LORD, all the earth; break forth into joyous song and sing praises." We sing our praises to the vine grower as branches of the vine, planted in the earth. When we pray we must not forget that we are part of God's creation. We may enjoy the praises that God's creation sings, and we pray together with all things he has made. Our relationship with nature would certainly improve if we realized that all the earth sings God's praise, and we are called to join in this song.

4. PRAYER *THROUGH JESUS CHRIST*

Early Christians believed in Jesus Christ and they prayed to God; how did they relate their prayers to Jesus Christ? They frequently used a formula taken from the New Testament: *through Jesus Christ,* or *in the name of Jesus Christ.*

The reason is that these phrases summarize concepts by which the New Testament relates the prayers of Christians to their teacher, lord, savior, king, high priest, sacrificial lamb, etc. Here is a short introduction to the rich variety of different but complementary concepts.

a. Prayer "In the name of Jesus" in the Bible

In the Gospels, especially in the Gospel according to Luke, Jesus is depicted as a pious man who prays often. Jesus often withdraws to lonely places to speak to his heavenly Father. When his disciples ask him (Luke 11): "[1]Lord, teach us to pray, as John taught his disciples," Jesus responds by teaching them to pray to *our Father in heaven.* Jesus, being truly human, teaches his disciples like a master teaching his apprentices. Jesus prays, and he is a teacher of prayer. Together with their teacher Jesus Christ, the disciples stand in the presence of God.

When teaching about prayer, Jesus, like any human teacher, often spoke simply of *God* (Luke 18): "⁷And will not God grant justice to his chosen ones who cry to him day and night? Will he delay long in helping them?" Thus, with his prayers and with his teaching about prayer, Jesus continued the language of prayer *to God* long used by his people. What was new was Jesus' way of addressing prayer to his *Father* and teaching the disciples about their *Father* in heaven.

The letter to the Hebrews says (Heb 2): "¹¹ For the one who sanctifies and those who are sanctified all have one Father. For this reason Jesus is not ashamed to call them brothers and sisters." Jesus wants us to be his brothers and sisters, but he is certainly not just a brother among brothers; he is the one who sanctifies them. Nobody in the New Testament writings dares to call the Lord *brother*, which would insolently ignore that it is grace when Jesus, our king, Lord and master, addresses us as his brothers. Still, Jesus prays together with human beings to the Father.

Moreover, Jesus is not merely a teacher who instructs his students and sets an example. His prayer is at the center of the narrative about his sacrificial death on the cross. After the resurrection, the risen Christ encouraged his disciples to understand the events of the three days (Luke 24): "⁴⁴These are my words that I spoke to you while I was still with you—that everything written about me in the law of Moses, the prophets, and the Psalms (!) must be fulfilled.⁴⁵ Then he opened their minds to understand the scriptures, ⁴⁶ and he said to them, Thus it is written, that the Messiah is to suffer and to rise from the dead on the third day. . . ."

So the death and resurrection of Jesus Christ fulfills the law and the prophets, but also the prayer of the Psalms. We read about Jesus praying Psalms on the cross; according to Matthew he prays (Matt 27:46 / Ps 22): "⁴⁶My God, my God why hast thou forsaken me"; according to the Gospel of Luke he prays (Luke 23:46 / Ps 31:5): "⁴⁶Father, into your hands I commend my spirit." His prayer is part of his sacrificial death for us on the cross. When we pray Pss 22 or 31, we accept Jesus' prayer for us and the guidance of the crucified Lord who leads from lamentation to glorification; praying, we follow Jesus' way through suffering with the certain hope for glory.

In John's Gospel, Jesus' own words explicitly lead beyond the understanding of Jesus as a mere teacher of prayer. For the time after Easter, Jesus had promised that he himself would perform miracles when the disciples pray *in his name* (John 14:14);[17] thus he promised that prayers in his name would be backed by his divine power. In John 4 Jesus says, "²³ But the hour is

---

17. It is doubtful that Jesus actually says, "If in my name you ask me." Some important manuscripts do not have the word *me*, and as a rule, the shorter version is authentic.

coming, and is now here, when the true worshipers will worship the Father in spirit and truth, for the Father seeks such as these to worship him. ^{24} God is spirit, and those who worship him must worship in spirit and truth." The meaning of the phrase *in truth* is found in Jesus' farewell speeches (John 14): "⁶I am the way, and the truth, and the life; no one comes to the Father, but by me." In contrast to the worship of the Jews in the second temple of Jerusalem or of the Samaritans on Mount Gerizim, Christians pray *in Spirit and truth*, meaning *in Jesus*, or, in Saint Paul's words, *in the body of Christ*. Jesus is certainly not just another historic religious leader.

In the Book of Acts and in the New Testament letters, we find only a very few examples of invocations to Jesus the risen Lord. Addressing Jesus in prayer appears to be rather the exception. In the Pauline letters, we find 45 prayers addressed to God,[18] and the only doxology clearly addressed to Christ is found in 2 Tim 4:18. In Acts 4, the early church prays to the Father in the name of Jesus (cf. Chapter 2.IV.2. about Acts 4). In the Epistles, thanks is offered to the Father *in the name of our Lord Jesus Christ* (Eph 5:20) or *through* him (*the Lord Jesus*; Col 3:17). In Rom 1:8, Saint Paul gives thanks for the congregation *through Jesus Christ our Lord*, and so he does at the end of this letter (Rom 16): "²⁷ to the only wise God, through Jesus Christ, to whom be the glory forever! Amen." In the thanksgiving for the congregation in Corinth, Saint Paul writes (2 Cor 1): "¹⁹ For the Son of God, Jesus Christ, whom we proclaimed among you, Silvanus and Timothy and I, was not 'Yes and No'; but in him it is always 'Yes.'²⁰ For in him every one of God's promises is a 'Yes.' For this reason it is through him that we say the Amen, to the glory of God."

The meaning of those formulas—*through Jesus* or *in the name of Jesus Christ*—can be understood through examining various complementary concepts in the New Testament: According to 1 Tim 2:5, Jesus Christ, the human being, is mediator (μεσίτης) between God and man; Jesus is the head of the church (Col 1:18; Eph 5:23); he is our advocate (= παράκλητος 1 John 2:1); Jesus is at the right hand of God and intercedes for us (Rom 8:34); in Hebrews, Jesus is the eternal High Priest who always intercedes for those whom he saves (Heb 7:25), who passes through the heavens and sympathizes with our weaknesses (Heb 4:14–16). According to John 16:26–27, the intercessions of Jesus Christ (*on your behalf*) are not said as a substitute for the prayers of the people, but they ask *in (my) [Jesus']*

---

18. Whether the description of Christians as those "who call upon the name of Jesus" (Acts 9:14; 1 Cor 1:2; Rom 10:12) actually implies that they *pray to Jesus* is still under discussion; this wording is most likely just a label for Christians given by outsiders. There are also some places where the doxology may or may not address Christ; in Rom 9:5, for example, it is more likely that God is praised.

name. Here again, the idea is probably that Jesus Christ presides over his people as their High Priest, and thus their prayers come before God through him. The typical Pauline formulas *in Christ* or *body of Christ* belong in this context: The people of God pray *in Christ* or as *the body of Christ*.

In 1 Peter, we find a similar thought (1 Pet 2): "[4] Come to him, a living stone, though rejected by mortals yet chosen and precious in God's sight, and [5] like living stones, let yourselves be built into a spiritual house, to be a holy priesthood, to offer spiritual sacrifices acceptable to God through Jesus Christ." God is called the head of Christ (1 Cor 11:3), and the Father of our Lord Jesus Christ (Eph 1:3; Col 1:3; 1 Peter 1:3). That we are allowed to address God as Abba, Father, is possible only through the mediation of Jesus Christ, God's only Son, who has taught us to do so.

The prayer of Jesus for his people, and thus the people's prayer through him, has educational and moral implications. As Christians adapt their prayers to those of Jesus Christ, they will pray more and more in accordance with Jesus, the head of the church. Jesus' intercession purifies the prayers of the people. Their petitions, but also their thanks and praise, will be transformed by Jesus' praying and thus acceptable (1 Pet 2:5) to God the heavenly Father. To summarize it: the meaning of the phrase *through Jesus Christ* is that he relates our prayer to God as God's Son, mediator, High Priest, advocate, head of the body.

But there are indeed some places where Jesus Christ himself is worshipped. According to Matthew, Jesus refused to be worshipped before the Resurrection (Matt 20): "[28] just as the Son of Man came not to be served but to serve, and to give his life as a ransom for many." Later, the risen Christ did not refuse to be worshipped (see Matt 28:9,17), and in John 20 we read: "[28]Thomas answered him, 'My Lord and my God!';" so it is in Luke 24 and Acts 1: The disciples worship the ascending Lord. In Acts 7 we read: "[59]While they were stoning Stephen, he prayed, 'Lord Jesus, receive my spirit,'" which perhaps mirrors Jesus' prayer on the cross (Luke 23:46). In his letter to Timothy the author (1 Tim 1:12) gives thanks to Jesus Christ.

b. Development in the early Church[19]

The basic form of the invocation in the New Testament has been retained throughout the Church for centuries. Prayer has long been addressed to God *through Jesus Christ*. Prayers seldom have been addressed to Jesus. Polycarp (died AD 155) addresses God: "O Lord God Almighty, the Father of Your beloved and blessed Son Jesus Christ, *through whom (δι' οὗ) we have*

---

19. Josef A. Jungmann's *Christ in Liturgical Prayer* is a thorough study on this topic.

received the knowledge of You, the God of...."[20] Cyprian (died AD 258) writes about the Lord's Prayer: [21] "therefore, brethren beloved, pray as God our Teacher has taught us. It is a loving and friendly prayer to beseech God with His own word, to come up to His ears in the prayer of Christ. Let the Father acknowledge the words of His Son when we make our prayer, and let Him also who dwells within in our breast Himself dwell in our voice. And since we have Him as an Advocate with the Father for our sins, let us, when as sinners we petition on behalf of our sins, put forward the words of our Advocate." Following the examples of the New Testament, Christ was frequently called High Priest (ἀρχιερεύς); the Christian people are priests under him, as they appear in the Book of Revelation (Rev 1:6; 5:10; 20:6). The literature until the fourth century quite often refers to the priesthood of Christ, who governs our actions and prayers. On a regular basis prayers concluded with praising *The Father of all through Jesus Christ in the Holy Spirit,* or, more elaborately: *The Father of all through Jesus Christ in the Holy Spirit in your holy church,* so that the church is mentioned in connection with the Holy Spirit. The phrase *in the spirit* indicates that the Spirit is understood as the atmosphere in which God's people pray.

The observation that the praise of *God the Father through Jesus Christ in the Holy Spirit* was the common doxology is confirmed by the fact that in the fourth century the followers of a certain heresy, Arianism, referred to this formula, though misinterpreting it, to support their theology. The heretics tried to prove that God's Son was ontologically subordinate to God the Father. (The philosophical and theological rationale of the various forms of Arianism do not matter here.) The traditional prayer formula *to the Father, through the Son, in the Holy Spirit* was abused by the heretics to make their case: the wording *through Christ* would indicate subordination of the Son to God. The answer of the church to this error was that we must distinguish between speaking in terms of theology proper—meaning the teaching about God himself—and speaking in terms of the economy of salvation, meaning the way of the Son from the Father through suffering, death, resurrection and ascension at the right hand of the Father. As for God himself, the Son is coeternal with the Father and of the same divine being. As for the history of salvation, the Son *emptied himself taking on the form of a slave* (cf. Phil 2). To safeguard belief in the Triune God—Father, Son and Holy Spirit—the church from the fourth century on praised "the Father *with* the Son *and* the

---

20. *The Apostolic Fathers.*
21. Cyprian, *Treatise 4: On the Lord's Prayer,* chap. 3.

Holy Spirit," or "God the Father *and* the Son *and* the Holy Spirit," referring of course to the baptism formula in Matt 28, Jesus' own words.[22]

Belief in the triune God allows us to have absolute confidence in prayer: Jesus Christ is the only begotten Son of God, and is true God from true God, perfect image of God. Therefore, the words taught by the Son of God and spoken in the church to his Father, words that come from God and go to God, are absolutely certain to be heard and answered. The prayers we pray in the name of Jesus are not an experiment that might work or fail; these prayers in the name of Jesus are as certain to be heard and answered, as Jesus Christ is true God from true God.

5. CONCLUSION: JESUS PRAYS FOR US, WE PRAY WITH HIM, WE WORSHIP HIM

Saint Paul speaks about Jesus' intercession for us (Rom 8). Jesus calls his disciples to stay with him, to watch and to pray with him, and he promises (John 15): "[16] . . . the Father will give you whatever you ask him in my name." After the Resurrection, the disciples worship the risen Christ (Matt 28, John 20, Luke 24, Acts 1) on their knees.[23] Hence (a) Jesus is praying for us, (b) we pray together with Jesus, and (c) we offer our praise to Jesus.

a. Jesus prays for us and together with us

Saint Paul teaches (Rom 8): "[35]It is Christ Jesus, who died, yes, who was raised, who is at the right hand of God, who indeed intercedes for us." Jesus is lifted up to heaven, and there he is with the heavenly Father and speaks on our behalf to God. We have an advocate (Saint John), a high priest (Hebrews), one who intercedes for us (Saint Paul), a mediator (1 Tim 2:5) in heaven, who brings all our needs, all our petitions to God. Christians believe that the Lord sitting at the right hand of God prays for us (cf. Chapter part 2, IV,3).

---

22. Since the book by Basilius about the Holy Spirit in the middle of the fourth century and the First Council of Constantinople (AD 381), the traditional formula, *praise to the Father through the Son in the Holy Spirit*, which was, after all, based on the New Testament, fell victim to misinterpretation by the Arians. There has been criticism, however, that the formula used subsequently no longer shows the Son, Jesus Christ, as the mediator of our prayers and has weakened awareness of the distinction between Father, Son, and Holy Spirit (cf. Hans-Martin Barth, *Wohin—woher mein Ruf?*).

23. The word for *worship* in the original Greek is again προσκυνέω, meaning *kneeling before* him.

This belief in Jesus' intercession at the right hand of the Father in heaven does not contradict belief in Jesus' presence with us. Jesus has promised his presence among his praying friends (Matt 18:20): "For where two or three are gathered together in my name, there am I in the midst of them." Jesus' presence is also suggested by the images for the church: the vine and its branches, the body of Christ and its members, as well the temple and its living stones (1 Pet 2:5; 1 Cor 3:17).

Jesus is God's own Son and therefore close to the Father's heart, and God the heavenly Father will listen to prayers in the name of his son. Jesus is also truly a human being, born among us on earth, who shared our suffering and woe, bore God's righteous wrath against our sin, bore our illness and suffered our death; therefore we are close to his heart. Jesus Christ is the perfect intercessor for us on God's throne, next to the Father, close to his Father's heart, and bearing us in his heart. Jesus speaks on our behalf.

How is this done, that Jesus prays for us? It happens whenever two or three are assembled in Jesus' name. Whenever the Church prays, God listens. Every Sunday we pray for the Church, for the government (1 Tim 2:2) and for all people in need. Whenever we bow our knees in the name of Jesus, we pray with Jesus and Jesus prays with us, and the heavenly Father listens to his beloved Son. Whenever we say *our Father in heaven,* God listens to the intercession of his Son. Whenever we pray for our loved ones, for the Church, for the needs of our neighbors, for the needs of this society and for the needs of all people on earth, Jesus carries our prayers to the heavenly Father, at whose right hand he sits.

b. We pray together with Jesus

Jesus calls his disciples to stay with him and to pray with him (cf. Chapter 2.I.2). Christians want to pray together with Jesus, the king at God's right hand. We know well the prayers the Lord Jesus prays. We know the Lord's Prayer; we know Jesus' prayer in John 17, which is called his priestly prayer; and we know that Jesus prayed the Psalms.

The book of Psalms in the Bible was and is the prayer book of the Jewish community. As a faithful Jew, Jesus prayed the Psalms, along with a community who had prayed and meditated on them for centuries—and continues to do so. When we want Jesus to lead us in prayer, the best way to start is by reciting Jesus' own prayers, those contained in the Holy Bible. The Psalms remain an inexhaustible source of powerful and consolatory prayers. With the first Psalm of the Bible's prayer book, we pray: "Happy are those who do not follow the advice of the wicked, . . . but their delight is in the law of the LORD, and on his law they meditate day and night." Meditating on the word of God is a delight, and doing so we are called *happy* (Ps 1). When we pray the Psalms, we participate in Jesus' prayer; he leads us in prayer to the Father, and we follow by repeating his words, savoring the spirit of those prayers.

Happy is she or he who meditates on God's word day and night. Ps 1 is an introduction to the whole Psalter; it gives us the tenor of the whole prayer life nourished by the Psalms: Happy are those who take delight in God's word; they flourish and bear fruit. The Psalm gives a beautiful image for those who meditate on God's word: they are like a tree planted by streams of water. The tree is watered and nourished, grows and flourishes. In the hot and dry, stony and arid region of the holy land, a tree planted by a creek is a surprising and amazing sight. While we are living in a spiritually arid land, in the spiritual drought of this time, we are planted by the stream of freshness and nourishment, because we are watered by the never-ceasing stream of God's word. We are fed with the life-giving water that is made to sustain and keep all of God's creation alive. We are planted close to the river, the stream that makes us prosper and makes us bear fruit in due season.

Though we are planted by the streams of water, we might lose its effect if we rip out our roots and leave the life-giving river. Even a cactus cannot live without water in the long run, and we should not be so arrogant as to believe we are a cactus. We are in dire need of the continuous nourishment of the flowing waters, so that we can grow and green and bear fruit. We are planted by the flowing waters, and our roots must stay in the moist soil, irrigated by the stream of God's word, sacrament and prayer.

When we are nourished by this flowing water of God's word, when we participate in the prayers of Jesus and the church, first of all the Lord's Prayer, the Psalms, and the other prayers of the Holy Bible and also of the community of the faithful, Jesus prays with us and for us. When we pray the words Jesus prayed, Jesus, sitting at the heavenly Father's right hand, speaks with us and on our behalf to the Father. Thus, God our Father listens to Jesus when he leads us in prayers.

c. *The church worships Christ*

It is true that invocations addressed to Jesus are rare in the New Testament. But as already mentioned, we still have some powerful testimonies to the worship of Christ. Saint Luke, who writes about Jesus' ascension at the end of his gospel and the beginning of Acts, gives us his own interpretation of Jesus' ascension: The Lord blesses his disciples with his human hands; he sends them, and they worship him (προσκυνήσαντες) on their knees. Jesus ascended to heaven to be King of the universe and is worshipped as the Lord. On the fortieth day of Easter, according to the timeline of the Bible (Acts 1:3), the Church celebrates Ascension Day. We celebrate that Jesus is lifted up to heaven and is seated at the right hand of the Father. Therefore the creed of the Church confesses that Jesus ascended to heaven, and *He is seated at the right hand of the Father.*

In heaven, Christ takes the throne to rule with God, the Father, as king forever and ever. The tradition of the Church has rightfully applied enthronement Psalms, which celebrate the Lord's (יהוה) kingship, to the ascension of Jesus Christ.[24] With the Psalm the Church sings: "God has gone up with a shout, the LORD with the sound of a trumpet" (Ps 47:5). In Eph 1, we read about Jesus' kingship in heaven: "[20] God put this power to work in Christ when he raised him from the dead and seated him at his right hand in the heavenly places, [21] far above all rule and authority and power and dominion, and above every name that is named, not only in this age but also in the age to come."

God's rule over the whole cosmos does not mean that he is far away. The Old Testament praises God as the ruler in heaven, yet his presence in the temple was celebrated (cf. 1 Kgs 8; Isa 6). In one of the Psalms we hear the chant (Ps 84) of the Korahites, "[1] How lovely is your dwelling place, O LORD of hosts!" The Korahites were servants in the temple, singing of God's dwelling place, i.e., the temple. Thus, both God's rule in heaven over all the earth and his presence in the temple were proclaimed.

Accordingly, Jesus' enthronement, his ascension to heaven, does not mean that he wants to get away from us. As the right hand of God is present everywhere, so Jesus Christ, at the right hand of the Father, can be everywhere. According to Saint Luke, Jesus' ascension means sending his disciples, blessing them with his human hands and being worshipped by them.

Hence, the story at the end of Saint Luke's Gospel about the ascension of Jesus to heaven gives the same promise about which we read at the end of Matthew's Gospel. Jesus meets his disciples on the mountain, proclaims that he has all power in heaven and on earth, and promises (Matt 28): "[20]I am with you always, to the end of the age." Jesus is with us at all times and in all places. His omnipresent power is manifest and present in the sacrament of baptism (Matt 28:20), and the disciples worship the present Christ on their knees (Matt 28:17). Likewise Jesus Christ has come near us, is with us in the word of forgiveness (Matt 16:19) and the sacrament of the altar (Matt 26:26) and in the praying community (Matt 18:20).

---

24. Pss 47; 93; 96–99.

At the end of the Gospel according to John, it is Thomas who touched the wounds in the body of the risen Lord Jesus and said (John 20): "[28] My Lord and my God!"

II

Prayer to God the Father

JESUS HIMSELF PRAYED TO his Father and so set an example; he taught about prayer; and he led his disciples in prayer. Therefore, prayer is for Christians mainly prayer to the Father of Jesus. In everyday reality, however, prayer to God is not always recognizably based on the example, teaching and guidance of Jesus and not necessarily recognizable as prayer to this Son's Father in heaven. Therefore we need to ask: What makes prayer a Christian prayer?

1. WHY DO PEOPLE PRAY?

Most people involved in any local church pray, but you may meet more and more non-church-goers who pray as well. Some cultural milieus seem to prefer spontaneous prayers motivated by accidental situations in a person's life and world, or by certain moods of the soul.

I used to visit an elderly lady. She never had the opportunity for a higher education but was highly intelligent, devout and caring for family and neighbors. She showed me a piece of paper with a prayer she had composed years ago and had used every night ever since. While the content was quite orthodox, the wording certainly was her own. Once, it had been a spontaneous prayer; she perhaps did not put down all the parts of the text at the same time. But now it has become a written prayer, faithfully used for years. As a pastor and fellow Christian, I had nothing but respect for this wonderful old lady. Still, thinking about prayer, I have to wonder: why do people actually pray? There are certainly various reasons.

a. Prayer as Expression of Faith?

Many people, when asked about the reason and meaning of prayer, will answer that prayer expresses their faith. That this answer is honest, genuine, and sincere should not be questioned. It still needs to be pondered in the light of God's Word. The concept of prayer as an *expression* of faith seems to be plausible; only, there is no place in the Bible that would define prayer as an *expression*, be it of faith or of other thoughts and feelings.

It is certainly possible to interpret biblical prayers and stories about praying people in such a way that the prayers appear to be spontaneous *expressions*. It is, for example, possible to view a Psalm like Ps 23 as a spontaneous *expression* of the faith of some unknown individual more than two thousand years ago. The fact, however, that we learn from this Psalm very little about the author does not support this understanding. If we assume that this prayer is the record of a spontaneous *expression* of faith in a particular situation, we would expect to learn from the Psalm something about this situation, but the diversity of the metaphors (valley, table, shepherd, house of the Lord) does not allow us to place the Psalm in a specific historical context.[1] With the concept of *expression* the Psalm's words about enemies would be understood as the *expression* of someone's fear and hate, which for many readers will then be quite disturbing, or so I hope. The interpretation of a biblical prayer in terms of *expression* may be more or less plausible, but there is no way to prove that this particular understanding of biblical stories and prayers is more appropriate than any other explanation. In fact, to interpret a biblical prayer through the concept of *expression* might very much depend on a particular understanding of the human soul.

If we understand a prayer of the Holy Bible as a spontaneous *expression*, it is of course not necessary for us to employ its words at all. At best, a Psalm may serve as a model or example, and not a very relevant example if it is an *expression* of someone who was living in a very different time, different country, and different culture.

We perhaps want to speculate about the origin of Ps 23, and a lot of historical research has been invested in this question, without convincing success. It is, however, certain that for two thousand years the carefully composed poem has been prayed by innumerable people who found guidance and consolation in the ancient words.

If the words of the Bible—and the Church—are dismissed as records of what people, often unknown, in the distant past and in distant places *expressed*, it remains an open question what the content of our own prayers

---

1. Walter Brueggemann, *The Message of the Psalms*, 273–74.

today is to be. That which is *expressed* might be faith or cynicism, loving intercession or selfish wishes, hatred or Christian love, petitions of faith or just selfishness. It is obvious that the concept of *expression* provides no guidance for the content of our prayers. And this absence of guidance sometimes appears to be the very purpose of the concept of prayer as *expression*.

If we conceive prayer as personal expression, prayer would be constrained by the limitations of the self-expressing individual. The needs of strangers and far-off people, the needs of the world, and the hopes and visions of the faith community would be relevant only as far as they happen to affect my personal peace of mind.

The concept of *expression* expects prayer to be genuine and truthful. Hence, doubts about the self-expressing *ego* are not allowed, otherwise its *expressions* would be questionable, and consequently prayer couldn't be confident. So the whole concept of *expression* would collapse. But does it make sense that the faithful put their trust in themselves while standing or kneeling in the presence of God's majesty? Isn't God's glory always greater than our expressions? Don't we always owe God more thanks than we feel and desire to express?

The idea of prayer as a form of expression is obviously inconsistent when applied to prayers of penitence. Prayers of penitence, if understood as *expression,* would be limited by the praying person's sensitivity for his or her sin, or more likely by the lack thereof: the more reckless a person is, the less penitence needs to be *expressed*. Prayers of penitence would be completely perverted if the worshipper tried to express his or her own ingenuity. There is no such thing as a "beautiful prayer of penitence." Prayers of penitence, if understood as *expression*, would have no real standard as to what faults need be confessed, unless the sole standard was the arbitrary moral sensitivity of one individual.

Another test for the concept of *prayer as expression* is the comparison of biblical prayers to what might be *expressed* by human beings. Which of the seven petitions of the Lord's Prayer would come up as a spontaneous *expression*? In our times, probably just the petition for bread, and not any of the first three petitions which refer to God's name, kingdom and will. If prayer is primarily comprehended as an *expression* of individuals, it is hard to explain why the Bible provides us with hundreds of prayers, the Psalms, the Old and New Testament canticles, the hymns in the Epistles and more. The concept of *expression* has indeed already undermined the use of the biblical prayers in many congregations.

Jesus' disciples asked the master (Luke 11): "[1] Teach us to pray." They obviously understood prayer as something that can be taught and learned. If prayers are understood as the *expressions* of individuals, it needs to be explained why *expression* can be taught. Whatever explanation can be given, it is certain that Jesus answered the request of his disciples neither by teaching them about themselves, nor by teaching them a spiritual technique, but by giving them a specific liturgical text, saying: "When you pray, say: . . . ." A concept of prayer as *expression* hardly needs a prepared text, even if taught by the Lord himself.

Furthermore, it is often hard to show whether those *expressions* are specifically Christian, if the invocation of Jesus Christ or of his Father has any impact on the content. To say it bluntly: if we understand prayer as an expression, do we need an addressee at all?

b. Prayer as one-to-one conversation?

The quest for the addressee seems to be solved in the common understanding of prayer as a one-to-one conversation. This seems to be an acceptable way to describe prayer, and yet there are inconsistencies in this view as well.

A passage in the Bible that clearly speaks about a one-to-one conversation between God and man is the dialogue in Gen 18 between Abraham and God about his judgment on Sodom. But is this story really a teaching about prayer? Abraham tried to convince God not to destroy Sodom by arguing that there were perhaps a few righteous men in the city to be found. Abraham failed, and Sodom was eventually destroyed. Not repentance but the righteousness of humanity is Abraham's argument, and therefore his whole "prayer" was doomed from the beginning. The whole story reflects on humanity's and God's righteousness, and perhaps on the problem of collective punishment. If we read this passage as a story about prayer, it is obvious from both the basis of Abraham's prayer and the result that this prayer is hardly a positive example to follow.

Still, many prayers in the Holy Bible can rightfully be understood as a dialogue between persons. A beautiful poem in the book of Isaiah calls upon God (Isa 51): "⁹ Awake, awake, put on strength, O arm of the LORD; awake, as in the ancient days." Here God is anthropomorphized; i.e., God is depicted as a human person. It is still true (Ps 121): "⁴ He who keeps Israel will neither slumber nor sleep." The Old Testament people called upon God to awake his arm, but they knew very well about God's unceasingly active power. What appears to be a contradiction is in fact appropriate, even necessary language about the mystery of prayer: the almighty and all-knowing God allows us and encourages us to address him in a human way. The wealth and beauty of this biblical way to address God foreshadows what would be revealed in Jesus Christ (Matt 8): the almighty God in human flesh sleeps in the ship; he is called upon by the disciples to wake him up, and then even the winds and the sea obey his mighty word! Hence we are certainly allowed to speak to God as we speak to a human person.

However, we must not forget that addressing God is also very different from any conversation with human persons. Though we may speak to God as we would another person, he does not answer as human persons do. Viewed from the outside, prayer appears to be more a monologue than a dialogue. When in confirmation class a pastor hides in a closet and, impersonating God, answers to frightened students, it might be funny—for him—but it completely misses the point. Christians pray to respond to God's word, given once and forever in Jesus Christ, to whom the Holy Bible gives witness.

While the Bible does employ the image of a conversation between human beings, we need to realize that this communication is never a dialogue between equals. But (Isa 33) "[22] the LORD is our judge, the LORD is our lawgiver, the LORD is our king; he will save us." Even if we understand prayer as a one-to-one conversation, we need to respect God's majesty.

The analogy of prayer with a one-to-one conversation is acceptable only if we keep in mind its inadequacy, which becomes even more evident when we think of God's qualities: God is Lord, uncreated, infinite, eternal, almighty, omnipresent, omniscient, always loving. The praying human being has none of those qualities.

The understanding of prayer as a one-to-one conversation is qualified by God's omnipresence. It is true that we pray (Ps 22): "[19] But you, O LORD, do not be far away! O my help, come quickly to my aid!" But we do not pray to ask God to come to our place because he would otherwise be absent. As we invoke God, we pray to the one God who always waits for us, wherever we might be (cf. Ps 139).

This understanding of prayer as a one-to-one conversation is qualified by God's omnipotence (Ps 135): "[6] Whatever the LORD pleases he does, in heaven and on earth, in the seas and all deeps." When we pray to the almighty God, we do not ask God to withdraw his allegedly limited power from another issue and turn it to our problems. God's omnipotence is certainly more than the power to react to a given situation or request. God, who created and sustains heaven and earth, is in control of every individual life already.

The understanding of prayer as a one-to-one conversation is also qualified by God's eternity. The Psalmist prays (Ps 90): "[2] Before the mountains were brought forth, or ever you had formed the earth and the world, from everlasting to everlasting you are God." When we pray, we do not ask God to change our present situation, because our present would not have been foreseen by him. But we pray to him who says (Rev 1): "⁸I am the Alpha and the Omega, ... who is and who was and who is to come, the Almighty" (cf. The excursus *God and time*).

The understanding of prayer as a one-to-one conversation is further qualified by God's omniscience: We do not talk to God to let him know what he would not know already. Rather, we pray to him who knows everything, who knows our needs before we pray and even before we are aware of them ourselves, and he knows them better. When Jesus teaches about prayer, he teaches about God's omniscience (Matt 6): "⁸your Father knows what you need before you ask him." Thus he transcends the simple analogy of prayer and a one-to-one conversation.

It is certainly still legitimate to apply the analogy of a conversation between human persons to the prayer of humans to God. But it is necessary to understand the metaphorical character of this simple analogy.

Excursus: Person

- ### Introduction

If we view prayer as a dialogue between persons, we need to explain our understanding of what a person is.

Surveys on religion in society sometimes simply ask about belief in a *personal God*, usually without explaining the presupposed theology. And if anyone questions the sentence *God is a person*, the response will probably be emotional and polemical. But what does that mean? Browsing the internet for an actual definition of the term *personal God*, one will find explanations the likes of: *God is not an impersonal force*. A double negation, however, does not explain anything.

Person is widely believed to be a traditional way of speaking about God; but as far as I know, discussion of a *personal God* came up only in the late 18th century when the concept came under attack and theologians began to defend the term, thus accepting what is perhaps a false dichotomy. At least the reformers, including Calvin, did not use the phrase *personal God*.

- ### The term "person"

Derived from the Latin *persona*, the term *person* is not biblical. It doesn't even have an equivalent in the biblical languages of Hebrew, Aramaic, and

Greek. It has its origin in Latin jurisprudence, describing both natural persons and juristic persons (e.g. a company).

If one looks up the word *person* in English Bibles, one finds only a few places where it has a qualified meaning. Sometimes the word *person* is just required by the English language and does not translate any word in the original text. The King James Version, for example, calls Esau a *profane person* (Heb 12:16). But the original text reads just *a profane;* the word *person* is added by the translation to adjust the text to the English language. Nowhere(!) in English Bibles is God is called a person![2] There is only one context in the King Jes Bible where the word *person* has a qualified meaning: The Pharisees, seeking to flatter and trap Jesus, say (Mark 12:14): ". . . Master, we know that thou art true, and carest for no man: for thou regardest not the person of men, but teachest the way of God in truth." Impartiality is indeed a Christian virtue, as Gal 2:6 proves: "God accepteth no man's person (πρόσωπον = face): for they who seemed to be somewhat in conference added nothing to me." This context, *God does not regard the person,* hardly encourages us to employ the concept of a conversation from person to person to understand prayer.

In Latin or English, without theological reflection, *person* can be intuitively said about the man Jesus, the Son of God. The Holy Spirit is, in the original Greek of the New Testament, of neutral gender (τὸ πνεῦμα) and turns male (*spiritus*) only in the Latin translation. The Latin term *persona* has been introduced into the language of the Latin church by the lawyer Tertullian in about AD 200, specifically to distinguish between the three persons of the Holy Trinity.[3] The traditional terminology of the West accordingly speaks about God as *one being* in *three persons*.[4] The intuitively

---

2. Jesus Christ is called by the King James Bible a *person* only in two places. The first place is 2 Cor 2:10, where the word *person* is the translation of the Greek word for *face*. The second place is Heb 1:3, where the word *person* is the translation of the Greek word ὑπόστασις (= subsistence), which in philosophical Greek theology is the term for the eternal Son of God. He is, in the traditional Latin terminology since the third century, the second *persona* of the Holy Trinity. Therefore only the later Latin theological terminology motivates the translation: ὑπόστασις = person.

3. Tertullian, Adversus Praxean, 27. The somewhat suitable Greek word for *person* is πρόσωπον, the meaning of which is *face* or *theater mask*. Thus, translated into Greek, the three *persons* of the Holy Trinity seem to be just three faces or appearances of the same individual. There was actually a heresy in the West that thought along those lines (Sabellianism). Tertullian is fighting exactly this heresy. Still, the Greek Church remained suspicious about the terminology of the Latin Church, which apparently fails to distinguish carefully enough between Father and Son. Both the oneness of God and the biblical testimony to a conversation between Father and Son need to be preserved.

4. *The Athanasian Creed (quicumque vult)* says, ". . . *We worship one God in Trinity and the Trinity in unity, neither confusing the persons nor dividing the divine being*

obvious understanding of Jesus as a person is now applied to the Father and the Holy Spirit. Therefore, whoever speaks about God just as a *person* must know that he/she disregards the traditional theological terminology. This is perhaps acceptable if alternative concepts are presented—perhaps. The question, however, as to how we speak about God the Father, God the Son, and God the Holy Spirit—one God—must be answered if we want to speak about prayer as a dialogue between persons.

- ### *The historic understanding of "person"*

Some clarification of the term *person* is necessary, precisely because the meaning is intuitively obvious.

The most influential definition of *person* was given by Boethius in the sixth century: A person is "an individual substance of the rational nature;" that is, angels, humans, and God. Boethius based his definition on an analysis of the factual usage of the word[5]. Boethius' definition of *person* defines, i.e., delimits, a person against other persons. If, however, the meaning of *person* is therefore an individual, the personal God would not be infinite and eternal, not encompassing all creation. So it's hard to explain why one should believe creation could not exist without this individual.

Boethius' statement is a *genus–differentia* definition: A person is an individual of the family of rational beings like gods, men, or angels. According to this understanding of *person*, God would be one individual of many. Thinking in terms of *genus–differentia*, this implies polytheism, even if the number of individuals of the family is just one; at least it is difficult to explain why there would be only one god-person of the genus *persons*, why the one universe would be made by the one God, or why I have to decide for only this person. The tendency to refer to God as an individual, whom logic suggests may be only one of a group of god-persons, perhaps contributes to the seeming randomness of choices one can make in a multireligious society, including no choice at all. Slencska[6] points out that inconsistencies in the traditional definition appear even in pre-modern theology.

A really troubling problem with the word *person* in the context of prayer is that the term implies a distinction between what is a *person*, in

---

(*neque substantiam separantes*). For the Father is one person, the Son is another, and the Spirit is still another. But the deity of the Father, Son and Holy Spirit is one. . . ."

5. Boethius, *Theological Tractates*, 72: "*Rationalis naturae individua substantia.*" The Latin expression *rationalis natura* perhaps refers to the Greek definition of man as an animal gifted with language or reason and therefore with freedom of will (ζῷον λογικόν). For the following, cf. Notger Slenczka, "Einleitung."

6. Notger Slenczka, "*Einleitung*," 4.

the sense of a rational being, and what is not a *person*: God, angels, and human beings are supposedly persons; the rest of creation is not—including the sheep of the shepherd. But this undermines a much more important biblical distinction: the distinction between creator and creation. There is no third category besides creation and creator. Whatever can be and must be said about the special position of humanity in creation (Gen 1:26) will not change this fundamental distinction between creator and creation. The term *person*, however, categorizes God and humans as *persons* as opposed to all non-human creatures on earth. The most fundamental biblical distinction between *creator* and *creation* is thus superseded by that of *person* and *non-person*. Our reckless disregard for our fellow creatures is perhaps due to the fact that we forget we are creatures among creatures, standing together with them in the presence of the creator. Isaiah praises God (Isa 55): "¹² the mountains and the hills before you shall burst into song, and all the trees of the field shall clap their hands."

Saint Augustine, in his famous *Confessions*, addresses God: "Man, who is just a small portion of your creation, wants to praise you."[7] The prayer book of the Bible ends with the line (Ps 150): "⁶Let everything (!) that breathes (כל הנשמה) praise the LORD! Praise the LORD!"

- ## The Term God

Blaise Pascal (1623–1662) in his *Memorial* proclaims: "God of Abraham, God of Isaac, God of Jacob, not of the philosophers and savants".[8] It is true that religious conscience speaks to God and about God as a person, i.e., as an individual, as a *someone*, as a *you* who is able to communicate. After all, religion is not about an explanation of the world and not mainly about ethics, but takes place in certain activities like prayer. Then again, religious and philosophical understandings of who or what God is have always existed side by side. Philosophers, speaking about God as the *being* (ὁ ὤν), or the first *cause* (τὸ αἴτιον), the one and all (τὸ ἕν καὶ πᾶν) or *the whole* (τὸ καθόλου) of the world, have always insisted that they speak about the same God religion is speaking about. Usually philosophers claim to enlighten the religious understanding of God, which tends to objectify and anthropomorphize God and speaks about his partiality. Early Christian philosophers, like Justin (martyred † AD 165) and Athenagoras as well, were absolutely sure

---

7. Augustine, *Confessions*, 1.1.1: *Et tamen laudare te vult homo, aliqua portio creaturae tuae.*

8. *Dieu d'Abraham, Dieu d'Isaac, Dieu de Jacob, non des philosophes et des savants Certitude. Certitude. Sentiment. Joie. Paix.* Pascal, *Pensées*.

that their philosophical way of speaking about God would deepen and enlighten the faith but not replace it.

This enlightenment, however, is suspected of stripping religion of its capacity to counsel, to console, and to enable people to cope with life, which largely depends on anthropomorphic images of God (cf. Slenczka, 5f.) Then again, the beautiful hymn of the pagan stoic philosopher Cleanthes teaches stoic philosophy and still invokes Zeus as *first cause and ruler of nature*[9]; which proves that it is simply not true that the God of philosophers cannot be invoked and trusted, obeyed and loved. And there are indeed people who tell me they would pray to the universe. There is truth to the claim of philosophers that they speak about the same God religion is speaking about, in an enlightened way. Religion itself knows about the inadequacy of its objectifying and anthropomorphizing manner of speaking about God and to God, and is thus interested in transcending this language. Isaiah (chapter 44) mocks his pagan opponents: "[15] Then he makes a god and worships it, makes it a carved image and bows down before it. [16] Half of it he burns in the fire; over this half he roasts meat, eats it and is satisfied. He also warms himself and says, 'Ah, I am warm, I can feel the fire!' [17] The rest of it he makes into a god, his idol, bows down to it and worships it; he prays to it and says, 'Save me, for you are my god!'" Hence the philosophical way of speaking about God, which transcends any man–made image of God, is born from religion itself.

Giving up on the traditional conjunction of philosophical enlightenment and the anthropomorphizing language of *person* will seriously jeopardize any meaningful conversation between religion and philosophy and science.

- ***The copula "Is"***

If we say *God is a person,* we have to explain our understanding of the copula *is.* Some theory of symbols or metaphors is, consciously or not, applied whenever we say *God is . . .* because only human language is available to speak of the divine.

---

9. Παγκρατὲς αἰεί . . . φύσεως ἀρχαγέ. *Cleanthes' "Hymn to Zeus."* The editor says the poem clearly manifests the form and motifs of a traditional cult hymn (page 8). The hymn concludes with the prayer:
    deliver human beings from their destructive ignorance
    disperse it from their souls; grant that they obtain
    the insight on which you rely when governing everything with justice
    . . . .
    Always to praise the universal law in justice.

The origin of the word *person* in Latin jurisprudence does not necessarily mean that it would be illegitimate to employ the metaphor *person* as we speak about God and speak to God; but we need to keep in mind that it is just a metaphor taken from the terminology of a specific culture and from a terminology that speaks about a specific form of human interrelationship; that is to say, in terms of law. Therefore if the term *person* and thus the concept of *personal relationship* dominates our thinking and prayer, we run the risk of involving the original Latin context of the word, meaning we perhaps describe the interrelationship of God and humanity in the framework of law.

The word *person* is a metaphor taken from the realm of human interrelationships and applied to the relationship between God and men. So far, this metaphor is as legitimate as any biblical metaphor, as long as we are aware of the metaphorical character of the term. The Holy Bible, however, is full of other images of God which imply different modes of interaction between God and humanity. Metaphors are, of course, never completely consistent with what they describe, nor with one another. Therefore the metaphor *person* as well is not completely consistent with the wealth of the biblical language. This is true for the more abstract, theological metaphors of the Bible, for example Isa 12: "[2] Surely God is my salvation; . . . the LORD GOD is my strength and my might; he has become my salvation" (similar: Exod 15:2 and Ps 27:1). We have no reason to assume that these biblical terms would be just metaphors, whereas the non-biblical term *person* would be less metaphorical. The metaphor *person* is certainly not consistent with the more concrete biblical metaphors: In Ps 18, God is called a *rock* and a *fortress*, my *buckler*, and the *horn of my salvation*, and *my high tower*, a *lamp in the darkness*; in Ps 84, *sun and shield*; in Ps 28, *strength and shield*. In Ps 118, the Lord is *my strength and song*; in Lamentations 3:24, the Lord is *my portion*. In Ps 23, the Lord is the shepherd of the lambs, which again is imagery hardly consistent with the concept of two persons. In the Gospel of John, Jesus is both the *good shepherd* (John 10) and the *lamb of God* (John 1:29 +36), and in the book of Revelation this lamb sits on the throne and paradoxically shepherds those who washed their robes in the blood of the lamb (Rev 7). Hence, not even the *good shepherd* can really undergird the concept of *persons* as the exclusive means of describing how we address God. All the examples mentioned above are taken from biblical prayers and thus show that we should not limit our prayers to the anthropomorphic image of God as a person and thus suffocate the wealth of the biblical language: God is a *person* just as *a mighty fortress is our God*.

- *Person as God's hiddenness and freedom?*

As we speak about the *person* of God, one would at least preconceive that Jesus is a person.

Some authors, however, seem to see the meaning of *Person* in God's historicity, hiddenness, and freedom.[10] Even Spinoza, almost identifying God and nature (*deus sive natura*), distinguishes between the *nature naturing* and *nature natured*, so that God is the free cause of all things, and is in this way somehow hidden behind the scenes.[11]

In modern times, following the end of the eighteenth century, philosophers began to oppose the Church's concept of God. The German philosopher Fichte, for example, identifies the divine with the moral order of the universe, of which every rational subject is a part, and by which he/she is motivated against instinct and the individual desire for happiness. The moral order of the universe is identical with any moral subject; hence Fichte objected to a personal God behind and above the moral order of the universe. To the reproach that this concept would mean atheism, he returns the compliment by responding that objectifying and anthropomorphizing a God behind the moral universe would mean creating an idol.[12] So Fichte opposes a *personal* god in the sense that this person would be someone hidden behind the universe. Is God a person hidden, like an actor speaking through (in Latin: *per-sonans*) a theater-mask? If we return to the traditional terminology, i.e., God as one being in three persons, *person* is—as is intuitively obvious—our God made visible in Jesus Christ, and therefore *person* is not the hidden God (*deus absconditus*) but the visible, audible, touchable word of God in human form, the *God-with-us*, the one whose deeds and suffering we know, who is obedient to his Father, whose miracles are done to reveal the kingdom, and who was not rescued from the cross by prayer and a miracle.

Criticism of a concept of God that objectifies and anthropomorphizes him somehow ignores the traditional teaching that God has anthropomorphized himself when his word became flesh in Jesus Christ. Jesus Christ is God's human face. With Jesus Christ, the Old Testament ceremonial law

---

10. Rosenau speaks of "Geschichtlichkeit, Lebendigkeit und Unverfügbarkeit," Rosenau, "Gott höchst persönlich."

11. (*Natura naturans* and *natura naturata*.) Cf. Rosenau, "Gott höchst persönlich," 58.

12. In an answer to Fichte, Jacobi claims, "*God is outside me, an independent living being. Hence God is before and outside any knowledge and gives value to all knowledge and reason.*" Jacobi distinguishes between what appears to reason and the one who appears. Cf. Jacobi, "Jacobi to Fichte (1799)."

to make no image of God is obsolete because Jesus is "the visible image of the invisible God" (cf. Col 1:15; εἰκών... τοῦ Θεοῦ τοῦ ἀοράτου): God in person.

In 1 Tim 2 we read: "⁵ For there is one God; there is also one mediator between God and humankind, Christ Jesus, himself human." We need to make sure that the abstract concept of *personal relationship with God* does not replace Jesus Christ as the one who relates us to the heavenly Father, teaching and leading us in prayer. Prayer as a one-to-one-conversation can describe the dialogue between the Father and the Son, and we are called to join in the words the Son is praying.

- ### *Person as God's Freedom?*

Wayne R. Spears criticizes Robert Simpson: "Such a view of prayer does not regard God as personal in the sense that He would respond to prayer in an objective way apart from the change of orientation in the one who prays."

For Spears, *personal* obviously means that it's not humanity but God who has to change his ways. Here, the almost blasphemous consequences are drawn from a concept of prayer that is based neither on obedience, nor on repentance, nor on the acceptance of the cross, but is just a kind of wishbone to gain personal advantages and temporal goods. Jesus (Matt 6) connects prayer with fasting, i.e., giving up goods of this world, and with the call to bear the cross. Jesus connects the prayers of intercession with giving alms (again Matt 6), i.e., taking responsibility for our neighbors.

Saint Paul does not refuse the possibility that God answers prayer in such a way that human wishes are fulfilled. But he tells his own story about answered prayer in 2 Cor 12: Three times he prayed that the thorn in his flesh might leave him, but the answer was: "My grace is sufficient for you." Whether or not this answer came as a special revelation or via meditation on the already given revelation does not matter, because Saint Paul certainly tells his story not just as some autobiographical anecdote, but rather to speak of his authority as the Lord's apostle, which is precisely *not* based on special power (δύναμις) and answered prayer. Saint Paul views this denial of his wish not simply as bad luck; rather he finds meaning and strength precisely in this seemingly unanswered prayer: "for power is made perfect in weakness." Saint Paul tells his story certainly not simply as a particular event, but as a normative teaching: followers of the suffering Lord will not live on the hope of fulfilled wishes but bear the cross of their Lord.

c. Prayer as an Experiment?

The idea that prayer would be some kind of experiment looks, at first glance, almost blasphemous. But it is actually not uncommon that the attitude towards prayer is like experimentation: *"Let us pray and find out; perhaps God helps . . . or not."* A biblical story could be interpreted as a scientific experiment: In the story of Elijah and the prophets of Baal (1 Kgs 18)[13] the prophets of Baal pray to their god for rain, but they fail; Elijah prays to the God of Israel and rain begins to fall. Thus Elijah has proof that his God exists and provides rain, but the theory of Baal's prophets is wrong. The question remains whether this is an appropriate interpretation of the biblical story.

Scientific experiments need to meet certain requirements. A scientific experiment serves to confirm or to falsify a theory. Any scientific theory must be considered true only provisionally, and is therefore always subject to new tests. Scientific theories are generalizations, and therefore any experiment must be reproducible. An experiment must be a risk for the theory. The scientist must be ready to have her/his theory tested and possibly falsified by a new experiment; he/she must keep distance from his/her favorite theory and must base all scientific work on methodological doubt.

How do these requirements of scientific experimentation apply to prayer? According to Jesus' teaching about prayer, the answer to disappointment is *not to lose heart"* (Luke 18:1). Therefore disappointment is exactly *not* a falsification of a theory but a challenge to our faithfulness. The worshipper cannot be detached from his or her prayer as a scientist is required to maintain detachment and objectivity. Hence *doubt*—methodological or not—cannot be the attitude for prayer.

Brümmer[14] insists that there is a difference between scientific experiments and prayer, because the former deals with causal necessities, whereas the latter refers to a personal God making free-will decisions that are never inevitable. But this argument seems to introduce exactly the doubt and uncertainty that is incompatible with prayer, unless one wants to admit that the world of scientists is more reliable than God—an attitude that indeed undermines the prayer life of many people. Brümmer does not give any definition of the term *personal* besides the concept of God's free will. He argues prayer is not like running machinery: prayer does not influence God with causal necessity, like handling a machine. But again, isn't our confidence in prayer necessarily correlated to the reliability of God's doing? Brümmer argues that the requirement of reproducibility in experimental

---

13. Vincent Brümmer gives this example. Brümmer, *What Are We Doing When We Pray?*

14. Brümmer, *What Are We Doing When We Pray?*, 1.2.

science would not be applicable to prayer—Elijah would not accept the competition with Baal's prophets a second time. Only Brümmer already presupposes a concept of prayer that doesn't rely regularly on given texts and forms such as the Lord's Prayer, the Psalms and canticles. The very fact that these prayers are provided by the Bible implies repetition. As strange as it might seem to modern people, two biblical morning prayers (Ps 57:8 and 108:3) say: "I will awake the dawn." These prayers presuppose that the sun rises every morning and that every morning, in some way, prayer is connected with the rising sun. To non-Christians this will look like absurd magic that purports to make the sun rise. But the Bible does not speak about prayer simply in terms of cause and effect, so that prayer would be a willful action of humans to cause an effect on God and on the course of nature. But Christians understand this word of the Bible, "I will awake the dawn," as the word of God, which is said by God the creator, is written in the Bible to be read by us, and is to be prayed by the Church. Therefore we can indeed understand this invocation to raise the sun as repeating the word of the creator who makes the sun to rise by his word and who wants us to join in and pray his word. This *experiment* can be and shall be reproduced, every morning.

Brümmer's *philosophical inquiry* never refers to the specifically Christian concept of prayer, the concept of Trinitarian prayer, which is grounded in the belief that the word of God created heaven and earth (John 1), was made man in Jesus Christ, and is present among us in the word that we both hear and pray in the Holy Spirit.

d. Prayer to acquire grace?

In some Protestant groups, prayer is considered as a means of grace next to word and sacrament. Lutheran tradition has always reserved the term *means of grace* for God's means by which he acts on human beings. This might appear as a mere dispute about words. But it becomes a practical problem when preachers recommend personal prayer to souls afflicted by sin. The advice just to pray could lead to the dangerous error that a terrified soul thinks God's work of reconciling the world with himself through Jesus Christ is not yet complete, and therefore a sinner can and must do something in addition to trusting in God's grace in Christ. If prayer is thus misunderstood as a human effort to acquire God's mercy, the afflicted sinner, when being counselled only to pray, is tempted to focus again on him- or herself. The result may be that their doubt about God's mercy only grows worse. Or, if prayer is misunderstood as a meritorious work, it may lead to ruinous haughtiness. Sinners who feel their sin and yearn for God's grace need the clear word of forgiveness and need to receive the Body and the Blood of Christ.

We are certainly welcome to pray the fifth petition of the Lord's Prayer, the penitence Psalms or other prayers of repentance. Christians know that they are sinners, and by joining in those prayers they are members of the community created by God, the community of sinners, who prays together, guided by the only sinless one.

2. PRAYER AS OBEDIENCE OF FAITH

We ask again: Why do Christians pray? The answer to this question should be simple: Prayer is what Christians do. She or he who prays need not justify prayer, and we know, especially in prayer, that in the presence of God's majesty we cannot justify ourselves but must depend on God's grace; this grace is exactly what we pray for. It is still helpful to consider the question of what Christians actually do when they pray. It is wholesome for Christians to clarify for themselves what they do, and it is good for the world when Christians are ready "to give account of the hope that is in them" (cf. 1 Pet 3:15).

Jesus tells us to pray, and when we pray obedient to his word, (a) Jesus promises that God will hear our prayer, so we are encouraged to pray; (b) Jesus teaches prayer, so we have guidance in prayer; and (c) God's name is holy, so we pray with humility.

a. *The meaning of obedience*

Jesus called his disciples to stay with him, to watch and to pray (Matt 26), and Jesus' disciples followed him, who lived in obedience to God (Phil 2:8).

Readers perhaps feel uncomfortable with the phrase *obedience of faith* (Rom 1:5), but we should realize that the commandment to pray is actually the only motivation for prayer the New Testament speaks explicitly about. The introductions to the Lord's Prayer are:

Matt 6:9: "Pray then in this way: Our Father in heaven..." (cf. Matt 26:41 and 42).

Luke 11:1-2: "one of his disciples said to him, 'Lord, teach us to pray, as John taught his disciples.' ² He said to them, 'When you pray, say: Father....'"

In Gethsemane, on the eve of his suffering and death, Jesus told his disciples (**Mark 14:38**): "Watch and pray that you may not come into the temptation; the spirit indeed is willing, but the flesh is weak."

In all three places, Jesus' commandment to pray is connected with his example. Jesus prays, teaches to pray, and tells us to pray, and accordingly in church, discipleship and obedience have become important motivations for prayer. The word *obedience* might appear offensive to many people. But we need to understand that *obedience* is in fact expected in various areas of life.

Children need to be obedient to their parents for the sake of their own safety: "Do not touch the hot stove!" "Do not run across the street!" "Call me when you need help!" Following the New Testament, we pray to God *our Father*. The analogy of obedience to loving parents is appropriate to understand the commandment to pray.

Students and disciples need to obey their teachers to learn and to strive for perfection. In the New Testament, Jesus is frequently called *teacher*. He is the teacher of his disciples, meaning his students; he sets an example and he orders them to pray.

Patients are given orders by their doctor, and for their health's sake they should obey their doctor's prescriptions about diet, exercise and medication. In Exod 15 we read: "[26] If you will listen carefully to the voice of the LORD your God, and do what is right in his sight, and give heed to his commandments and keep all his statutes, I will not bring upon you any of the diseases that I brought upon the Egyptians; for I am the LORD who heals you."

Servants and soldiers need to obey the orders of their superiors; otherwise the whole system will not work. This principle is true for revolutionary armies as well. Jesus is called *King* and *Lord*; the letter to the Ephesians employs the language of the military (Eph 6).

A client should follow the advice of his or her lawyer. In a capital trial, it could be a matter of life and death to have the jury hear the right words as instructed by the defense attorney. In the Gospel of John, the Holy Spirit is called *advocate* (John 14:16), and in 1 John 2 we read: "[1] Jesus Christ the righteous is advocate with the Father." Rom 8 speaks about prayer and refers to the imagery of a court of law (Rom 8:1). The advocate speaks on our behalf, and we, when called to testify, want to say to the judge what our counselor has advised us to say.

Finally, a friend might be given advice by a friend which is helpful to obey. Jesus says (John 15): "[14] You are my friends if you do what I command you." So *obedience* doesn't necessarily mean mindlessly observing a merciless law, but rather following a friend's advice. We are called to be Jesus' friends and want to obey his good counsel that calls us to pray.

Despite all reservations modern people hold against *obedience*, it is still true that the more God's majesty is honored, the more the commandment to pray will appear as merciful permission. As we obey Jesus' advice, prayer revives our hope while we are on our journey on earth, until we reach the end of our pilgrimage and can offer full adoration.

As we obediently pray the words of the Bible, the value of the biblical prayers is not limited by our ability to understand them. In his explanation of the Lord's Prayer, (1519) Martin Luther writes: "There is such a great measure of grace in the word of God that even a prayer that is spoken with the mouth and without devotion (with a sense of obedience) becomes fruitful and irritates the devil."[15] The common Protestant bias against prayers that are allegedly spoken with the mouth only and not with the heart jeopardizes the nourishment of our prayers from the Bible and the community of the faithful. Only the practical use of biblical prayers and prayers inherited from the faith community makes it possible for us to understand them. If, for example, we delayed praying the Lord's Prayer until we fully understood all its petitions, we would have to wait forever—at least in this life—until we could pray the words Jesus wants us to pray. *Understanding* is not a precondition but the result of praying the prayers of the Bible. Without the guidance of the Bible, our prayers could soon turn into either uneducated prattle without much specifically Christian content or die of starvation. Besides, why should the mouth stop praising God when our soul and mind fail to do so?

Obedience to the majesty of God, however, would be completely perverted if the idea sneaked in that we could earn merit through our prayers, which God would have to take into account. Jesus teaches about obedience in general, which is certainly right for prayer (Luke 17): "[10]So you also, when you have done all that you were ordered to do, say, 'We are worthless slaves; we have done only what we ought to have done!'" He or she who prays does not want to earn merit, but acknowledges our dependence on God's mercy. Obedient prayer might require abandoning the hope of getting our wishes fulfilled. Mystic thinking in the late Middle Ages occasionally spoke about a willingness to accept even damnation (*resignatio ad inferum*) in order to let the love for God's honor prevail.[16]

b. Encouragement

Following Jesus' example and obedient to his word, we can experience this obedience as liberating, freeing us to forthrightly speak to God. In prayer we need neither grudgingly follow orders, like a child compelled to say "please" and "thank you," nor are we called to crawl, grovel, and beg. God's own

---

15. Luther, "An Exposition of the Lord's Prayer for Simple Laymen," 20 (WA 2,82).

16. For example, Thomas à Kempis, *The Imitation of Christ*, II,11,5, and the anonymous book *Theologia Deutsch*, chap. 11.

Son authorizes and encourages us to approach his Father, to address him candidly and to ask him for what we need. This encouragement means, on the other hand, that we need not cling to illusions about ourselves, our powers and freedoms, but we can acknowledge the reality of our dependence on God, who gives us all we need and keeps his promises.

Christian prayer is an act of obedience to Jesus' word (Matt 7): "⁷ Ask, and it will be given you; search, and you will find; knock, and the door will be opened for you." With three imperatives, *ask—search—knock*, Jesus encourages us to pray. These imperatives encourage us to speak up, and each of them is backed by the promise that our prayers will be answered: *it will be given, you will find, the door will be opened*. The absoluteness of the promise allows absolute confidence. We need not view prayer as just an experiment that may or may not work; neither does Jesus promise a merely probable fulfillment of particular wishes. This word of Jesus makes sense when we know that all prayers are already heard by the eternal and omniscient God and included in his plans for us. The letter of St. Peter continues Jesus' encouragement to pray when he advises us (1 Pet 5): "⁷ Cast all your anxiety on him, because he cares for you." The letter says *all* anxiety; obedient prayer does not necessarily expect the fulfillment of particular wishes, but professes faith in God who always provides *all* we need. This profession of this faith is best done in form of petitions.

Jesus has told us to pray and to pray confidently. The confidence we have in prayer is based not on human skill, effort[17] or worthiness, but on the biblical concept of the omniscient God (Ps 94): "⁹ He who planted the ear, does he not hear? He who formed the eye, does he not see?" (cf. Matt 6:8 about God's omniscience). Luther writes about the address of the Lord's Prayer in his Small Catechism: "With these words God wants to attract us, so that we believe he is truly our Father and we are truly his children, in order that we may ask him boldly and with complete confidence, just as loving children ask their loving father."

Obedient prayer in Christ is not a submissive resignation to fate. We are encouraged to maintain the belief that Jesus Christ sits at the right hand of the almighty God, who rules over all people and things that try to usurp control of our thinking, feeling, and hoping. Thus obedient prayer can be an act of resistance and an armor against those who, by fraud or sword, want to gain power over our souls. For Christians, their prayer based on obedience to God can be an act of resistance so that they can maintain their integrity when social and economic pressure—or opportunity!—endeavor to

---

17. With the popular the phrase *praying hard*, the answer to prayer seems to depend on human effort. If so, *praying hard* would mean not to pray at all.

overthrow Christ and usurp power over our hearts and minds. In his book of Acts, Luke tells us that the Apostles, when thrown into prison, actually praised God (Acts 12; 16). Prayers—even for material goods—will create an openness to God's plans. Therefore, with prayer we can hold up our resistance against hopelessness and against the erosion of our commitment to a better life for our neighbors. Prayer can strengthen our dedication to serve. The prayers of the Bible and those inherited from our faith community lead us who "do not know what[18] to pray as we ought" (Rom 8) to new trust and hope.

If prayer is understood as obedience of faith, the question about answered and unanswered prayers is no longer the main focus. Obedience and devotion are already the beginning of the answer, because in prayer we surrender to God and accept God's gracious will, knowing that he has listened to our prayer already. While we are on our pilgrimage on earth, we have in prayer a foretaste of the praise and thanksgiving in heaven.

In prayer, the Psalmist recalls God's promise to the faithful (Ps 50): "[15] Call on me in the day of trouble; I will deliver you, and you shall glorify me." This means that those who pray remind God of his promise. As we speak about God's caring providence, we need to understand that God acts in mysterious ways and not just where human judgment agrees with God's doing. On the contrary, a confrontation with God can be terrifying. A few challenging examples may illustrate this:

When Jacob was renamed "Israel," meaning a *fighter against* (!) *God*, he professed the miracle (Gen 32): "[30] For I have seen God face to face, and yet my life is preserved." God calls Moses to serve him (Exod 3) and then (Exod 4): "[24] it came to pass by the way in the inn, that the LORD met him, and sought to kill him." The Bible dares to say that God himself hardens the heart of Pharaoh (Exod 4:21; cf. Rom 9:17). God himself caused the fight about the census in David's kingdom (2 Sam 24): "[1] Again the anger of the LORD was kindled against Israel, and he incited David against them, saying, "Go, count the people of Israel and Judah." The story of Jesus' temptation shows that it is God's spirit who leads into the desert of temptation (Matt 4). The sixth petition of the Lord's Prayer makes it unmistakably clear that God permits if not causes temptation against God. Those mysterious stories show that an encounter with God is shocking and awe-full; and they show that God's providence is indeed beyond the obvious chain of cause and desired effect, and surpasses our understanding, our sense of comfort, and certainly our wishful thinking. But these disturbing stories show, as well, that in and

---

18. The original text says indeed "*what to pray*" (in the original Greek: τι) and not "*how to pray.*" Cf. the chapter IV,3 about Rom 8 in this book.

by means of apparently evil events, through our enemies and his enemies, even when God seems to fight against us, God's love and providence are still at work. Knowing this, we can pray confidently in the darkest of times. God's answer surpasses human prayer, surpasses even what is humanly possible to expect from God (Jer 33): "³ Call to me and I will answer you, and will tell you great and hidden things that you have not known." When we invoke God and hope for his answer to prayer, we trust in God's providence that surpasses our understanding and exceeds all expectations.

Tradition has given various answers to the question of in what ways God answers prayer. Traditional Protestant doctrine tried to describe God's providence by distinguishing different ways that God might act: God prevents causes from having an effect; God redirects the course of events so that the causes have effects different from those intended by humans; God sets limits to the evil effects which a cause might bring about; God permits bad things to happen without actually being the cause of evil.[19] The beauty of this concept is that most biblical stories can be described plausibly. In another concept, teachers of the Church have distinguished between the first cause of all events and the secondary causes. The secondary causes form the chains of cause and effect in this world, of all events of nature, of history and of human actions. The first, uncaused cause is God, who is mysteriously at work both in all regular processes and in all apparently extraordinary events. Prayer belongs to the secondary causes, but addresses the first cause, i.e., God, immediately. Still, prayer belongs to the processes inside God's creation, which remain under the continuous control of God's providence. In other words: God uses our prayers to reach his goals. Compared with the stories of the Bible, this concept looks at first sight quite abstract, but the beauty of this concept is that the basic biblical idea of God's almightiness and his love working in all things, both ordinary and extraordinary, pleasant and evil, including defeat and disaster, including his enemies (!), including the prayers of the faithful, is maintained.

Prayer that simply expects a godless world to continue its good or bad path—and only asks God to intervene in isolated cases by modifying a few of the effects the world's powers cause—has a smallish idea of God's providence. In prayer, we may trust that all things in God's creation are made, sustained and governed by God. Even Satan can do nothing without God's permission, as the book of Job shows (Job 1–3). Satan, though unwittingly,

---

19. The Latin terms are *impeditio, directio, determinatio, permissio*. The concept is problematic in two respects: First, the term *permission* only describes God's almightiness, without giving a satisfactory answer to anyone who suffers and prays. Second, the whole concept is developed without referring to any of the Christological teachings of the New Testament about creation, for example John 1, Col 1:15–20, etc.

even contributes to God's plan of salvation, as the story of Judas shows. Believing this, we can pray in spirit and truth against appearance.

The poets of the lamentation Psalms, and all people who ever since have used these Psalms in their own pain and need, praying these words of lamenting and rebelling, bargaining, and complaining, testify to faith in God's providence in times of trial. The suffering of Christ is then the ultimate revelation of God: On the cross, Jesus prays and surrenders his life into his Father's hands (Luke 23:46). So we, while bearing our crosses, may pray confidently, knowing that our pain and prayer are part of God's plan.

c. Guidance

As followers of Jesus, God's Son, we are allowed, taught and encouraged to pray to his Father. So is this call to confident prayer a license to expect the fulfillment of any wish?

Jesus' word (Matt 7) "[7] Ask, and it will be given you; search, and you will find; knock, and the door will be opened for you," is, as already mentioned, encouragement, but not without guidance. Within the Sermon on the Mount, this promise follows the main instruction about the content of prayer, the Lord's Prayer, and it follows Jesus' warning not to strive for food, drink, and clothing (Matt 6:31) but to strive for the kingdom of God (Matt 6:32).

In the Gospel according to Luke, Jesus' comparison of prayer to the persistent asking of a friend (Luke 11:5) follows Jesus' institution of the Lord's Prayer, which again shows that Jesus first taught about the content of prayer, then about confidence and persistence in prayer.

In the Gospel of John, Jesus encourages prayer and also sets standards for the content (John 14): "[13] I will do whatever you ask in my name, so that the Father may be glorified in the Son. [14] If in my name you ask me for anything, I will do it."[20] The term *in my name* is explained by the next verse (John 14): "[15] If you love me, you will keep my commandments." Jesus' words encourage prayer said, first, *in Jesus' name*, and second, aimed at glorifying the Father. Therefore confident petitions are not meant to be expressions of selfish wishes but are part of a life *in Jesus' name*, meaning a life of love to Christ, a life lived by his commandments, a life for the greater glory of God and therefore a life in the community in Christ.

Also in the Gospel of John, we find the bold promise (John 15:7): "If you abide in me, and my words abide in you, ask for whatever you wish, and

---

20. Cf. also 1 John 5:14: *"this is the boldness we have in him, that if we ask anything according to his will, he hears us."*

it will be done for you." The disciples will be granted *whatever you wish*, on the condition *if you abide in me*. The term *abide* is frequent in the Gospel of John and explained, for example, through the image of the vine and the grapes (see above 2.I.4.). This *abiding* certainly has ethical implications, as Jesus says a few lines later (John 15): "[10] If you keep my commandments, you will abide in my love, just as I have kept my Father's commandments and abide in his love." This *abiding* implies our abiding in the community of the faithful. Jesus' promise encourages not self-centered wishes but a confidence that is consistent with our abiding in God's word and community.

Saint James ascribes power to prayer itself. He writes (Jas 5): "[16] Therefore confess your sins to one another, and pray for one another, so that you may be healed. The prayer of *the righteous is powerful and effective.*" The power and the effectiveness of prayer is promised to the *righteous*, which means this prayer presupposes a confession of sin that reconciles us with Christ and thus with his community; for this reason, Saint James writes first: "confess your sins to one another." Those who have thus received righteousness before God in Christ are brought back into the praying community; for this reason, Saint James writes: "pray for one another." With confession and intercession, we return to communion with God and to the communion of all who pray to him. As prayer aims at community, prayer itself is effective indeed, because it causes what it prays for: praying obediently, we are in communion with God and in communion with his praying people. Many people experience the blessing of a prayer chain, of a community of people praying for them in times of need or illness. Saint James is obviously not too concerned with the question of whether the prayer really *works* healing. Those who pray believe that God is gracious and that he continuously cares for his own in Jesus Christ. He or she who prays trusts that God has included all the prayers of the righteous in his plans. Thus we find guidance in the community with God and with his people in Jesus Christ.

d. *Humility*

It takes humility to accept guidance. It appears that in the time of the New Testament, only Christians considered humility a virtue. Nowadays humility is again not exactly a popular character trait. Some people pretend to be humbled by the approval of their voters or customers only in moments of extraordinary success. Pride, in turn, is no longer considered a vice and is frowned at only if it is too obviously out of proportion with actual accomplishments. Pride is today seen as a source of happiness.

It's understandable to have reservations about the idea of humility. If we speak about prayer merely in terms of a one-to-one relationship, humility perhaps appears as submission to superior power. If prayer is understood as a dialogue with an overpowering individual, a mere human would not be entitled to any answer to his or her prayers, and God would be obligated to nothing. You can almost hear a Sunday school teacher telling you off: 'You should be seen, not heard!' If prayer is mainly viewed as addressing a superior individual, the formula *for the sake of Jesus* would indicate that the worshipper knows about his or her condition as a sinner, and that he or she would not be entitled to anything prayed for. Humility in a one-to-one conversation with an invisible, powerful tyrant would mean being dragged by force rather than being guided by authority. Under that kind of thinking, prayer indeed appears to be servile begging and a substitute for responsible work. Prayer understood as a dialogue with a superior individual will, when wishes are fulfilled, lead to false security and pride: "Oh, I am on such good terms with my personal God." With prayers understood as personal relationship, disappointment may lead to despair or rebellion. In such a one-to-one relationship with an overwhelming power, humility serves the function of somehow keeping pride or despair, rebellion or false security under control. So in the framework of such a personal, one-to-one relationship the whole idea of humility is hardly attractive.

Christians, however, do not pray because they want to beg favors or claim entitlements; they pray because God's own Son prays, teaches them to pray and authorizes them to ask his Father for the necessary provisions for their life and work on earth, to which God has commissioned them. The phrase from the Psalms *for your name's sake* may illustrate this attitude: Such a prayer is not begging for alms but reminding God of his honor and promise to support us in our work for his goals.

Humility means joyously accepting Christ's encouragement and guidance. Those who use the prayers of the Bible and perhaps of the faith community need not worry about whether those words are appropriate and suited to convince God, but can simply accept them from Jesus' hand and humbly and boldly offer them to his Father.

As God's Son authorizes us to pray, both encouraging and guiding us, prayer cannot be our own work and merit; we will invoke God but not expect to be rewarded for the quantity or quality of our prayers. Believing in the Father's power and authorized by his Son, we have a firm basis for our trust and hope. We may pray as God expects us to pray, obediently and trusting in his mercy. We can give up on asserting ourselves—even on asserting ourselves by means of obedience(!)—and can be certain of the love of Jesus' Father.

We pray with humility; we pray for things not by claiming them as a reward that we have earned, nor by begging like slaves, but because God's own Son has called us *friends* (John 15:15) and is "not ashamed to call us brothers" and sisters (Heb 2:11), and told us to pray for what we need for our work on earth; and we can trust that he will fulfill his promises. With our petitions and intercessions especially we acknowledge that we receive everything from God, including our potential, acquired skills, and opportunities. In prayer we can give up delusions about ourselves, our powers or merits, and acknowledge the creator. Thus God is honored as the one who gives everything.

We need to pray with humility for the sake of our suffering brothers and sisters. Certainly, an overwhelming number of witnesses testify to their prayers being answered, and there is no reason and no decent way to reject those testimonies. There is, however, also the silent sadness of those who feel that their prayers remain unanswered and usually do not talk about that experience. Testimonies of those who witness to their answered prayers can increase the pain of those who are disappointed. To deal with the problem of seemingly unanswered prayers, we need recall God's love revealed by the suffering Christ: Jesus did not walk the way of *answered prayers* and quick fulfillment of his wishes, but wrestled with God until he said, "Not my will but thine be done." Facing pain and death,[21] Jesus asks us: "stay with me, watch and pray."

We need to pray with humility because we are part of the church, of society, and of creation. Individual experiences with prayer have to be taken seriously, but the prayers of individuals also take their place in a larger context. We cannot simply ignore the challenge of reconciling individual experiences with the needs, hopes, and pains of the church, of society, and of the whole creation. Triumphant prayers of thanksgiving for being saved in a disaster while thousands miserably perished will be seen as repulsive, and rightfully so. We need to remain humble, knowing about the majesty of God and the dignity of our suffering brothers and sisters.

We pray with humility, because we pray for God's glory. The prayers for things of this world—for material goods, for health, life, success and social standing—are transcended when we aim at God's glory. Elijah's prayer for rain on Mount Carmel was said in a time of a severe drought, in a parched and devastated land. But Elijah knew that this material disaster was caused by God's wrath. Therefore, his prayer for rain was focused not so much on the rain itself but on the demonstration of the true religion (1 Kgs 18): "[39] When all the people saw it, they fell on their faces and said,

---

21. See part 2. I 2 about Jesus' prayer in Gethsemane.

The LORD indeed is God; the LORD indeed is God." The examples of helping miracles in the New Testament, which indeed responded to concrete needs of individuals, are still meant to reveal the kingdom of God. Saint Augustine says (Exposition on Ps 77): "He doth indeed hearken to thee at the time when thou dost seek Himself, not when through Himself thou dost seek any other thing."[22] We pray humbly as members of the kingdom and serve our king with pride.

3. THE TRADITIONAL PRAYER TO THE ALMIGHTY GOD

Most Christians rightly believe that God answers prayer. Popular belief and sometimes philosophical thought presuppose that there is some kind of causal connection between prayer to the powerful, loving, personal God and desired events. If this presupposition is valid, it should be possible to verify the effectiveness of prayer empirically. The effectiveness of prayer is undoubtedly evident in the experience of many individuals, but there seems to be no statistical proof; at least insurance companies do not take prayer into account.[23] Still, the language of many contemporary prayers suggests that we need to tell God what he seems not to know, and that we need to motivate God to do what he seems not to desire. Thus prayer is supposed to cause an effect on God. The prayers of the Bible, however, speak in very different ways, and Jesus' reminder that the heavenly Father knows already what we need (Matt 6) demands deeper reflection. The tradition of the church has mostly followed Jesus' teaching about the loving, all-knowing, and almighty God, who needs not to be informed of our world and life, nor to be encouraged to change his activity. Jesus' teaching in Matt 6 (see above 1.1.II) about the caring providence of God is a great consolation and the basis for our confidence that God listens to our prayers. Because of his omniscience, God hears and understands clearly our unclear, ill-thought-out, mumbling, often self-centered prayer; God has understood our needs even before we did, heard our prayer already before the idea of praying ever popped up in our confused and sinful hearts. Rather, the worshipper defines in prayer his or her attitude towards God and His doing. In prayer we acknowledge God as the loving Father and we surrender to God's will. Thus we may understand the petition *Thy will be done*. We consent with God's powerful will always being done, rather than vaguely hoping that we

---

22. Augustine, "Psalm LXXVII: Exposition."

23. I describe the problem by employing Brümmer's book *What Are We Doing When We Pray?*

may convince him of a better plan. Jesus teaches (Matt 10): "[29] Are not two sparrows sold for a farthing? And one of them shall not fall on the ground without your Father." The prayer *Thy will be done* leads us to accept God's will and to commit to do God's will.

Augustine (around AD 400), referring to Matt 6, writes in his letter to Proba (chapter 17): "Why this should be done by Him who 'before we ask Him knoweth what things we have need of,' might perplex our minds, if we did not understand that the Lord our God requires us to ask not that thereby our wish may be intimated to Him, for to Him it cannot be unknown, but in order that by prayer there may be exercised in us by supplications that desire by which we may receive what He prepares to bestow. His gifts are very great, but we are small and straitened in our capacity of receiving."[24] We say in prayer what God most certainly knows already. This is even more obvious when biblical Psalms and liturgical texts describe God's qualities and deeds and present them to God himself. The collect, a form of prayer used for centuries, always begins with recalling God's qualities and deeds. In the evening prayer of the Anglican *Book of Common Prayer*, a prayer by John Chrysostomos (AD 400) is recited that first of all speaks of God's deed and promise: "Almighty God, who hast given us grace at this time with one accord to make our common supplications unto thee: and dost promise that when two or three are gathered together in thy name thou wilt grant their requests: fulfill now, O Lord, the desires and petitions of thy servants as may be most expedient for them; granting us in this world knowledge of thy truth and in the world to come life everlasting."

Christians have traditionally prayed to render homage to the all-knowing, almighty and loving God, and to report for duty. It was a welcome and even intended side-effect when those prayers shaped the minds and souls of God's praying people.[25] Martin Luther, in his Small Catechism, says about the fourth petition of the Lord's Prayer: "God gives daily bread, even without our prayer, to all wicked men; but we pray in this petition that He would lead us to know it, and to receive our daily bread with thanksgiving." God is not in need of our prayer, but we are. In prayer we acknowledge, foremost, God's gracious will and unfailing power to execute his will. Prayer leads us from dwelling on our wants and wishes to contemplating God's actual doing. Christians of all times have contemplated God's marvelous deeds and meditated on God's word. Methodical meditation (see Ps 1) has always been important for Christian prayer life (for example, *lectio divina*).

---

24. Augustine, *Letter 130* (to Proba).

25. H. M. Barth and Brümmer, in their books about prayer, give numerous examples of both Catholic and Protestant theologians who spoke about prayer in this way.

Many Christians of our times are suspicious of certain methods of meditation and contemplation, presuming that those activities involve some kind of magic. But we must not forget that in any kind of methodical reflection—this is most certainly true for science!—*method* is supposed to protect the subject matter from possible manipulation by the studying person. Therefore, methods of contemplation, methods of prayer guided by scripture, or methodical meditation[26] on God's word are exactly not magic but, on the contrary, a way to reduce possible misuse of God's word by humans[27] and thus allow God's word to provide teaching and challenge, consolation and guidance, as 2 Tim 3:16 suggests, which is an obvious example for a spiritual method—in a sense a four-step program—to use the Bible.

Traditional prayer and meditation focus on God's word rather than on our wants; traditional prayers are based on the belief in God's omniscience, almightiness and love.

• *Excursus: God and time*

As God is almighty and foresees all future (Matt 6), the question arises how he relates to time. The Bible describes God's doing often in terms of time, of human life stories, and of history. Christian teaching, however, also maintains the biblical statement that God is the creator *in the beginning* (Gen 1, John 1) and therefore the creator of time itself. Hence, God is beyond the timeline, while his actions in this world are still experienced in the course of time, in history and in biographies. An ancient image of this insight (by the Christian Philosopher Boetius, AD 480–525)[28] is that God oversees events

---

26. In traditional terminology, *meditation* is strictly the meditation on God's word, as opposed to *contemplation*, which is a religious reflection with or without specific texts or images. Cf. Pennington, *Lectio Divina*.

27. Cf. Manfred Josuttis, *Religion als Handwerk*.

28. Brümmer reproaches Boethius for teaching a deterministic universe. But Boethius dedicates the whole fifth book of his *Consolation* to the problem of the freedom of the will and God's providence, repeatedly making reference to prayer.

Brümmer writes that it would be "*logically impossible to perceive the past or future.*" Here Brümmer seems to ignore that Boethius discusses the problem within a reflection on a theory of knowledge according to which every judgment is an act formed from the capability of the person who judges, not from the capability of any other. (*nam cum omne iudicium iudicantis actus exsistat, necesse est ut suam quisque operam non ex aliena sed ex propria potestate perficiat.* [Boethius, *Consolation*, book 5, prose 4]). It seems to me that Brümmer presupposes that space and time are not created by God but beyond God's control.

Brümmer writes that if God is beyond time, then he could not be the kind of being who could have temporal relation with the world and with human persons (page 47). Brümmer obviously constructs a God without any reference to the fact that the eternal,

in the course of time like someone sitting on a high mountain looking over the wide land. Thomas Aquinas, the great theologian of the Middle Ages (died 1274), distinguishes the acts of God's will from their effects: Whatever happens at a certain point in time, God wanted from eternity that it would happen at that point in time.[29] The criticism that this concept teaches some kind of determinism misses the point: As we live this life forward, we still look at an open future; at the same time, faith in God's sovereign providence is a great consolation in distress and gives confidence that God has taken our prayer already into account.

4. THE CHALLENGE TO THE TRADITIONAL UNDERSTANDING

The traditional view of prayer is, however, being challenged. In many contemporary prayers, God is addressed as an individual, like a human person. This is certainly a legitimate way to phrase our prayers (s.o. 2.III.1b.). But if the *relationship with God* is understood only in analogy to human relationships, it is possible to view the relationship with God, just like any other relationship, as more or less important, and therefore it is hard to demonstrate why a relationship with God is necessary at all, unless one is threatened with hellfire.

Another consequence of thinking in terms of *relationship* is that prayer would require a double contingence:[30] Prayer seems to presuppose that God may or may not act on a request, because it would make no sense to ask God for what is inevitable. This double contingence seems to be a consequence of what is called *personal relationship*. However, if we understand prayer only as a conversation with an anthropomorphic individual person, we must assume that God randomly reacts to given situations or requests. Those contingent events would then appear to be outside and independent

---

omnipotent, and omnipresent God made himself subject to space, time, and suffering in Jesus Christ, who is still truly God. Brümmer ends up with a God who has just relatively better foresight. Again, Brümmer wants some degree of uncertainty to be part of prayer.

29. Thomas Aquinas, *Summa Theologica*, the second part of the second part, "Treatise on the Cardinal Virtues," question 83, article 2. In the context of a discussion about prayer, Thomas distinguishes three errors: (1) All things would happen out of necessity, (2) there would be no providence at all, (3) God's plans could be changed. Brümmer wants to reproach Thomas for something that Thomas himself (!) called *error*. Cf. Brümmer, *What Are We Doing When We Pray?*

30. For the following reflection again I refer to Brümmer, *What Are We Doing When We Pray?*

from any perpetual providence. In a sense, the world is viewed as deserted by God, and then he has to be called in to take care of some isolated issues. For all practical concerns, this understanding of prayer views this world as a world without God.

- ### *Excursus: "relationship"*

In this book I have mostly avoided the phrase *relationship with God*. The reason is that with the word *relationship* a lot of unbiblical ideas can intrude.

First, the word *relationship* in everyday language is oddly unclear; often it describes, for example, an uncommitted love–affair of people who feel that they are not ready to get married. This usage of the word *relationship* is hardly appropriate when we speak about prayer.

Second, the word *relationship* summarizes various concrete ways to relate to God: To the creator, king, lord, judge, loving father, etc., in the ways of fear and trust, of rebellion or accepting God's judgment, of confession and forgiveness, of lamentation and praise, of petition and thanksgiving, etc. Therefore the summarizing term *relationship* can easily make us forget what this relationship actually involves.

Third, Christians believe in the Triune God, Father, Son and Holy Spirit: empowered by the Holy Spirit, we speak to the Father through Jesus Christ. The term *relationship* has actually belonged to the traditional terminology of the Western church since Saint Augustine. Saint Augustine employs the term *relationship* (in Latin *relatio*), when he speaks about the Father, the Son and the Holy Spirit, the three persons of the one Godhead. So if we want to speak just about a *relationship with God*, our words would be, at least, inconsistent with the traditional language that distinguished between the three relationships of the Holy Trinity, one God.

Fourth, according to biblical teaching about the mediator ($\mu\epsilon\sigma\iota\tau\eta\varsigma$, in 1 Timothy and Hebrews), the high priest (Hebrews), the sacrificial lamb (Saint Paul and the Gospel of John), the advocate (Gospel of John and Saint Paul), the teacher, role model, leader in prayer (Gospels of Matthew, Mark, Luke), etc., Jesus is the one who relates us to God the Father. We must not use the word *relationship* as a replacement for Jesus Christ and his various ways to relate us to his Father.

Fifth, when Jesus says, "be perfect as your Father in heaven is perfect," he confronts us with God, the reliable and certain standard for our striving for perfection, the rock and fortress for our trust and confidence. *Relationship*, however, is something in between persons or things, and thus implies some kind of mutual dependence. The word *relationship* suggests that everything receives its measure only in the encounter with something else; therefore, there is no absolute measure. Consequently, in any encounter between man and someone or something, humanity will claim to be the measure of all things. Eventually the subjectivity of the human soul will be the standard for everything.[31] Consequently, God is no longer the sole standard for our life and prayer. Rather, the standard will be what is between him and us. Thinking in terms of *relationship* will then make us think that the experience of human beings and not the reliability of God is what makes prayer genuine and truthful. The standard for our prayer will no longer be God but rather our sense of well-being, the intensity of our prayer, or other feelings. Then both God's will and the needs of our fellow creation are relevant for us only insofar as they affect our feelings. In the church, neither the truth of God nor the needs of our fellow creation, but the wishes of the majority of people—or, worse, the wishes imposed by the informal power of a few individuals—will then determine common prayer.

The presupposition is, in a sense, that truth is not solely divine but comes into being only in the meeting between the divine and the human partner. If we adopt the concept of *relationship*, the biblical teaching that the human soul is sinful and needs to have a standard to be measured by, judged and forgiven is hard to understand. We turn truth into something relative, and sin into merely subjective discomfort. With the concept of *relationship*, the confidence of prayer is no longer based on God's reliability but is a work of human beings.

5. THE NAME OF GOD

It is beyond the scope of our reflections to speak about what natural capacity is contained in common sense and philosophical reasoning to know God and to live with him, given that we have fallen from what we were created to be. But in any case, we are in dire need of Jesus to lead us to our Father. When God speaks to us through Jesus Christ, he enables us to speak to him. The prophet Zephaniah aims at reforming our language of prayer (Zeph 3): "⁹ I will change the speech of the peoples to a pure speech, that all of them may call on the name of the LORD and serve him with one accord."

As praying Christians, we must think of the *name* of Him to whom our prayers are addressed. With the *name*, Jesus begins his teaching about

---

31. One can easily relate this discussion to the philosophical discussion between Socrates and Theaitetus about the nature of knowledge. Here, Thaitetus starts out with the thesis that knowledge would be the same as perception.

prayer (cf. I.3.1). Saint Paul expects that in the name of Jesus every knee shall bow (Phil 2; cf. 2.I.3).

We need to be aware that different times have preferred different images of God for their prayers. Nationalistic preachers in the late 1800s—of all nations!—loved the images of a king and military leader (Ps 44:4). Nowadays, the father figure in the contemporary nuclear family shapes the common understanding of the Father in the Lord's Prayer (see above part 1, III, intro). Pietists loved to call upon Jesus as their *friend*, which is nice, though not biblical.[32] More elaborate liturgical traditions seek to avoid one-sided addresses: With the *Kyrie* we call for mercy to the *Lord* because only the mercy of him who is Lord can help (cf. Matt 20:31). Together with the angels we praise God: "Glory to God in the highest." Some churches use the biblical hymn "This is the feast" (Rev 5): "[12] Worthy is the Lamb that was slaughtered to receive power and wealth and wisdom and might and honor and glory and blessing!" Thus the faithful praise the helplessly suffering Jesus, the Lamb of God (cf. John 1:29), who is the mighty one. In the beginning of the Eucharist, Jesus is welcomed with "Hosanna" like a king entering his capital city (Mark 11:9); and God is praised with the Sanctus, the "holy holy holy," taken from Isa 6. Here the prophet experiences painful cleansing from sin when he realizes the sublime and consuming majesty of the eternal God. Jesus leads us in prayer to *Our Father in heaven,* and finally Jesus is adored as the sacrificial "Lamb of God" (cf. John 1:29,36).

In the Psalms, images like that of the mighty fortress (Pss 18, 31, 91, 144) allow us to take part in God's strength. Thus we are called (Ps 81): "[1] Sing aloud to God our strength." The Bible provides us with a wealth of titles and images of God, which may enrich and deepen our prayer life.

6. MARANATHA, THE PRAYER FOR GOD'S PRESENCE

Prayer first of all means that we spend time with God. All other considerations, as true as they may be, must not supersede the primary focus, which

---

32. In John 15:15, Jesus calls his disciples *friends* and *not slaves*. But the verse follows Jesus' word about his sacrifice and 15:14: *"You are my friends if you do what I command you."* The disciples are friends, not slaves, because Jesus tells them what he has heard from his Father. Hence Jesus hardly establishes an equal relationship with his disciples that would allow us to call him *friend*. The same is true for the word *brother*. (Heb 2) "[11]*For the one who sanctifies and those who are sanctified all have one Father. For this reason Jesus is not ashamed to call them brothers"* and sisters. Here again, it is not about an equal relationship, but Jesus is the one who sanctifies, and we are to be sanctified. Nowhere (!) in the New Testament is Jesus called *friend* or *brother*.

is God. If religion appears to be a means to an end, it will be rightfully perceived as disingenuous. When well-meaning Christians want to explain the usefulness of their faith and prayer for daily life, for family, job, ethics, politics, etc., they unwittingly suggest that there are other, perhaps more efficient means to reach the preset goals. In contrast, the traditional collect-prayers first speak about God, his qualities and deeds; thus they are a good exercise in focusing on what matters most (cf. 3.IV.2).

Meditative practices of prayer like *lectio divina* or even the rosary direct our attention on the divine mysteries. Protestants criticize these practices for various reasons, but they have to ask themselves if it is advisable to give up these alternative lenses designed to focus our view on the Bible.

a. Praying for God's presence

Next to prayers for material or spiritual goods, the Bible knows prayers for God himself. After Israel's political disasters (722 BC, cf. 2 Kgs 17, and 586 BC, cf. 2 Kgs 25:2-4; Jer 39:2, 52:7; Ezek 33:21, 40:1), when all national hopes and prayers were painfully disappointed, the promised land was lost, the king's palace and the temple destroyed—in those times the praying community needed to gain a deeper understanding of prayer. In the misery of their exile, Israel found consolation in God's presence, especially God's word (Isa 40): "[8] The grass withers, the flower fades; but the word of our God will stand forever." Jesus' teaching continues this tradition when in the Sermon on the Mount, after his counsel about charity, prayer and fasting, he says (Matt 6): "[33] But strive first for the kingdom of God and his righteousness, and all these things will be given to you as well." In the parallel passage in the Gospel of Luke (11:13), the answer to prayer is God's Spirit.

Prayer asks for God's grace, love and forgiveness. God can be understood as the giver of spiritual gifts and also as the one who gives his own self. Prayers for God's presence could culminate in the phrase (Ps 73): "[25] Whom have I in heaven but you? And there is nothing on earth that I desire other than you." The various goods we may pray for are indeed less and less significant when we pray for God's very presence. The Old Testament can go so far as to say that God's presence is more desirable not only than material goods but more than life itself (Ps 63): "[3] Because your steadfast love is better than life, my lips will praise you." The Psalms of the Old Testament prayed for God's presence; in the New Testament Jesus is God's word in human flesh amongst us (John 1).

A prayer attributed to Saint Benedict of Nursia (480-547) says: "Deign to give me, true and holy Father, understanding to understand you, sense to sense you, a soul to discern you, diligence to search for you, wisdom to find you, a soul to inquire into you, entrails to love you, a heart to think about you, deed to enrich you, hearing to hear you, eyes to see you, a tongue to proclaim you, conversation that pleases you, patience to endure you, perseverance to expect you, a perfect end, your holy presence, a good resurrection, recompense, eternal life. Amen."[33] There is a story told about Thomas Aquinas: He was praying one day and Jesus spoke to him from the crucifix: "You have written well of me, Thomas; what do you desire as a reward for your labors?" Thomas replied: "Nil nisi te," which means, *Nothing except for you*.[34] Martin Luther[35] explains the prayer of Mary, Mother of the Lord. Its first verse (Luke 1:46-47) is: "My soul magnifies the Lord, and my spirit rejoices in God my savior." Martin Luther writes: "Thereby she teaches us to love and praise God for Himself alone and in the right order, and not selfishly to seek anything at His hands. This is done when one praises God because He is good, regards only His bare goodness, and finds joy and pleasure in that alone. That is a lofty, pure, and tender mode of loving and praising God and well becomes this Virgin's high and tender spirit" (page 309). And a little later: "Such spirits fulfill what is written (Is. 30:21): 'You shall not stray from the even and right way of God, neither to the left hand nor to the right.' That is to say, they are to love and praise God evenly and rightly and not seek their own advantage or enjoyment. . . . Such a spirit is manifested here by Mary, the Mother of God. Standing in the midst of such exceedingly great good things, she does not fall upon them or seek her own enjoyment in them, but keeps her spirit pure in loving and praising the bare goodness of God, ready and willing to have God withdraw them from her and leave her spirit poor and naked and needy."

*

The church prays: "Maranatha, come Lord Jesus" (1 Cor 16:22, Rev 22:20), a prayer for the presence of the Lord. God wants to be present among his beloved people in Jesus Christ. This presence is experienced in

---

33. Handed down by Alcuin (735-804), *Oratio Sancti Benedicti*, in *Officio per ferias*, Patrologia Latinus vol. 101, col. 0553C. *Digneris mihi donare, Pater pie et sancte, intellectum, qui te intelligat, sensum qui te sentiat, animum qui te sapiat, diligentiam quae te querat, sapientam quae te inveniat, animum qui te cognoscat, viscera quae te ament, cor quod te cogitet actum qui te augeat, auditum qui te audiat, oculos qui te videant, linguam quae te praedicet, conversationem quae tibi placeat patientam quae te sustineat, perseverantiam quae te expectet, finem perfectum, praesentiam tuam sanctam, resurrectionem bonam, retributionem, vitam aeternam. Amen.* English translation by Frank Bahr.

34. Foster, ed. and trans., *Life of St. Thomas Aquinas*, 42.

35. *Luther's Works*, vol. 21, "The Magnificat," 311.

various ways. God's Son promised to be present in the community of prayer (Matt 18:20), which cannot be sufficiently understood in terms of a mere personal one-to-one relationship. Jesus has promised to be present in the sacrament (Matt 26:26), and Jesus' disciples experience the *abiding* of the risen Lord in the breaking of the bread (Luke 24:13). Jesus sent his disciples to spread the gospel and promised his servants (Luke 10): "[16] Whoever listens to you, listens to me." In the Gospel of John, Jesus speaks about his Church using images like that of the Good Shepherd with his flock, or the vine with its grapes.

The early Church knew about God's presence in the Holy Spirit. The Holy Spirit is both the giver and the gift. When we ask for the Spirit of God to come into us, we cannot possibly reduce our prayer to a dialogue between persons. Protestant tradition has emphasized God's presence in his *word*, which is understood as God's own speaking to the faithful: those who hear the word of God are touched by God's Spirit, his creative breath.

Traditional prayers ask that God himself may make it possible to meet him. For the opening of a prayer service, one would pray, for example (Ps 51:15): "Lord, open my lips and my mouth will proclaim your praise." As we pray for God's presence, we have the promise of an answer in the process of prayer itself. This is most obvious when Jesus, the Son of God, is among us to lead us in prayer to *Our Father in heaven*. As we pray for God's presence, God will not refuse this prayer. In a sense, this prayer is already the answer to prayer, because only with God, the Son, being present among us and leading us, is this prayer to the Father possible.

The spacial metaphors of the Bible transcend the concept of prayer as a mere person-to-person dialogue (Ps 139): "[5] You hem me in, behind and before, and lay your hand upon me."

The confidence given by God's presence accompanies the worshipper in all of his or her activities: doing one's job, living one's private life and in all public activities. God's presence grants freedom. Saint Paul—in words borrowed from Stoic philosophy—describes what it means to love God above all other things (2 Cor 6:4-10): "[4] as servants of God we have commended ourselves in every way: through great endurance, in afflictions, hardships, calamities, [5] beatings, imprisonments, riots, labors, sleepless nights, hunger; [6] by purity, knowledge, patience, kindness, holiness of spirit, genuine love, [7] truthful speech, and the power of God; with the weapons of righteousness for the right hand and for the left; [8] in honor and dishonor, in ill repute and good repute. We are treated as impostors, and yet are true; [9] as unknown, and yet are well known; as dying, and see—we are alive; as punished, and yet not killed; [10] as sorrowful, yet always rejoicing; as poor, yet making many rich; as having nothing, and yet possessing everything."

Praising God above all things, we can experience independence from the world. This freedom is strengthened by the hope that eventually Jesus comes to heal and to restore, and (Rev 21): "⁴ he will wipe every tear from their eyes. Death will be no more; mourning and crying and pain will be no more, for the first things have passed away."

b. Prayer as a Spiritual Self-Care

Saint Paul writes (2 Cor 12): "⁷ Therefore, to keep me from being too elated, a thorn was given me in the flesh, a messenger of Satan to torment me, to keep me from being too elated. ⁸ Three times I appealed to the Lord about this, that it would leave me, ⁹ but he said to me, 'My grace is sufficient for you, for power is made perfect in weakness.'"

Obviously Saint Paul suffered pain and did not get his wishes fulfilled. Still when we pray to God, our prayer is helpful even if the answer does not satisfy our longing. When we pray, the mere presence of the gracious God is liberating, healing, and encouraging. Therefore with prayer we care for our souls.

Prayers in God's presence include some reflection on the realities of this life. Prayer includes reflecting, narrating, and situating.[36] In Hezekiah's prayer (2 Kgs 19:15ff.), the king ponders the political situation before he turns to his petition: "¹⁷ Truly, O LORD, the kings of Assyria have laid waste the nations and their lands, . . . ¹⁹ So now, O LORD our God, save us, I pray you. . . ." The famous Ps 23 ponders our situation in God's presence and finds orientation in this world. Jesus, after his baptism (Luke 3:21), retreated for prayer to reflect on his commission. Because prayer to God includes critical reflection on our situation in this world, the Bible connects prayer frequently with words like *wait* (Ps 37): "³⁴ Wait for the LORD, and keep to his way, and he will exalt you to inherit the land." The Bible connects prayer with being *sober* and of *sound mind* (1 Pet 4): "⁷ be ye therefore of sound mind, and be sober unto prayer"; with keeping awake (Mark 14): "³⁸ Keep awake and pray."

We do not pray to convert God or to teach God, but we pray to gain for ourselves an understanding of reality, of what we have been given and of what we fall short of, of what to thank and of what to hope for, of opportunities and limits.

For this reflection and meditation, he in whose presence prayers are said determines the content of our prayers. What happens if the content of

---

36. Cf. Walter Bernet, *Gebet*. He uses the German terms *Reflektieren*, *Erzählen*, and *Situieren*.

a prayer is not consistent with the one to whom the prayer is addressed is shown in Janis Joplin's sarcastic song "Mercedes Benz," with lyrics written in the form of a prayer[37] The song targets consumerism and not necessarily prayer, but we can learn from it that only in the presence of God can we be realistically aware of our whole self and our place in the world.

*

First, prayer, even if it does not expect a concrete answer, provides psychological relief. The mere act of articulating an issue is a first step to regaining control. The worshipper no longer suppresses his/her anxieties but becomes aware of them and admits them. The lamentation Psalms or Jesus' prayer in Gethsemane provide words to address suppressed fears.

Second, a prayer that confesses guilt, indecision, and failure, and that admits fear and anxiety helps to recognize potential and opportunity, to articulate hopes and desires, and can thus be a decisive step toward overcoming the paralysis caused by guilt and fear.

Third, prayer can help us gain a better sense of reality, because the person who prays to the Lord of our whole lives and the whole world will contextualize his/her desires. In prayer, we will view our present desires in the context of our whole biography, in the context of society, history and the kingdom of God. Prayer can clarify what we can rely on. Thus, prayer has a cleansing function: It can clear our mind of false hopes and delusional *positive thinking*.

Fourth, having gained through prayer a new sense of reality, of our selves and of the world, prayer can give us an impulse to take action. Thus prayer can help make us contributing members of the kingdom of God. The criticism that prayer might become a substitute for responsible work is proven wrong by a cloud of witnesses throughout history.

*

This brings up the question of whether prayer aims to change God or change us. The traditional answer remains predominant, that God is faithful and just, so that it is not the goal of prayer to change God but to adore him. We may pray and know that God listens, has already listened, knows our

---

37. Janis Joplin, with a lot of self-irony, gave an introduction to the ironic song; "I'd like to do a song of great social and political import." Car maker Mercedes actually used this song for an ad in 1995. Lyric writer Bob Neuwirth, who helped Joplin write "Mercedes Benz," was "well, totally cool about the whole deal. 'It was never meant to be taken seriously,' he said recently. Don't forget, he pointed out, Janis owned a Porsche." (Phil Reeves, "Now Janis is a friend of the Mercedes Benz," *Independent*, March 19, 1995).

needs already, and knows them better than we do. There has always been the expectation that prayer would change the praying person. Prayer can, however, change us only because it reaches beyond ourselves and reaches out to God in petitions, thanks and praise.

From the viewpoint that God is almighty, omniscient, and good, that he is in need of nothing and needs not to change, both Greek philosophers (Plato, Laws 10) and the Old Testament prophets have criticized the practices of sacrifice and prayer often superstitiously misunderstood by believers. It is not God who needs to change his ways, but us. Penitence Psalms are most obviously guides that reshape the soul of a worshipper. Ps 51 is a prayer of penitence and probably underwent some stages of development before becoming the text it is now. Verse 16 of this prayer adopts the prophetical criticism of sacrifice: "¹⁶For you have no delight in sacrifice; if I were to give a burnt offering, you would not be pleased." Then the Psalm leads us to repentance and guides us to know God: "¹⁷The sacrifice acceptable to God is a broken spirit; a broken and contrite heart, O God, you will not despise." Only then, after repentance and with a purified understanding of sacrifice, the Psalmist goes on to express a renewed hope that sacrifices will be offered in God's house: "¹⁸Do good to Zion in your good pleasure; rebuild the walls of Jerusalem, ¹⁹then you will delight in right sacrifices, in burnt offerings and whole burnt offerings; then bulls will be offered on your altar." The understanding of the prayer in this Psalm is obvious: God remains faithful to his plan and purpose. According to this Psalm, the right understanding of prayer and sacrifice is not that they are an attempt to influence or to bribe God so that he would yield to our wishes, but a means of knowing God's plans, repenting and returning to God's ways.

7. TO WHOM DO WE PRAY? (GOD'S EXISTENCE, CARE AND FAITHFULNESS)

Jesus Christ, God's word made flesh, teaches, encourages and guides our prayers to the Father, and he allows us to join in the prayers which he prays, which we find in the Bible and which are prayed by Christians at all times and in all places. Following Jesus Christ, Christian prayer presupposes three things: First, that God actually exists (a); second, that he cares both for the whole world and for individuals (b); and third, that he is faithful and reliable (c).

a. God's Existence

The teaching that God exists seems to be a matter of course for Christians. But if we honestly search our hearts, our daily lives do not always recognize God's existence. Most Christians—when asked—would never doubt God's existence in a theoretical way. But if we invoke him only when we covet something, if we give thanks only when we happen to feel thankful, if we only praise him when we experience extraordinary events, then we practically accept that the world functions—or dysfunctions—on its own. In a sense, we accept the materialistic view of the world.

The fact that God's existence often is simply ignored and the temptation to live essentially atheistic lives is not necessarily prompted by contemporary atheistic theories or by the lifestyle of the modern world. Even in antiquity, quite a few philosophers (Atomists) thought that the world was just a product of matter and chance, and that the order and shape of the cosmos, including the human soul and whatever is going on in the human mind—thought, belief, faith, art, etc.—are just the product of coincidental combinations of material elements (cf. Saint Paul "elements of the world," Gal 4:3: τὰ στοχεῖα τοῦ κόσμου). It's somewhat naïve to assume a continuous development from antiquated religion toward a modern, materialistic worldview. But religious practice—along with any intellectual effort—tends to fade as we yield to material desires.

It takes some effort to keep up the belief that the order of the cosmos, that that charity and reason, that art and virtue are the forces moving the material world, or, in terms of anthropology, that the soul controls the body and that they are therefore more basic than the matter moved by these forces. The belief that the universe is not just a mix of matter and chance but is moved by some plan and purpose, and that we are challenged to know God's plans and live accordingly—this belief is persistently challenged by the way our perceptions deceive us, by the cravings of the flesh, and by lazy thinking. But persistent prayer nourishes our faith in God's perpetual care.

Christians pray to the heavenly Father and believe that he unceasingly cares for his creation; but this faith is challenged by our experience of suffering and injustice. It is certainly easy to bring the beauty of God's creation into contempt by pointing out the suffering of God's creatures. In the story of Job, Satan challenges Job's faithfulness by questioning his motives and inflicting countless pains on him. In modern times, just as in the early years of the Church, theological systems (Gnosticism) have tried to marginalize belief in the goodness of the creator and to separate a redeemer from the allegedly merciless creator and judge whom we would experience in a dark and cruel world. Following such thinking, we are tempted in prayer to withdraw from the material world and consequently to dodge responsibility for God's creation. But we must maintain that the experience of injustice and suffering is at the core of the foundational Christian story, the story of Jesus' passion.

The early Church, employing the creation Psalms and Jesus' parables, saw the marvels of God's creation and the beauty of God's creatures as parables for God's kingdom. Christians believed in the goodness of the creator. Therefore the criticism of sacrifice found in the Old Testament prophets and the criticism of prayer by Greek philosophers (Plato, Laws X), as mentioned above, led them to the understanding that praising the creator should be the main purpose of worship and prayer, not changing God's ways. The human soul, although spoiled by original sin and pressured by persistent temptation, is nevertheless called to praise God and to participate responsibly in the order of God's creation. The witnesses of the Bible do not view the world as a bad, godforsaken place in which good people are incarcerated. Rather, they suggest that, though humanity has fallen, we sinners continue to live in God's beautiful creation, which suffers from the sin of humans (Rom 8:21). In the tradition of this belief stands a statement attributed to Isaac Newton: "Sir Isaac Newton, when asked what he thought of the infatuation of the people, answered that he could calculate the motions of erratic bodies, but not the madness of a multitude."[38] Both parts of the Bible give witness to the praise hymn of all creation, in heaven and on earth (Isa 6): "³ Holy, holy, holy, is the LORD of hosts: the whole earth is full of his glory." (Hab 3): "³ His glory covered the heavens, and the earth was full of his praise." (Rev 5): "¹³ And every creature which is in heaven, and on the earth, and under the earth, and such as are in the sea, and all that are in them, heard I saying, Blessing, and honour, and glory, and power, be unto him that sitteth upon the throne, and unto the Lamb for ever and ever."

It is true the Bible speaks mainly about historic revelations to God's people, but it does not deny God's revelation in the marvels of his creation. Sin, however, has damaged the ability of human beings to perceive God's beauty in his creation. Therefore we need God's word; it is the source from which to draw our knowledge about prayer, and we need teachers to explain this knowledge. The meditation on that which has been given to us may guide us. Thus we participate in that which precedes our own thoughts and feelings. Contemplative prayer is a way to sustain this faith in the creator's goodness.

Despite suffering and despite our continuous destruction and exploitation of the world which God has made good, faith is permanently called to

---

38. Quoted first in *Church of England Quarterly Review* (January 1850) 142.

sustain the view of God's glory being present in his creation. Christians follow Jesus, who both praised the creator and suffered in this world, committing his soul to his Father with a prayer from the Psalms (Luke 23; Ps 31).

b. God's Care

The second presupposition of praying Christians is that God cares both for the world and for all individual creatures. This belief in God's gracious care faces three major challenges:

First, we see innocent people suffer and wicked people succeed. If this experience does not challenge our belief in God's existence altogether, it certainly puts our trust in God's care to the test. The Bible, throughout all its books, tells us about this challenge: about Joseph who was betrayed by his brothers but would become their savior, about persecuted prophets, about the struggle of Job with his friends and the crisis of Ecclesiastes, and foremostly about Jesus' innocent suffering and death, then about the persecuted Church. The experience of suffering is not an argument against Christian prayer, but is in the core of the Christian way to speak about God and to speak to God. Prayer means to live out faith in God's care in the midst of challenge. The experience of many generations shows that, paradoxically, people who suffer the most are most firm in their belief in God's care. The proverb "there are no atheists in foxholes" has been confirmed again and again.

The other challenge for the Christian belief that God cares for the needs of each creature is that we confuse human wants with real needs. The revelation in Jesus Christ not only reveals his Father to us but also confronts our human nature corrupted by sin. Our true needs might be hidden from our awareness in a cloud of wants, which may come from our own heart or be induced by commercials.

The third challenge for our prayer life is the question of whether God actually cares both for all the little things of our daily life and for the whole world. Many people readily accept that God is the creator and sustainer of the world in general but find it hard to believe that he actually worries about little things like the lilies of the field or the sparrows. On the other hand, because of our self-centredness and attitude of entitlement, our heart has a hard time perceiving our personal wants in the larger context of the Church, of society and of the world in need. But why wouldn't God, who knows, sees and hears everything, care for the small things? We cannot believe that God is negligent. As for the other possibility, that it would not make a difference for the whole if some small parts were neglected, the Bible clearly witnesses to God's care for marginalized, individual members of his people. Jesus indeed speaks about God's care for the sparrows (Matt 10:29) and the lilies of the field (Matt 6:28), and the Gospel tells us that the Son of God gave bread to hungry individuals and he gave healing to individuals. Although these stories are meant to reveal the kingdom, they can still legitimately be read as stories about God's help for individuals. Various parables for the church, the vine and its grapes (Gospel of John), the body and its members (Saint Paul), the temple and its stones (Saint Peter) speak about the whole and its parts. An ancient image for the importance of every little portion of God's creation is the temple wall built of big and small stones. In a wall, all the big stones will not hold together unless the gaps are filled with small stones, even with grains of sand. According to this image, God will care for the smallest portion of his creation; he will not think of any prayer as petty so that he would ignore it. The smallest contribution, the seemingly unimportant worker in God's kingdom, contributes to the beauty and perfection of the whole. Each single creature and its labor has its dignity as a portion of God's beloved creation. Christians are called to view all of God's creation and all that is in it as dignified by God's plan and purpose and treat it with respect. The prayers of the Bible guide us to know God, to know and acknowledge God's caring love for the whole world and for each single creature.

Of course, it is easy for God in his almightiness to pursue his plans and to do his work of care. The presence of evil in the world does not reveal weakness or carelessness on God's part. When we perceive injustice in God's plans, when the wicked succeed through their evil deeds, we still need to know that they have in fact contributed to the whole—though unwittingly and subject to the coming judgment. God will eventually provide the reward for evil or good intent (see above III.2.b).

c. *God's Faithfulness*

The third presupposition for prayer is: God is faithful. No law or force will compel our minds to love or to hope. But when we trust that God keeps immutably and faithfully listening to the prayers of his Son, actually has already listened to them before we ever speak the words, we will want to abide faithfully in the prayers, hymns and liturgies of the Holy Bible.

The Holy Spirit uses the prayers of the Bible to fashion our souls, so that we become more and more accustomed to God's plans and faithful goodness. Because we believe that God is faithful to his word and plan, we want to know, to love, and to be guided by God's plans through the prayers provided by God in the Bible.

The Bible teaches that God provides for us not only when prayers are miraculously answered, but always; God cares even though his helping and giving is mediated through creation, through sun and rain, through a farmer who tills the soil, a tailor who makes clothing, a builder who builds housing, or through a doctor who cures diseases. Prayer cannot refer to extraordinary miracles only, which would mean to events of which we have no proper explanation—yet. Prayer cannot be reduced to a simple dialogue with a mighty individual who affects the world and is being affected by the world, and this only in extraordinary situations. Prayer should not be turned into a magical tool to change God's will and the course of nature. Christian prayer addresses God, who is the creator in the beginning and who continues to sustain and to govern the world.

Knowing that my will, plan and longing are part of God's will, plan and longing, I can put my wishes into prayer. God's will might then appear as an opposing will; prayer is the place where our longing is being transformed into surrender. Accepting God's will is not resignation, dullness or bland imperturbability, but the power to integrate the opposing will in one's own life, or rather the power to integrate one's own life into God's plan.

Tradition used to subdivide prayer into the categories of *petition*, *thanksgiving* and *adoration*, a hierarchical order, from the most self-centered to the most selfless form of prayer. Prayer ascends from the desire for material items to the praise of God's glory and honor alone, to the prayer of the angels and those in heaven, to the vision of God's beauty and goodness. From petitions for help and health and saving deeds, for spiritual goods like community and consolation, through the prayers of thanksgiving for particular goods and for *all* material and spiritual goods, we may reach the contemplation of God's faithful love itself.

III.

Prayer in the Holy Spirit

Saint Paul writes (Gal 4): "⁴But when the fullness of time had come, God sent his Son, born of a woman, born under the law, ⁵in order to redeem those who were under the law, so that we might receive adoption as children. ⁶And because you are children, God has sent the Spirit of his Son into our hearts, crying: Abba! Father!"

Moved by the Spirit of the Son, we pray to the heavenly Father. The Holy Spirit is God himself and must not be confused with our own spirit, our excitement or reason. Saint Paul calls this the *Holy Spirit* (Rom 5:5) or *Spirit of God* (Rom 8:15; 1 Cor 2:7,12). The spirit is the Spirit of Jesus Christ (Rom 8:9), the Spirit of the Lord (κύριος, 2 Cor 3:17). Jesus, who is the last Adam, is himself the live-giving spirit (1 Cor 15:45). The spirit is the *Spirit of Truth* (John 14:17; 15:26; 16:13), is even the truth itself (1 John 5:6), and the truth will make us free (John 8:32). From water and Spirit, we are born again (John 3:17). It is the Holy Spirit who stirs up the human spirit to speak to the Father. In the Gospel of John, the Holy Spirit is called an *advocate* (in Greek: παράκλητος, transcribed: *parakletos*), who speaks on our behalf to God, and who comforts and strengthens us by defending us in the court of our conscience. This Spirit dwells in us (1 Cor 3:16; Rom 8:11; Jes 4:5), drives and moves us (Gal 5:18; Rom 8:14). But the Holy Spirit is never our possession but a mere deposit (ἀρραβών 2 Cor 1:22; 5:5; Eph 1:14) or a *first portion* (ἀπαρχή, Rom 8:23, usually translated as *first-fruits* with reference to the Old Testament).

The Holy Spirit is not our property, which we could employ for our own purposes, but rather Lord and leader who leads us in the truth. We believe, hope and pray *in spirit and truth* (John 4:23): Revealed truth is the home where Christians live. The apostolic greeting prays for the Spirit (2 Cor 13): "[13] The grace of the Lord Jesus Christ, the love of God, and the communion of the Holy Spirit be with all of you."

Christian life is guided by God, the Holy Spirit. The Holy Spirit is given to us, but we are still God's creation and therefore infinitely different from the creator. The gift of the Holy Spirit makes us understand exactly this; that we are but creatures, and as created beings together with other creatures we stand in the presence of our creator. The Holy Spirit confronts us with God's majesty and reminds us of God's presence. Confronted with God, we realize that we are but creatures among creatures—failing, even rebellious creatures. Gifted with the Spirit, we confess that we are still God's sinful creatures, and, being sinners, we violate the common good of all creation. We cannot approach God through our own understanding and power (cf. Luther's Small Catechism about the third article), but the Holy Spirit calls us through the Gospel. Thus adopted as brothers and sisters of God's only Son, we are allowed and enabled to invoke his Father as our Father.

In all the ambiguities of our existence and despite our sin, the Holy Spirit assures us that we are the beloved children of the Heavenly Father. Thus we stand in God's presence as a community of believers who are taught, allowed, and encouraged to invoke our Father in Heaven.

Following Jesus Christ, the Son of God, we are free children of God. The phrase *children of God* suggests that spiritual life is not just a life of exceptional moments but continuous life. Being God's children, we are called and welcomed to continue in prayer. There is, of course, always the danger that we drop out of spiritual life, or more likely that we doze off. When Jesus prayed in the Garden of Gethsemane, the best disciples fell asleep, and we are certainly not better than they were. But Jesus continues to pray to his Father, he stirs up his disciples in the garden, and he keeps waking us up. Thus we may rejoin Jesus' prayer. Jesus, at the right hand of the Father, continues to pray for us (Rom 8:34) and to lead us in prayer, and some portion of his chosen people all over the world will always participate, and God will always find ways to wake his disciples up again to rejoin his prayer.

The church has received and uses the prayers of our Lord Jesus Christ, the Our Father, the Psalms, canticles etc.; and it is the work of the Holy Spirit, who has inspired the Holy Bible to put its words into our hearts and onto our lips. The Holy Spirit leads us to participate in the communication between the Father and the Son. (Rom 8): "[29] For those whom he foreknew he also predestined to be conformed to the image of his Son, in order that he might be the firstborn within a large family." Therefore, being brothers and sisters in Christ, we may ask from one another (1 Thess 5): "[25] Beloved, pray for us."

The Holy Spirit is God himself. With the Nicene Creed, the Church professes that the Holy Spirit with the Father and the Son shall be adored and glorified[1]. Because the Church believes that the Holy Spirit is God himself, she can address the Holy Spirit in prayer: "Come Holy Spirit." The tradition of the church provides us with beautiful hymns about this topic. (In order to search for music, it is helpful to know the Latin words: *Veni sancte spiritus*).

1. THE HOLY SPIRIT LEADS IN PRAYER (ACTS 2)

In the second chapter of Acts, we read about the outpouring of the Holy Spirit. The central part of this chapter is a sermon about the Holy Spirit by Saint Peter, who explains two Psalm prayers.

The wider context of Saint Peter's sermon is the history of the apostles and the early Church, beginning with the ascension of Jesus Christ. The first twelve chapters mostly speak about Saint Peter and his ministry, mostly in Palestine; the following chapters tell mostly about Saint Paul and the mission of the church to the ends of the world, in fact to the regions belonging to the *Res Publica Romana*.

The immediate context in Acts is the beginning of the Church, starting with the ascension of Jesus Christ (Acts 1:6–11): Here he blesses his disciples and they worship him. We read about the convention of the apostles when the vacant twelfth position is given to Matthias (Acts 1:12–26). In Acts 2, we find the story of Pentecost: the outpouring of the Holy Spirit and the sermon of Saint Peter; then we read about the first converts and the life of the church, followed in Acts 3–6 by various reports about Saint Peter and the other apostles, their miracles and the Church persecuted by the Jews.

The story in Acts 2 speaks about the outpouring of the Holy Spirit. The church gathered at the festival called Pentecost, thus observing the festival calendar already established in the Old Testament faith community.[2] The church was assembled in one place, in a building (2:2) as the Bible explicitly says. The people were sitting. They could hear a wind and see divided tongues as of fire, so that a fiery tongue rested on each of them, which means the individual gifts of the Holy Spirit have a single origin. This imagery is consistent with Saint Paul's remark that there are many gifts but one Spirit and one Lord (1 Cor 12). The Spirit who guides our prayers is one, and the one to whom we address our prayers is one. The Holy Spirit comes from

---

1. The classic text about this topic is Basil the Great († 379), *On the Holy Spirit*.
2. Pentecost is the Greek name for the Jewish harvest festival, HaShavuot, literally Festival of Weeks: Exod 34:22, Deut 16:10; Exod 23:16, Num 28:26.

heaven; therefore we must not confuse the Holy Spirit with the excitement and feelings of our flesh. The people learned to understand foreign languages. Outsiders mocked these Christians, who spoke in various languages, for being drunk. According to Acts 2:14-21, after the Holy Spirit had been granted, Saint Peter preached a sermon not from his own heart but based on the Bible, the word inspired by the Holy Spirit; namely he preached from a prophetic book, Joel 2:28-32. Later, in the same sermon, he speaks about two Psalm-prayers (Pss 16 and 110).

First, Saint Peter speaks about the prophecy of Joel concerning the Holy Spirit. This prophecy, like most of the Old Testament prophetic writings, is in poetry (only Ezekiel is mostly in prose), similar to the Psalms and thus probably meant to be recited and chanted. The gift of the Holy Spirit is accordingly very much connected with poetry and therefore with the recitation of words given by divinely inspired prophets. Saint Peter says about the day of Pentecost (Acts 2): "[16] this is what was spoken through the prophet Joel: [17] 'In the last days it will be....'" The events in this assembly of the church after Easter were the fulfillment of the prophecy. The prophecy for the *last days* (Acts 2) said: "[19] ... blood, and fire, and smoky mist. [20] The sun shall be turned to darkness and the moon to blood, before the coming of the Lord's great and glorious day." This prophecy is now fulfilled. After this special coming of the Holy Spirit on Pentecost, Saint Peter does not deliver a new prophecy but preaches about Joel's fulfilled prophecy.

Saint Peter continues his sermon in Acts 2:22-36 by speaking about Jesus Christ, his death and resurrection. In verse 25, Saint Peter says "David says concerning him" (= Jesus). When David is cited, the citation usually refers to one of the Psalms which are said to be composed by David.[3]

Saint Peter, in his sermon on Pentecost, refers not only to the prophetic books of the Bible but also to the prayer-book of the Bible, Psalms. Regular prayer of the Psalms had been observed by the Jewish community, and the early Christian Church just continued the Jewish custom. The sermon of Saint Peter shows that the Psalter is an acknowledged authority. Saint Peter's

---

3. Acts 4: "[25] *it is you who said by the Holy Spirit through our ancestor David, your servant: 'Why did the Gentiles rage, and the peoples imagine vain things?* [26] *The kings of the earth took their stand, and the rulers have gathered together against the Lord and against his Messiah.'"* = Ps 2. Rom 4: "[6] *So also David speaks of the blessedness of those to whom God reckons righteousness apart from works:* [7] *"Blessed are those whose iniquities are forgiven, and whose sins are covered;* [8] *blessed is the one against whom the Lord will not reckon sin."* = Ps 31:1. Rom 11: "[9] *And David says, 'Let their table become a snare and a trap, a stumbling block and a retribution for them;* [10] *let their eyes be darkened so that they cannot see, and keep their backs forever bent.'"* = Ps 63:23. Heb 4: "[7] *God ... saying through David ... Today, if you hear his voice, do not harden your hearts."* = Ps 95:7.

sermon, however, establishes the new, Christian concept of praying the Old Testament Psalms.

Saint Peter cites Ps 16. The heading of Ps 16 is *a miktam of David*. *Miktam* is a special genre of the Psalms. The phrase *of David* was thought to mean that David was actually the author. Now Saint Peter relates life, death, and resurrection of Jesus Christ immediately to Ps 16, saying: "David says concerning him (= Jesus) . . . ."

St. Peter's argument is this: David, praying to God with the words of the Psalm, says that God does not abandon him to Hades, meaning *to the place of the dead*, or let his faithful see the pit, meaning *the grave*. Saint Peter shows that it does not make sense to relate David's words to David himself, because (Acts 2:29) "David . . . both died and was buried, and his tomb is with us to this day." Therefore, St. Peter argues that in speaking about eternal life, David cannot have been speaking on his own behalf but must have represented someone else. Therefore, he says, it would be obvious that David spoke as a prophet on behalf of Jesus Christ, so that the words of the Psalms are Jesus Christ's own words spoken through the mouth of David. Of course, David lived hundreds of years before Jesus, but David spoke as prophet foreseeing the story of Jesus and praying Jesus' words. The context of this argument is Saint Peter's sermon in the first worship service of the church on the festival of Pentecost, amid the outpouring of the Holy Spirit. The Holy Spirit has given us the gift of the scriptures, specifically David's book, the Psalms, which are understood both as prophecy and prayer.

In terms of history we can say about the prayer of the Psalms: Jesus, following Jewish custom, prayed the Psalms inspired by the Holy Spirit. The early Church, following Jewish customs and Jesus' example, continued to pray the Psalms. Hence, we may simply follow the example of the Jews, of Jesus and of the early Church. In terms of Saint Peter's teaching, we can say that the Psalms are composed by David, who, empowered by the Holy Spirit, spoke prophetically about and on behalf of Jesus Christ. Therefore the Psalms can be understood as the words of Jesus Christ himself, first spoken through the mouth of the prophet David, then by Jesus Christ during his life on earth, and now spoken by the Christian Church in the same Spirit of Jesus Christ. The Church listens to Jesus and repeats Jesus' words and thus prays to the heavenly Father in the power of the Holy Spirit.

Saint Peter continues his sermon in verses 34b–35. He again says *David says*, which indicates he is quoting again from a Psalm: Ps 110. Saint Peter assumes that the Psalm confesses him, Jesus Christ, as the king in heaven. He focuses on one verse of Ps 110, the most frequently quoted piece of the Old Testament in the New Testament: "The Lord said to my Lord, Sit at my right hand, until I make your enemies your footstool." The explanation is that David did not ascend to heaven to sit at God's right hand; so the Psalm must be speaking about someone else—so it speaks about Jesus' ascension to heaven. Again, Saint Peter presupposes that those words are the words of David, and they make perfect sense when understood this way: The Lord (= the Father in heaven) says to my Lord (= David's Lord = Jesus Christ) sit at my (= the Father's) right hand.

Saint Peter has thus preached about both Jesus' resurrection and his ascension with two Psalm-prayers as the basis for his sermon[4]. So the Church prays the Psalms both as prayers of Jesus and as praises to Jesus, the Lord. The Holy Spirit has inspired the prophet David, who composed the Psalms, and we, when praying the Psalms, follow the lead of the Holy Spirit.

2. THE HOLY SPIRIT EMPOWERS US TO PRAY AND TO PREACH (ACTS 4)

Saint Peter, in his sermon on Pentecost (Acts 2), taught about the Holy Spirit and referred to the prayer of the Psalms (Pss 16 and 110). The Holy Spirit, through God's word, also guides our prayer in special times of need and suffering. The book of Acts tells various stories about the help of the Holy Spirit for the suffering and praying church. In Acts 4, the prayer of the persecuted church for strength and courage is again based on a Psalm (Ps 2). The Psalm is God's inspired word, gift of the Holy Spirit, so that the Holy Spirit is already given, when the church prays the Psalms. In our story, the prayer is answered when the Holy Spirit is in a special way granted again (Acts 4:31).

This prayer in Acts 4 is the most extensive prayer in all the New Testament and is probably meant to be a model for the prayers of the church. This prayer employs an invocation from the Old Testament: Ps 2. First, the church accepted the Psalm as Jesus' own word and used it for a prayerful reflection on God's qualities and God's deeds, specifically a reflection on the passion of Christ. Only then are specific petitions about the immediate situation voiced, the actual supplication of the church in the given situation.[5]

Context: The context of this prayer in Acts 4:24–37 is a report about the worshipping assembly when the church was suffering from persecution by the Jews. Saint Peter and Saint John had been arrested and then released,

---

4. This is actually a nice literary device to summarize the reports about Jesus' resurrection and ascension in Luke's books.

5. The church's collect prayers have their strict form, and to some degree they follow the pattern of this early model prayer. Cf. Below the chapter about the forms of prayer (3.IV.2).

under the condition that they must stop preaching about Jesus Christ. The prohibition on preaching was backed with threats.

After the prisoners' return from jail to their friends (verse 23), the church offered a common prayer; we read that "they raised their voices together." We read the expression *in one accord* in other places of the New Testament, in Acts 1:14 and 2:46, and in Rom 15:6. The Church raised their voices *in one accord* because all assembled there agreed with the apostles that it is right to obey God rather than human beings. The members of the assembly agreed, and this collective prayer is based on scripture. Thus the basis of this prayer is scriptural truth and community, rather than an individual expression. The prayer in Acts 4 invokes God in a particular situation of trouble and is still based on praying the words of the Bible.

Form: The form of this prayer has parallels in Jewish prayers of the time: Invocation > qualities of God > historical reference > transition to the actual petitions.[6] The prayer has a clear structure, in two parts. The first part begins with the address *sovereign* (verse 24b): "Sovereign Lord, who made the heaven and the earth, the sea, and everything in them." The second part turns to the present and immediate needs of the church; this part begins in verse 29 with the address *Lord:* "And now, Lord, look at their threats, and grant to your servants to speak your word with all boldness." The first part can again be subdivided (Acts 4:24-25) into two parts, first: "[24] Sovereign Lord, you made the heaven and the earth. . . ." and then: "[25] it is you who said by the Holy Spirit through our ancestor David . . . ." Two times, God is explicitly addressed with *you*, and two words tell about God's actions: the words *make* in verse 24 and *speak* in verse 25. The two parts of the prayer speak about God's deeds as the creator of the universe and about his revelation in history.

Form of address: God is addressed as *sovereign*. The address *sovereign*, in the original Greek, is actually *despot* (δεσπότης). The meaning of this Greek word is *owner of slaves* (cf. 1 Tim 6:1-2; Titus 2:9; and other places). In the Greek version of the Old Testament the word *despot* is used for the sovereign of all things (Job 5:8). Both Greeks and Jews used this word to speak about God, the sovereign ruler of all creation. Knowing that we are God's servants, we are free from other despots on earth. And this is the very issue in our story: shall we obey the Jewish leaders, or shall we obey God? Therefore the address *sovereign God* already reflects the topic of the prayer. The address *sovereign Lord who made the heavens and the earth* is adopted from biblical tradition; it is similar to the Greek versions of Exod 20:11, the story of Moses' meeting with God on Mount Sinai. The Church prays

---

6. Cf. Daube, *Prayer Pattern*.

to the "Sovereign Lord, who made the heaven and the earth." Hence the Church prays in the midst of all creation to the creator who is the ruler of all, including the enemies of the Church. Therefore this prayer-address already frees us from fear and self-centeredness, reminding us that we are God's creatures and a small portion of God's beloved creation. This creation is not just the visible world here; addressing this prayer to the *maker of heaven and earth* reminds us also of the world beyond, and this in a situation when the disciples have to face the possibility of martyrdom.

Verse 25 turns the view from cosmos to history (Acts 4): "^{25} it is you who said by the Holy Spirit through our ancestor David, your servant . . ." The Holy Spirit spoke the Psalms through the mouth of David, who is called *ancestor* or *forefather*. Hence our prayer is rooted in history. Both the cosmos and the world's history are in view when the Church prays in a particular situation, a situation of immediate danger. For this prayer, the church has the book of Psalms, gift of the Holy Spirit.

In verse 29, specific petitions for the given situation follow. God is again invoked and now addressed as *Lord*: "^{29} And now, Lord, look at their threats, and grant to your servants to speak your word with all boldness, ^{30} while you stretch out your hand to heal, and signs and wonders are performed through the name of your holy servant Jesus."

The prayer continues with the phrase *and now*. This word in verse 29 marks the transition from reflection on God, the creator of the universe and sovereign of history, to the actual situation of God's servants, the Church.

In this second part, the actual petitions, God is invoked with two imperatives: *look* and *grant*. The first imperative calls God's attention to the cause of God's servants, who relive the story of Jesus, *God's holy servant*,[7] and the story of his passion. The second imperative asks for the power to perform miracles that would support the disciples in boldly preaching the word. It is the Holy Spirit who grants the ability to perform healing miracles *in the name of Jesus*, as was previously mentioned in Acts 3:6 and 4:10. The disciples pray for those signs and wonders through the name of Jesus and for the ability to speak God's word with boldness in the presence of enemies.

Trinitarian: The prayer is clearly a Trinitarian prayer. The invocation is addressed to the sovereign God; then a Psalm prayer follows, which are

---

7. Saint Luke's book of Acts makes this identification of the church with Jesus Christ even more obvious in another place. In Acts 9:4, in the story of the conversion of Saul, who becomes the Apostle Paul, the risen Lord identifies himself with the persecuted Church (Acts 9): ^{4} "Saul, Saul, why do you persecute me?" The persecution against the Church is ultimately a persecution against Jesus Christ himself. Therefore the Church prays with the words Jesus Christ has prayed.

words given by the Holy Spirit and refer to the Messiah, Jesus; then follows the prayer *for* the Holy Spirit.

The Holy Spirit had spoken through David's mouth, the author of the Psalms. The praying community, the church, now recites the Psalms, praying them in a specific situation. Hence the congregation already experiences the Holy Spirit's support, as they employ the Psalm given through David and pray for the help of the Spirit, which is granted again when (Acts 4): "[31] they were all filled with the Holy Spirit and spoke the word of God with boldness."

It is possible to adopt the Psalm for the prayer of the Church because Ps 2 is viewed as a Psalm about the Messiah, Jesus Christ, and especially about the passion of Christ. Jesus is called the *holy servant* because he is anointed with the Holy Spirit (Luke 3:22; 4:1.14.18; Acts 10:38). The title *holy servant Jesus* connects this prayer in Acts 4 with Saint Peter's sermon in Acts 3 (verses 13b+14a+26). The prayer employs the messianic Psalm (Ps 2), places the situation of the praying church in the context of the history of salvation, and asks for boldness in the Spirit. The persecuted church identifies itself with the suffering Lord and prays his words, applying those words prayed by David and by Jesus immediately to their own situation.

The answer: The answer to the prayer is told as an epiphany story, a story about God's appearance (Acts 4): "[31] the place in which they were gathered together was shaken." God's appearances cause earthquakes, as it was said in Exod 19, the story of God's appearances on Mount Sinai, or in Isa 6, the story of God appearing to the prophet Isaiah in the Temple of Jerusalem. Nature gives witness when its creator appears.

The story of the praying church in Acts 4 refers to the same people as the Pentecost story in Acts 2. The Church has already been given the Holy Spirit as she prays with the words of the Bible, gifts of the Holy Spirit; and this prayer is answered when the praying Church receives the Holy Spirit again. Thus, the Church continues to pray for the Holy Spirit to come to our help, and the Holy Spirit, who has given us the Holy Scriptures, is already present to aid our prayers.

3. THE HOLY SPIRIT INTERCEDES FOR US (ROMANS 8)

In Rom 8, Saint Paul[8] speaks about this aid of the Holy Spirit for prayer. The Apostle writes about the life of those who are *in Christ Jesus* (8:1), who in

---

8. I collected important exegetical information from Wilkens, *Der Brief an die Römer*.

their weakness are helped by the Holy Spirit (8:26), and about their actual prayers. Prayer is perhaps not the main topic of this chapter, but prayer is important for the life of those who are saved, and in Rom 8 it is mentioned several times, embedded in a teaching about creation and salvation.

Saint Paul uses the same words to describe the intercession of both the Holy Spirit and Jesus Christ. He writes: "[26] Likewise the Spirit helps us in our weakness; for we do not know what to pray as we ought, but that very Spirit intercedes (ὑπερτυγχάνει) with sighs too deep for words. [27] The Spirit intercedes for the saints according to the will of God." A little later, Saint Paul writes about the intercession of Jesus Christ: "[34] It is Christ Jesus, who died, yes, who was raised, who is at the right hand of God, who indeed *intercedes* for us." The reason for these parallel sentences about the Holy Spirit and Jesus Christ is that the Holy Spirit, who works in us and helps us to pray, is no other than *the Spirit of Jesus Christ* (Rom 8:9, Phil 1:19). In other words, Jesus Christ sits at the right hand of his Father and speaks to him on our behalf, and his Spirit is in us and makes us speak together with him. Gifted with the Spirit of Christ, we pray together with Christ. The spirit of Christ makes us pray the words of Christ.

- *We pray "in Christ" and "in the Spirit"*

We are *in Jesus Christ* (Rom 8:1); we are also *in the Spirit* (verse 9). The preposition *in* basically refers to a location; it indicates where Christian life takes place[9]. This expression *in Christ* is consistent with the idea of the body of Christ: We are members in the one body. Saint Paul writes several times that we are "members of the body of Christ." Since we are baptized *into* Christ (Rom 6:3; Gal 3:27), we are part of his body and we have received Christ's Spirit, who then is in us and helps us in our weakness. Hence "we pray in the name of Jesus," because having received the Spirit of Christ in Holy Baptism we are enabled to respond to Saint Paul's encouragement (Phil 2): "[5] Let the same mind be in you that was in Christ Jesus." Because we are in Jesus Christ and in the community of Jesus Christ, the Spirit of Jesus Christ is in us.

Because we are in Christ, we live and suffer together with him, and he together with us. Rom 8 teaches us that those who are saved still suffer from hardship, distress and persecution (Rom 8:35), and thus we pray. Creation suffers from futility, and Christ, sent into the likeness of sinful

---

9. Some scholars try to avoid the mystical thought and translate the word *in* as *through*. This translation is not impossible, but I do not see any good reason for presuming this rather unusual meaning of the Greek proposition ἐν.

flesh (Rom 8:3), suffered in and together with this creation. When we speak about our being *in Christ*, we need to speak about the whole story of Jesus, including his suffering and death.

Our being in Jesus Christ means, in regard to suffering and death, that the experience of hardship, distress, and persecution (Rom 8:35) does not separate us from Jesus Christ, but we suffer and pray together with Christ and with his people and with all creation. Our being in Jesus Christ means, in regard to the judgment of the law, that for those who are in Christ, the condemnation is over. Those who are freed from the condemnation of the law no longer have their place in the body of death (7:24), but *in Christ Jesus*, participating in both his death and resurrection.

The Apostle's consolation is that the sufferings of the present time are not of final importance in the light of the glory to come. *Glory* is the presence of God himself. Christians can hope to be glorified after their suffering. As "joint heirs with Christ," (Rom 8:17) the Son of God, they are children of God. The end will reveal what they have become already in Holy Baptism: They are joined to Jesus Christ, the risen Lord, so that he is the firstborn among many brothers and sisters.

- **The Holy Spirit in us**

Saint Paul writes (verse 9): "But you are not in the flesh; you are in the Spirit, since the Spirit of God dwells in you. Anyone who does not have the Spirit of Christ does not belong to him." The Spirit of God makes us Christians because this Spirit is the Spirit of Christ. This sentence does not speak so much about special moments but about the permanent presence of the Spirit in us and our obligation to live accordingly as Christians.

Saint Paul continues (Rom 8): "[16] God's Spirit testifies for our Spirit, that we are Children of God." The divine Spirit is obviously not the same as *our spirit*. The expression *our spirit* is usually identified as *our inner life* or *human reason*. The Holy Spirit is not an expression of our own spirit, but our spirit receives God's Spirit when we hear God's word and pray God's word. Just as it is in 1 Cor 2:1, *our spirit* can be here only a receiving vessel for the divine testimony and the divine spirit. The Spirit of Jesus Christ is added to our inner life. The Holy Spirit does not eliminate the human self; we do not remain passive, but we *walk*—as Saint Paul says[10]—according to the Spirit. The Spirit dwelling in us is the Spirit who raised Jesus from the dead. Therefore the Spirit will give eternal life to our mortal bodies as well

---

10. περιπατῦσιν, Rom 8:4.

(cf. Ezek 37; 2 Cor 5). With this hope, all those who are guided by the Holy Spirit, by the Spirit of the Son, pray as sons and daughters of God.

In baptism we have become children of God when we have received the *spirit of adoption*, which means that we have the spirit of adopted sons and daughters, as opposed to slaves. The effect of the spirit of adoption is that, "through him we shout: ABBA, Father!" The word translated as *shout*[11] is in the Greek version of the Old Testament (Septuaginta = LXX) the technical term for an urgent prayer, but also for the ecstatic utterance of a possessed person (Mark 3:11, Acts 16:17), or for prophetic inspiration (Mark 11:9, John 1:15, Rom 9:27).

"Abba, Father" is certainly a prayer. A number of scholars assume that it is the beginning of the Lord's Prayer, which in the version of Saint Luke simply begins with *Father*, which corresponds with the Aramaic Abba.[12] The call *ABBA* in Rom 8:15 would then be a residue of the original Aramaic version of the Lord's Prayer, preserved in Greek-speaking congregations. Other scholars assume that *shout* indicates an ecstatic outburst; then *Abba, Father* would be a spontaneous acclamation in worship, similar to *amen, maranatha* or *alleluia,* preserved in Aramaic by the Greek New Testament. These explanations do not necessarily exclude each other, for the Greek-speaking congregation must have learned this foreign-language word somehow. Hence even the isolated, spontaneous Abba-acclamation is best explained as inspired by the Lord's Prayer. Whatever we want to say in our self-made prayers, and whatever words we want to use, prayer is still best learned from the prayers we have once memorized or which we have heard in the worship of our faith community.

Our adoption, given to us by the Spirit, can be experienced in common prayer. When Christians suffer and pray as part of the Christian community, they participate in Christ's suffering and prayer, and accordingly they can be certain that they will also participate in the glory of the risen one.

- **We pray together with all Creation**

Saint Paul writes about prayer and hope in connection with the *groaning* of the whole creation. In the Bible, the word *creation* (κτίσις) primarily refers to the non-human creation, following the usage of the word in the Greek version of the Old Testament (Septuaginta = LXX); so it is in Rom 1:20.25 and all other places of the New Testament. The whole creation is affected

---

11. κράζειν.
12. אבא in Rom 8:15, transcribed as ἀββα.

by human sin; therefore the fate of creation depends on the situation of humanity.

The children of God pray and suffer from the futility of the world in its present condition. *Suffering from futility* is a Hellenistic idea, and the *groaning of creation* has plenty of parallels in Greek literature. All creation is still groaning under the weight of the misery described in verse 20: "for the creation was subjected to futility, not of its own will but by the will of the one who subjected it, in hope." We live in a time when misery and futility are still lasting. This misery again is the consequence of the tensions in the world once made as God's beautiful creation and now suffering from the curse imposed by God in response to Adam's sin.

We pray along with all groaning creation. Saint Paul does not view creation *per se* as a *vale of tears*, as a hostile environment, or just as tool and material for humans. But he bases his thinking on the biblical understanding that humans are part of creation, and that both human and non-human creation stand together in the presence of God, their creator. The deep divide is not between God and humanity on the one side and the world on the other. Rather, there is an infinite difference between the creator and his beloved creation, of which humanity is but a portion (cf. Augustine, *Confessions* I,1). Creation groans because it suffers from the discrepancy between its God-given potential and its actual condition. Creation lives in expectation and hope that God will solve this tension. Creation will indeed participate in salvation.

So the groaning of Christians is part of the groaning of all creation. Saint Paul emphasizes this fact by the repetitive wording: *ourselves also, . . . even we ourselves groan*. We are gifted with the Holy Spirit, the first fruit, and we expect the adoption that is already given to us but remains as yet hidden and real only in Jesus Christ (there is no contradiction to verses 14–16).

Christians groan as all creation groans, although they have the Spirit, which guarantees their salvation. Their having the Spirit does not separate them from creation but unites them with God's creation suffering from futility. Their own salvation will be freedom for the whole creation from the slavery of futility. Christians, who, empowered by the Holy Spirit, know of their salvation, experience all the more the pain of futility from which all creation suffers: they groan when all creation groans.

Salvation is granted to Christians as representatives of the whole creation. The community God's children have with all creation reflects the justice of God, who remains faithful to his works and justifies sinners in order to lead them together with all creation to that perfection for which he has destined his creation in the beginning.

Because God has given for his works an objective goal, Christians hope and pray, since they have the Spirit as a deposit and first-fruit of this hoped-for reality, the new world of salvation. Just as they in their suffering participate in the futility of all creation, so they voice in their prayers the silent yearning and hope of all creation.

- **What to Pray**

Verse 26f continues with the thoughts of verse 23 (KJV Rom 8): "²⁶ Likewise the Spirit also helpeth our infirmities: for we know not what we should pray for as we ought: but the Spirit itself maketh intercession for us with groanings which cannot be uttered."

The keywords connecting this verse with verse 23 are *Spirit* and *groaning*[13]. The Spirit intercedes for us and thus comes to our help in our weakness. What our weakness actually is explains the next phrase: *for*[14] *what (!) we do not know . . . .*" We are weak because we do not know what to pray; and we do not know what to pray because we do not know what is appropriate to pray for.

Two points need clarification. First, Saint Paul does not write about any perplexity of *how* to pray.[15] There is not a shred of evidence in the New Testament that there were any problems among Jesus' disciples or in the early church with the way of praying. This sentence is often misinterpreted as *how to pray hard enough, how to pray sufficiently,* or *in what manner to pray,* or *with what attitude to pray.* But Saint Paul does not say *how to pray* but he strictly says: "We do not know *what* to pray." The King James Bible translates correctly, *what to pray.* The problem addressed here is: What is it that God wants to be asked for?

Secondly, nothing in the text indicates that Saint Paul is describing some personal experience of uncertainty. Neither does he indicate that he is speculating about what might be going on in the souls of those who would someday read his letters. If this sentence was meant to be a description, anyone could question if this is a fitting description of his or her own experience. Saint Paul's sentence only makes sense if it is understood not as a description of the assumed state of someone's mind, but rather as a doctrinal statement. Saint Paul teaches: Man being born in sin is, on his own, unable to know what is appropriate to pray; that is, what God wants to be asked for and what he wants to be thanked and to be praised for. This teaching is

13. Τὸ πνεῦμα and στενάζειν.
14. γάρ.
15. The Greek word is τι not ὡς!

consistent with the disciples' question in the Gospel of Luke (11:1) as they asked Jesus: "Lord teach us to pray," and as a response Jesus Christ gave them the Lord's Prayer, which doesn't teach a manner of praying but rather the content of prayer. Jesus, with giving his disciples the Our Father, answers the question of what to pray. Saint Paul explains that on our own we do not know what to pray. With this understanding, the word *appropriately* (καθὸ δεῖ) makes perfectly sense: it means indeed: *as we ought* (KJV). The standard for prayer is not necessarily how ingenuous, how sincere, how intense or fervent a prayer is subjectively, but rather whether it is appropriate to the clarity and glory of God. Prayer should not correspond to the state of our poor mind or our supposedly ingenious and ever so pious—and self-righteous—soul, but to the reality of God's deeds. To pray, we need to know what God wants to be asked for, and we need to speak God's language, which alone is appropriate to his glory.

- **Conclusion**

In this time of ongoing suffering and groaning, Christians suffer from the futility of all creation. Their weakness is that they do not yet fully know the coming glory. In verses 24–25, Saint Paul states, "We hope for what we do not see." We could say we do not know what to pray for because we do not yet *see* what to pray for. We can only hope, and we need to be taught what to hope for because we do not see it. The terms *hope*, *patience*, and *prayer* are together opposed to *sight*.

God's answer to our prayer is always infinitely wiser than our wishes. Therefore we need to be taught to pray for what we on our own do not see, nor understand, nor feel, nor desire, like the holiness of God's name, his kingdom, and his will. In this persistent time of suffering and groaning, the weakness of Christians is that they still walk only by hope and not yet by sight.

In this weakness, the Spirit comes to help and intercedes for us with a groaning in words that remain un-understandable and unspeakable for the world in its present condition. Saint Paul uses the foreign word *Abba* (verse 15), an Aramaic word in a letter to a Greek-speaking church. The early Christians were obviously reluctant to replace this strange word with new, familiar, contemporary words. This fact perhaps illustrates the fact that only the Spirit can give us the language to speak to God in an appropriate way. The Spirit of God's Son teaches us to pray for what his Father wants to be asked.

Verse 29 finally states the goal and purpose of our praying in Christ and in the Spirit (Rom 8): "[29]For whom He foreknew, He also predestined to be conformed to the image of His Son, that He might be the firstborn among many brethren." Jesus Christ is the image of God (2 Cor 4:4; Col 1:15; Heb 10:1).[16] Hence we are to be transformed to become images of God's Son, the image of God. The same idea is found in 2 Cor 3: "[18]And all of us, with unveiled faces, seeing the glory of the Lord as though reflected in a mirror, are being transformed into the same image from one degree of glory to another; for this comes from the Lord, the Spirit."

4. A PRAYER FOR THE HOLY SPIRIT (EPHESIANS 3)

Rom 8 teaches about the Spirit's help for our prayer. In the letters of the New Testament we find also an actual prayer which prays that the church may be strengthened by the Holy Spirit. Here the Holy Spirit is the desired good of the intercession prayed *by* the church, *for* the church.

This prayer is found in the introduction of the letter. Most letters in the New Testament have an introduction: first sender and addressee, a greeting and then a prayer of thanksgiving. In the letter to the congregation in Ephesus, this introduction is quite extended; it comprises half of the letter and concludes only at the end of the third chapter. The verses 3:14–21 are a prayer for the Holy Spirit.

Structure: The main part is an intercession asking for the church's growth in strength and knowledge (verses 14–19); the prayer is concluded with a doxology (Eph 3): "[20]Now to him ... [21]be glory in the church and in Christ Jesus to all generations, forever and ever. Amen."

In the original Greek text, the main part of the prayer (verses 14–19) is one long sentence. This sentence is structured in three portions marked with *so that* (verses 16,18,19b)[17]. The first *so that* sentence states the topic: growing strength of the inner human being. The second portion (verse 18) states two dimensions of this growth in strength, marked by the words *to comprehend* and *to know*, referring to the wideness of God's kingdom and to his love in Christ. The third *so that* sentence (19b) prays for the congregation to be filled with the fullness of God. There is a certain climax in the sequence of these thoughts: growth > comprehension > fullness.

The prayer is, as usual, addressed to the Father. The posture of the body is kneeling, a gesture that expresses homage, obedience, adoration,

---

16. Jesus Christ is here actually called the *ikon* (εἰκών) of God.
17. ἵνα.

submission, imploration (cf. chapter 3.I.3, *postures and gestures of the body*). The address *Father* is clearly not the intimate expression of a child, but refers to God's greatness and power (cf. Chapter 1.III, about the invocation *Father* in the Lord's Prayer).

The Apostle writes (Eph 3): [14] I bow my knees before the Father, [15] from whom every family in heaven and on earth takes its name." The word in verse 15 translated as *family* is *patria* (πατριά), and together with the word Father (= *pater*) forms a play on words that cannot be translated. The meaning of *patria* is actually *nation, lineage* or *house*. Therefore, here again this word does not refer to the nuclear family of modern Western society. Eph 3:15 states that from the one God and Father, the creator and sustainer of the universe, of all that is created, all peoples have their one origin. With this address we approach the *Father* of the universe and all nations. God is the Father of the universe (Eph 4:6) and the God of Jesus Christ (Eph 1:17), the merciful God of love (Eph 2:4). Inside the Church, the walls between nations are torn down. This sentence also reminds us that this intercession prays for a community. The same God has created everything and in Jesus Christ restores the damaged world and brings it back to obey his sovereignty.

Petition: The actual petition of the prayer is that the church may be strengthened. The apostle asks the Holy Spirit to grant more and more knowledge and comprehension. The apostle obviously presupposes that the work of the Holy Spirit is to provide knowledge and comprehension (cf. Isa 11).

The Spirit already given to the church is not sufficiently at work yet. But instead of admonishing the congregation, the apostle prays for the Holy Spirit to come, and he trusts in the Spirit's power. Speaking the word to the congregation, the apostle actually sets in motion what he is praying for: by speaking the word to the church he conveys the Spirit. The apostle does not speak about moral consequences but about abilities, about inner strength. A Christian becomes an *inner man* when the divine Spirit takes possession of him/her, pervades, lives in, and strengthens him/her. The Spirit is the life–giving Spirit (cf. 1 Cor 15:45) that flows from Jesus Christ.

The letter speaks about the Spirit's *dwelling in the heart*, and the Apostle also says that the congregation shall be rooted in love. He actually mixes the metaphors of dwelling in a home and the growth of a plant. Neither image allows us to think that the Spirit would come in fits of excitement. But the prayer asks for abiding (cf. also John 15:7) and for growth. The wording *through faith* refers to the dwelling of Jesus Christ in us, which is consistent with Gal 2: "[20] and it is no longer I who live, but it is Christ who lives in me.

And the life I now live in the flesh I live by faith in the Son of God, who loved me and gave himself for me."

The Apostle continues (Eph 3): "[18] I pray that you may have the power to comprehend, with all the saints, what is the breadth and length and height and depth...." The goal of this growth in strength is to *comprehend* and to *know*. The words *what is the breadth and length and height and depth* are mysterious. Various attempts have been made to uncover the preceding tradition behind these words, which is beyond the scope of this book. It seems, however, certain that the horizon of the aspired knowledge has cosmic dimensions.

The letter says (Eph 3): "[18] I pray that you may have the power to comprehend, with all the saints, ...[19] to know the love of Christ that surpasses knowledge, so that you may be filled with all the fullness of God." The verse is intentionally a paradox: to *know love that surpasses knowledge*. That which is meant to be known is indeed of immeasurable and incomprehensible greatness. Prayer leads beyond human understanding and personal desires. The apostle writes that we *know* and *comprehend* and do so *together with all the saints*. The growth in strength, the growth in comprehension and knowledge is not a goal that can be achieved individually, but only in the community of the Church. The community of the faithful, studying together, listening to the word together, praying the Bible together, nourishes the growth of knowledge.

The passive form *you may be filled* indicates that it is God's grace which makes it happen.[18] However, the English translation "be filled with all the fullness of God" is not quite correct. The word translated as *with* is in the original Greek a word (εἰς) that would be better translated as *into* or *towards*; therefore the sentence also implies a *striving* or *quest*.

Trinitarian structure: In the Church, the Holy Spirit guides us to participate more and more in the fullness of grace in Christ, and thus we are led closer and closer to God the Father. The goal is strength in the Holy Spirit so that Christ dwells in us. Thus, prayer draws us into the life of the Triune God. This prayer does not respond to any specific situation; it is focused on the fruitful reception of the gospel.

The prayer concludes with a doxology: "[20] Now to him who by the power at work within us is able to accomplish abundantly far more than all we can ask or imagine, [21] to him be glory in the church and in Christ Jesus to all generations, forever and ever. Amen."

Consistent with the style of prayers in Judaism and in the Christian Church, this doxology is shaped by the normal form, which requires three

---

18. The form of the word in the original Greek is an imperative passive.

elements: the name of the one to be praised, the word of praise, for example *blessed be* or *glory to,* and some word that speaks about the eternity of the praise (Gal 1:5, Rom 1:25, 9:5, 1 Tim 1:17, 6:16, 1 Pet 4:11). The doxology in Eph 3 states that God is superior to our prayer and aspiration. God knows better than we do what we are in need of, and his giving is better than our praying. This verse speaks about the surpassing love of Christ, just as verse 19 had done, so that this doxology is closely intertwined with the main part of the intercession. With the word *we* the doxology turns the individual prayer of the apostle for the Church into a prayer said by the Church. The praise-hymn of the Church is sung *in Christ* to the Father.

The prayer concludes with the word *Amen,* which indicates that the Apostle expects that his prayer is actually read and prayed in the congregation of his addressees.

- **Appendix: The Prayer of the Psalms**

The Psalms and the canticles of the Old and the New Testament are special gifts of the Holy Spirit. This is not just a preconceived idea but the testimony of the Psalter itself.

Seventy-two Psalms are said to be composed by David; twelve by Asaph the choirmaster of David; twelve by the *sons of korah*, a choir serving under David; and two by Solomon, the son of David. Hence, all Psalms are written after David has been anointed king. Therefore the book of Psalms is under the authority of him who is anointed with the Holy Spirit, which is the meaning of the Hebrew word *Messiah* and the Greek Word *Christ* (cf. 1 Sam 16).

The Holy Spirit speaks through David, and David gives witness to Jesus Christ: Acts 2:25-32 (Ps 16); Acts 2:34-35 (Ps 110), Heb 5 (Ps 2), Luke 20:41 (Ps 110). Jesus Christ speaks himself in the Psalms, according to Heb 2:12 (Ps 22) and 10:5 (Ps 40). The Holy Spirit speaks in the Psalms: Heb 3:7 (Ps 95).

In Acts 12:5 the prayer of the Church for the imprisoned Saint Peter is called in Greek *proseuche* (προσευχή), a word frequently used by the Greek version of the Old Testament in the headings of Psalms (for example Ps 16:1, which Saint Peter explains in Acts 2) and other ceremonies—for example in 2 Chr 6-7:1, the dedication of the temple with prayer and sacrifice. Therefore it is reasonable to assume that the prayers of the church in Acts 12 offered for the imprisoned apostle included as well Psalms of the Bible, and that perhaps prayer (*proseuche*) in the New Testament always at least included a prayer of the Psalms.

Order of Prayer: Some verses in the Psalter indicate that the prayer of the inspired word—inspired by the Holy Spirit—was meant to be done on a regular basis.

Daily Prayer:

Ps 119: "[164] Seven times a day I praise you for your righteous ordinances." Ps 119: "[62] At midnight I rise to praise you, because of your righteous ordinances."

Morning prayer:

Ps 5: "[3] O LORD, in the morning you hear my voice; in the morning I plead my case to you, and watch."

Evening prayer:

Ps 141: "[2] Let my prayer be set forth before thee as incense; and the lifting up of my hands as the evening sacrifice."

Night prayer:

Ps 4: "[8] I will both lie down and sleep in peace; for you alone, O LORD, make me lie down in safety."

Using these Psalm-verses and honoring the hours in the passion story of the Gospels, monasticism has established regular prayer times kept to these days; the prayer services are called *horae*, the Latin word for *hours* (see below, Part 3.III.3). Protestant Christians do not obey these biblical counsels as a law that could earn salvation. But it is certainly healthy for the soul to keep a certain order of prayer. (1 Cor 14): "[33] for God is a God not of disorder but of peace. As in all the churches of the saints." Observing a common order for morning and evening prayer allows us to participate in the Spirit given to the church of all times and all places.

The Psalter is not just an anthology of Hebrew poetry but composed as a book, which suggests that it is meant to be used not just selectively but as a whole. In the first and last Psalms we find advice for the spiritual usage of the Psalter: *meditation* (Ps 1) and *praise* (Ps 150). The double introduction, *law and messiah*, (Pss 1 and 2) is a key that opens the prayer book of the Bible for our understanding.

Some topics of the Psalms:

Creation	Pss 8, 19, 104.
History	Pss 78, 105, 106.
Law	Pss 1, 19, 119.
The End	Pss 6, 17, 39, 90, 102.
Service	Pss 27, 42, 46, 48, 63, 81, 84, 87.
Church	Pss 46, 126, 137.

Suffering Pss 13, 31, 35.

Enemies Pss 5, 7, 9, 10, 13, 16, 21, 23, 28, 31, 35, 36, 40, 41, 44, 52, 54, 55, 58, 59, 68, 69, 70, 71, 137.

    Because it is Jesus Christ who prays the Psalms, the words of vengeance must not be used as a license to express our own anger. We are sinners and therefore probably those who deserve to suffer from the vengeance for which the Psalm prays. With these Psalms, we accept that God is judge over heaven and earth and hope for his mercy.

The seven Penitential Psalms: Pss 6, 32, 38, 51, 102, 130, 142.

The Messiah Psalm: Ps 22 (Matthew used the words of this Psalm to tell his version of the story of Jesus' suffering, death and resurrection. Hence, praying this Psalm, we may meditate on the story of Jesus Christ.)

PART 3

The Praxis
of the Praying Community

I.

Postures and Gestures of the Body

THERE IS, OF COURSE, no wrong posture for prayer. If we are sick, we may lie down and turn to whatever position makes us a little more comfortable, as King Hezekiah did (2 Kgs 20:1–4). The Holy Bible speaks about various postures and gestures of the body, but never in terms of a law that would demand mindless obedience.

It is still not a matter of indifference which postures and gestures we choose for our prayers. The human body does matter. In Jesus Christ the word of God has become flesh, a human being with a body. Jesus is not a ghost, as the disciples once suspected (Matt 14:26) when they saw him walking on the water; but in this story Jesus stretched out the hand of his body to save Peter's bodily life. God's Son has become flesh: a human being who suffered, died and rose again with his body, who then showed his pierced hands to the disciples (John 20:27).

There is a saying that, "A body without a soul is a corpse, a soul without a body is a spook." We are bodily beings, whether we think of man as a whole (holism) as opposed to a collection of parts; or a composite of two parts: body and soul (dualism); or a composite of three parts: spirit, soul and body (trichotomism), a view that Saint Paul seems to favor (1 Thess 5:23): "may your whole spirit, soul, and body be preserved blameless." Because we are bodily beings, our body is not just an instrument of our mind. Experience shows that the expressions of our body are more genuine than our words: cramped shoulders and clenched hands show how strained and stressed we are, despite all words of denial. When you loll around, let your toes play with your flip–flops and let your shoulders droop, you show no respect for yourself and for others. But the body is not just an expression of our soul, the body also affects our feeling and thinking. Anyone who experiences a toothache knows that. When we stand straight and upright, keep our feet together, pull back our shoulders, lift our chin, feelings about ourselves and our attitude toward the world around us will change. Some self-esteem problems could perhaps be solved by a good dancing class.

Therefore our posture has certainly an impact on our relationship with others. When I stand knock-kneed, look down at my feet, scratch my neck and mumble, I have a relationship towards the other person different from a relationship that is both expressed and shaped by a posture of standing straight, looking into the eyes of the partner and speaking with a clear, loud voice. As a matter of fact, unless one is a telepathist, we always relate to others by means of our body, its posture, its voice, its gestures, its looks.

To God as well, we relate as bodily human beings, so that our relationship with God is never without our body. God has made us with a body, and he will raise us from the dead with a body (1 Cor 15; 2 Cor 5). Therefore we find in the Holy Bible a wealth of examples that show how our body both expresses and shapes our attitude towards God. We may try out which postures and gestures feel most appropriate for the words we say in our prayers, for our petitions, or for our offerings of thanks and praise. We can try out which postures and gestures are most appropriate for the words we say to God, the lord, king, judge, merciful Father, etc. Saint Paul writes (Phil 2:10): "at the name of Jesus every knee should bow, of those in heaven, and of those on earth, and of those under the earth."

1. STANDING

Standing upright on two feet was, in antiquity, amongst both Jews and Greeks, the posture of the faithful who bring their offerings. It was a regular posture of prayer as we read in Mark 11:25 or Luke 22:46; pictures of the first century of Christianity found in the catacombs show that standing was a common posture of prayer. Since the earliest times of the Church, standing has been the preferred posture of worship, especially of the Eucharist.

In the prayers of the Old Testament the Psalmist confesses (Ps 40:2): "He drew me up from the desolate pit, out of the miry bog, and set my feet upon a rock, making my steps secure." The prophet Isaiah (7:9) warns us: "If you do not stand firm in faith, you shall not stand at all." In the imagery of the Bible *standing* is the posture of *faith*. Saint Paul writes (1 Cor 16): "[13] Keep alert, stand firm in your faith"; and (1 Cor 15) it is the Gospel "[1] in which you stand." In another letter he writes (Phil 4:1): "stand fast in the Lord, beloved." Hence *standing* corresponds with faith. We may stand with reverence and confidence in the presence of the heavenly Father (Gal 4:7; 5:1), *stand* on a firm rock (Exod 33:21), *stand* in God's grace (Rom 5:2). Christians are freed from the slavery of sin and death, and through Christ's resurrection we are lifted up, slaves no longer but sons and daughters.

Standing also corresponds with watching for the second coming of Christ (Luke 21:26). He or she who is baptized has been raised with Christ and expects to meet him when he comes again in glory.

If we do not just stand about but stand in awe in the presence of the Lord, we can experience a variety of things. Standing is the attitude:[BL 1–6]

- of being alert, vigilant and attentive (1 Cor 16:13);
- of deference and respect for God (Gen 18:22);
- of joy, free from depressing fear (Dan 10:9–11);
- of the readiness to listen (Ezek 2:1);
- of the readiness to receive a command and to serve (Isa 6:8);
- of the readiness to set off for a journey (Exod 12:11).

To experience what this *standing* means, we may try various ways to stand. Standing on my supporting leg and shaking the other leg, I will experience nothing special. Keeping my feet closely together, I stand unstable and insecure. Standing with my legs wide apart, I try to look strong, but in fact I can be tipped over easily. If I lift up my chin I appear arrogant. If I let my head droop I am in want of self-esteem and perhaps suffer from depression.

Reporting to God for duty, we stand upright and firm on both our feet; we may look up, forthright and candid. We may think of the revelation to Moses: "The LORD spoke to Moses face to face, as one speaks to a friend" (cf. Exod 33:11). The first prayer of the Psalter (Ps 1) gives us the image of a tree planted by flowing waters; standing on both our feet, we may visualize the nourishing water flowing through our roots; we spread out our hands like green branches to heaven.

2. BOWING DOWN

Bowing down is a gesture of adoration. We learn from the Psalms that people entering the house of God for morning prayer used to bow down (Ps 5): "But I, through the abundance of your steadfast love, will enter your house, I will bow down toward your holy temple in awe of you."

The hopes of God's chosen people for the whole world could be condensed in the prayer (Ps 86): "All the nations you have made shall come and bow down before you, O Lord, and shall glorify your name." In the New Testament, bowing down is a sign of conversion to God (1 Cor 14): "[25] After the secrets of the unbeliever's heart are disclosed that person will bow down before God and worship him, declaring, 'God is really among you.'"

Bowing down can be done in various ways. We may just bow our head and experience what effect this gesture has on us. We may bow head and shoulders. We may bow down deeply until the upper part of our body is at a right angle to our legs. We should try various ways of bowing and experience their effects. We can combine our bowing with various gestures of the hands: I may let them hang down, I may fold them over my chest, or put the palms together; each time, the gesture of bowing feels a little different. The various postures and gestures both express and shape our attitude towards God: love, grief about failure, humility or the pride of being a servant of the great king, or all of the above. The various postures and gestures for our prayers can help to protect us from distractions springing from our imagination, thoughts, or feelings, so that we may focus on the words of our prayers taken from the Bible, from the tradition of the church, or our self-made prayers.

3. KNEELING

Kneeling is mentioned quite often in the New Testament. It is a gesture of homage, obedience, adoration, submission, and imploration. The New Testament refers to the posture of kneeling in various wordings in Acts 7:60, 9:40, 20:36, 21:5, Mark 1:40, 10:17, Matt 17:14. The word *worship* in our English versions often translates a word from the original Greek which means concretely *kneel before* (προσκυνέω), in Matt 28:17, for example.

For many Protestants *kneeling* is unfamiliar, and it certainly affects our pride. But it was the great king Solomon who knelt before the Altar of the Lord (1 Kgs 8:54). The Psalter calls the community of the faithful (Ps 95:6): "O come, let us worship and bow down, let us kneel (LXX: προσκυνήσωμεν) before the LORD, our Maker!" Jesus, our master and leader in prayer, invoked his Father on the Mount of Olives on his knees (Luke 22:41). Throughout the Gospels, people kneel before Jesus Christ: the Magi in the Christmas story (Matt 2:11) open their presents for the divine child on their knees. Many people come to Jesus and (Matt 8:2, 19:18, 15:15, 17:14) kneel before the Lord, expecting his help. At the end of the Gospel, kneeling is the mockery of the soldiers who crucified him (Matt 27:29); but then in the

Easter story we read that the disciples worship the risen Lord on their knees (Matt 28:9.17).

After Easter the Christians of the early church prayed on their knees. In the Book of Acts we read about a speech of Saint Paul and (Acts 20:36): "When he had finished speaking, he knelt down with them all and prayed." Saint Paul's hope is (Phil 2:10) "[10] that at the name of Jesus every knee should bend, in heaven and on earth and under the earth, [11] and every tongue should confess that Jesus Christ is Lord, to the glory of God the Father."

We can combine the posture of kneeling with all gestures of our hands and our head. Kneeling is a posture of humility, a gesture that exposes ourselves helplessly to God accepting his word and his deed, his judgment and his help. Kneeling also means both humility and pride when you are to be knighted as a Christian soldier.

Kneeling, we may show our reverence to the altar and the cross. Some churches have kneelers which can help the faithful to kneel during the order of confession and forgiveness or during the Eucharistic prayer, and of course during our individual prayers.

4. WALKING

Walking uprightly is a symbol of human dignity. *Walking* is also a gesture of prayer, a gesture which we in fact practice all the time, though usually without realizing it.

Walking, we enter the church and thus approach the place where prayer, confession of faith and praise are offered. The psalmist says (Ps 122): "[1] I was glad when they said to me, "Let us go to the house of the LORD!" A number of Psalms have the heading *A Psalm of ascent*, which indicates that these Psalms were used for processions up onto the Mount of the Temple in Jerusalem. When we celebrate Holy Communion we walk up to the altar, and even people who find it difficult to get up and to walk often have the feeling that processing up to the altar is actually part of the Eucharistic celebration. We want to draw near to the altar, where the body of Christ is given and his blood is shed for us (Ps 43): "[4] Then I will go to the altar of God, to God my exceeding joy; and I will praise you with the harp, O God, my God." Processing into the church and up to the altar, we follow Jesus' call (Matt 11): "[28] Come to me, all you that are weary and are carrying heavy burdens, and I will give you rest." We walk to Jesus like the sick people who in the Gospel went to meet him with the expectation of healing.

Walking in procession can be a symbol for the journey of God's people. Walking, we meditate on our pilgrimage on earth, following Jesus' way to the cross and through death and resurrection to eternal life.

The various meanings of *walking* suggest that our walking, especially in the liturgy, should be not strolling, nor parading, nor running, but a self-controlled, dignified, graceful motion in upright posture.

5. SITTING

Sitting is a posture of calm and relaxation, also of attentiveness and of concentration.[1] Therefore the posture of sitting is not meant as a concession to human laziness and sluggishness but an opportunity to listen and to focus. Hence we should not sprawl in the pew but sit straight with open ears and thoughtful minds.

Sitting in worship has a double meaning. First, it is the posture of composure and concentration while we savor the divine word; it is the posture of focused, receptive, contemplative listening. We may picture the boy Jesus sitting amongst the teachers in the temple listening and asking questions (Luke 2:46). Or we may think of Mary, who sat at the Lord's feet listening (Luke 10:39). Accordingly it is the custom to sit during lessons, the Psalm prayers and the sermon.

Secondly, sitting was in the early Church the posture of the teacher. We read about Jesus teaching on the mount (Matt 5): "[1] When Jesus saw the crowds, he went up the mountain; and after he sat down, his disciples came to him." Accordingly the ministers in the early Church used to teach sitting on a chair, in antiquity called *cathedra*.

Judges also used to sit while officiating in a court of law. Accordingly, the judicial act of hearing individual confession and proclaiming forgiveness (absolution) is performed by a priest or a minister sitting on a chair (cf. John 8, the story of Jesus and the adulterous woman).

6. PRAYING WITH THE HANDS

The hand is specifically a part of the human body used to perform external actions, hence the metaphoric verb *to handle*. The Bible employs the word *hand* as a metaphor for *doing* in a general sense (Gen 20:5).

---

1. In the tradition of Christian worship, *sitting* was probably never related to *mourning*, as it was in the Ancient Near East (conf. Ps 137:1, Job, and the Lamentations of Jeremiah).

The symbol *hand* has various metaphorical meanings in the Bible: the right of disposal (Gen 16 KJV: "⁶ Abram said unto Sarai, Behold, thy maid is in thy hand"), human energy (Isa 35:3), victorious power (Gen 14:20), leadership (Num 4:28), etc. Often, a gesture of the hand has a symbolic meaning: when God instructs Moses and Aaron to perform miracles before Pharaoh and to bring about the Plagues of Egypt, every single instruction starts with the commandment: "Stretch forth thine hand toward heaven" (cf. Exod 8–10 and 14. 16. 26. 27 KJV).

For people in antiquity, the hand was a symbol of creative power, especially in the area of arts. Extending a hand means to connect with another person spiritually. Whenever we extend a hand to someone we do not only physically connect our own body with another body, but with this gesture we present our whole personality, our love, faithfulness, commitment and forgiveness. Extending a hand is a gesture that shows harmony and agreement (Augustine: *signum concordiae, signum consonantiae*).

In antiquity, many gestures of the hand have their origin in the rhetorical art, as statues of orators show.

- ## *Folding of the hands*

Folding the hands has been the common gesture of prayer among Protestants for a long time. It was already a custom in the twelfth century, perhaps under the influence of Germanic customs.

This gesture has no real biblical basis. It is still a useful gesture that prevents us from fidgeting around with our hands and allows us to focus. This gesture might express a spiritual wrestling. We may think of Jacob's wrestling with God all night (Gen 32:29) and of Jesus' wrestling with God in Gethsemane (Matt 26). Prayer can be a wrestling: seeking a way from rebellion to acceptance, from despair to hope, from helpless anger to confidence. Folding the hands is a gesture that corresponds with those wrestling prayers. Hence it is also understandable why this gesture has its place mainly in private prayer and has never been used in the liturgy.

- ## Lifting up the hands

Israel blessed his grandsons Ephraim and Manasse (Gen 48:14) with his hands. Aaron lifted up his hands and blessed the assembly of the people (Lev 9:22). Jesus blesses his disciples when he ascends to heaven (Luke 24): "⁵⁰ Then he led them out as far as Bethany, and, lifting up his hands, he blessed them." With the hands lifted up we bless both individuals and the whole community of the faithful.

In the Old Testament, a hand was lifted up to make an oath (cf. Num 14:30; Deut 32:40). Hands were lifted up for prayer (cf. Exod 17:11,12; 2 Chr 6:12,13,29; Ps 134:2 etc.); *lifting up the hands* is actually a common metaphor for prayer. Abraham says in Gen 14 (KJV): "[22] I have lift up mine hand unto the LORD, the most high God, the possessor of heaven and earth." Ps 141 says: "[2] Let my prayer be counted as incense before you, and the lifting up of my hands as an evening sacrifice." Lifting up the hands was, in the Old Testament (cf. Pss 28:2; 63:4; 134:2), the gesture for the sacrifice of thanks and praise. The Christian community continued to use those gestures of prayer and blessing. We read in 1 Tim 2 about prayer: "[8] I desire, then, that in every place the men should pray, lifting up holy hands without anger or argument."

A writer of the early Church, Origen, who died from the consequences of the persecutions in AD 250, considers this gesture of standing and lifting up the hands most appropriate for prayer: "Of all the innumerable dispositions of the body that, accompanied by outstretching of the hands and upraising of the eyes, standing is preferred—inasmuch as one thereby wears in the body also the image of the devotional characteristics that become the soul."[2]

There are various ways to lift up the hands. We can stretch the hands up and wave them in exultation. We can stretch out the hands (Pss 88:9; 143:6) and form a bowl or open vessel, a gesture of openness and readiness to receive. It is perhaps a good gesture with which to pray the Lord's Prayer.

Christians have connected the lifting up of the hands with the sign of the cross. We may extend our arms sideways to the level of our shoulders, and thus with our body and our arms we form a cross. Pictures of the early Church, in the catacombs for example, show this gesture of prayer. With this gesture of prayer we connect with Christ crucified; in a sense we are shackled to his cross. The meaning of this gesture is that Christian prayer is not just an expression of personal wishes and feelings. By so imitating the cross of Christ, we are made aware of the contradictions between our wishes and the necessities of life, of what we hope for and of what is inevitable, of our efforts and disappointments, of our yearning for joy and unavoidable suffering, of our longing for life and our mortality. We are connected with a suffering world: we acknowledge the pain we suffer in this world and the pain we cause others to suffer; we admit our guilt and suffering, and we also acknowledge our guilt that goes unpunished and yet afflicts our conscience.

---

2. Origen, *On Prayer*.

The gesture of the cross makes us feel helpless: we expose ourselves as vulnerable to God. In prayer, Christians accept God's will and the cross that God imposes on them.

- **Crossing the hands over the chest**

Once in a while, you see people crossing their arms over their chest. It used to be a common gesture of people walking up to the altar to receive communion. This gesture shapes and expresses dedication. Old paintings sometimes show the Mother of the Lord kneeling before the divine child with her arms crossed. With this gesture we tenderly and reverently cradle the divine child in our hearts.

- **Beating the Breast**

We read about an almost forgotten gesture in Luke 18: "[13] But the tax collector, standing far off, would not even look up to heaven, but was beating his breast and saying, 'God, be merciful to me, a sinner!'" Beating our breast is an appropriate gesture of repentance. We read in the passion story (Luke 23:48) about the crowd that had come to see Jesus die: "[48] And when all the crowds who had gathered there for this spectacle saw what had taken place, they returned home, beating their breasts." Watching the cross of Christ, we are reminded of our sins for which he suffered and died to save us. Hence it is appropriate to use this gesture in prayers of repentance before we receive Holy Communion. Beating our fist against our chest, we point at our heart, the center of our life. It is the heart that needs to be chastised for all we have done, according to the word of our Lord (Matt 15): "[19] Out of the heart come evil intentions."

- **The sign of the cross**

With the sign of the cross, we bless another person or we bless ourselves. We have testimonies of this custom going back to the second century (Tertullian, Corona Militis III = The Chaplet, cp.3). It is a visible confession of faith, a blessing and an expression of commitment in temptation. Everyone and everything can be blessed with the sign of the cross.

The common form of this gesture is this: Thumb, index–finger and middle–finger are outstretched, ring–finger and the little finger are bent. This gesture is sometimes called the Latin blessing, as opposed to the Greek blessing. The *Greek blessing* is like this: index finger, middle finger and the little finger are outstretched, thumb and ring finger are crossed. Thus the fingers show the Greek letters X and Σ, the abbreviation for CRISTOS = Christ. Some people interpret these gesture this way: The three upright fingers are a confession to the Holy Trinity, the two crossed fingers a confession to the two natures of Jesus Christ.

Martin Luther recommends to cross oneself in the small catechism, especially for morning and evening prayer.

- **Praying with the palms of the hands pressed together**

The custom of praying with the palms of the hands pressed together has perhaps its origin in the Germanic oath of allegiance, when the vassal stood with this gesture before his feudal Lord to receive from him the external signs of the fief. In secular custom, this gesture expressed dependence on and commitment to a superior lord. Hence it seemed appropriate to use this gesture when the faithful celebrated the Lord of lords. Putting the palms of the hands together is a gesture of submission and supplication, even of begging, hence it is quite appropriate for petitions. With this gesture the whole person, with all that is in him or her—opinions, wishes, thoughts and hopes—surrenders to the sovereign God and expects his mercy and shows readiness to serve.

The Bible does not present any of those postures and gestures of the body as a law that we have to blindly obey. But the guidance of the Bible and the experience of many generations of Christians can teach us to experience with our own body the presence of him who became flesh among us.

II.

Places for Prayer

As humans, we are bodily beings, and at prayer a body still exists necessarily at a certain time and in a certain place. Even when we pray up in the air, our prayer is still influenced by the excitement of traveling in an aircraft; we pray with our sadness or relief brought from the place of our departure; we pray with our hopes for or fears of what waits for us at our destination, perhaps with anxieties of our returning. Even when we try to participate in a worship service on TV or online, we are bodily beings in a certain place. As parts of God's creation, we pray as real, bodily beings in a real place in God's creation. The reality that our body is necessarily in a certain place will unavoidably affect us when we pray, and we should be aware of this reality.

It is a widespread idea that the Bible has disparaged all sacred places. However a survey of what the Bible says about places for worship and prayer does not confirm this view. On the contrary, many biblical passages strongly suggest that there are indeed special spiritual places.

The narrative of Jacob's vision in Bethel (Gen 28) provides an elaborate theology of the sacred place: the place is neither built nor chosen by Jacob but *found,* when Jacob was on the run and while he was sleeping; the place is a given reality even before it is recognized by a human observer, as Jacob says (Gen 28): "[16] Surely the LORD is in this place—and I did not know it!" The Bible gives witness to God's presence in the holy place and also to God's freedom from that place: Jacob calls this place Beth-El, a Hebrew word meaning *house of God,* and yet this place is not heaven but just the place where the ladder stands that reaches to heaven; Jacob also calls the place *gate of heaven,* which again teaches that there is access to God in some particular place and yet does not deny God's freedom and omnipresence.

Hence the concept that God is in heaven and yet present at a certain place on earth is expressed by the images of the ladder or the gate of heaven. This concept that God is in heaven and yet in some way present on earth will be found again in Solomon's prayer dedicating the temple (cf. 1 Kgs 8): God is in heaven but his name in the temple. Similarly, Ezekiel speaks about God's glory (כבוד) dwelling in the temple. Isa 6 shows the image of God sitting on his heavenly throne with his garment reaching down in the temple (Isa 6).

The fact that the Bible speaks about special holy places does not devalue the rest of the world; on the contrary, Jacob's Beth–El is a central point of the land promised to Jacob and his descendants; the blessing of this place is valid for all generations on earth. The place is found, not made by Jacob, but the Bible tells us also that this place is consecrated through anointing, through naming, building, confession of faith and vows (tithing). This concept of the holy place recurs in the enormous field of the biblical theology of the temple (cf. below).

The Bible obviously testifies to the existence of spiritual places. The idea that all places on earth are spiritually the same and devoid of divine presence is perhaps a kind of modern superstition.

1. THE MOUNTAIN

A pilgrimage Psalm prays (Ps 121): "[1] I lift up my eyes to the hills ... [2] My help comes from the LORD, who made heaven and earth." This verse shows that the special place of God's presence on the mountain does not limit God's universal power. Only the misunderstanding of the gentiles can say so (1 Kgs 20): "[28] Arameans have said, 'The LORD is a god of the hills but he is not a god of the valleys.'"

Still, in biblical tradition the *mountain* is an important place. Exod 3:1, for example, speaks about the *mountain of God*. The law was revealed on the mountain (Exod 19), and again, when Israel was about to start the new life in the promised land, Moses repeats the law teaching on a mountain (Deut 34); actually the whole book of Deuteronomy is designed as one long speech of Moses on the mountain. The tradition of the *holy mountain* is closely connected with the names of Moses (Exod 18ff) and Elijah (1 Kgs 19), which tradition is adopted by the New Testament, i.e., in the story of Christ's transfiguration (cf. Mark 9 and parallels): Jesus met with the lawgiver and the prophet on the mount. Here the disciples' desire to build dwellings is actually not refused by Jesus. As it was in the Old Testament, so in the New Testament the mountain is a place for revelation of the law (Sermon on the

Mount: Matt 5:1,18), and on a mountain the mission of God's people to the gentiles begins: the Great Commission (Matt 28:16ff; cf. also Heb 12).

Because the mountain is of such great spiritual importance, it is plausible that the mountain is a special place for prayer. Jesus withdrew alone to a mountain for prayer (Matt 14:23). Jesus gave his last instruction about prayer to his disciples on the Mount of Olives (Luke 22:39); and in this context Saint Luke explicitly remarks that Jesus prayed on the mountain according to the custom (κατὰ τὸ ἔθος).

Many people report that climbing a mountain is good physical preparation for prayer. The physical exercise provides an elevation above our everyday work and distraction. Climbing a mountain provides distance from the various entanglements of our everyday existence and gives the opportunity for a view over our daily life, both literally and spiritually.

2. THE RIVER

Saint Luke reports (Acts 16): "[13] On the Sabbath day, we went outside the gate by the river, where we supposed there was a place of prayer." Obviously the apostles did not select or manufacture this place but made an assumption about a given reality: at the river they expected to find a place for prayer. Perhaps it is not a coincidence that the prayer book of the Bible, the Psalter, starts with the image of a tree flourishing by the river to describe the meditation on God's word. The river is an image full of biblical meaning.

In the Bible, the river marks the borders of the good land, the land to live in, and this obviously already in paradise (Gen 2:10–14; Gen 15:18). It was God's command for Israel to seize the Promised Land (Deut 11; Josh 1) by crossing the river.

The river indicates separation and transition. Crossing a river means to separate from the past. Jacob had fled from his father-in-law, leaving behind a phase of his life to return to the land of his fathers (Gen 31:21). After crossing the River Jabbok, Jacob wrestles with God all night, which leaves him both bruised and blessed. We find the prayers of Moses and Miriam (Exod 15) at a point in the narrative when Israel has fled from captivity through the Red Sea. The persecuting army has been drowned, and the Israelites are about to begin their journey back to the land of their fathers. Another prayer we find in the second hymn of Moses (Deut 32); the situation here is that Israel is about to cross the Jordan River to enter the land promised to the fathers, and Moses himself faces his end. River and prayer mark the transition.

That the river is a place especially suited for prayer becomes more evident when we consider the biblical images of salvation through the deadly flood. Noah, his family and all kinds of animals were saved from the punishment of the flood. Moses was preserved in a basket of papyrus from being drowned in the Nile, and eventually saved by an Egyptian princess (Exod 2:5). The prophet Jonah was saved from drowning in the sea (Jonah 2) and "[1] Then Jonah prayed to the LORD his God from the belly of the fish."

Water stands, of course, for nourishment. In the dry climate of the Middle East, the availability of water was a matter of survival. Therefore, water was literally a necessity of life and thus a symbol of life and nourishment. The Temple, the house of prayer, was strong because (Ps 46): "[4] There is a river whose streams make glad the city of God, the holy habitation of the Most High." Water is a symbol of God's blessing, hence the Psalmist prays (Ps 65): "[9] You visit the earth and water it, you greatly enrich it; the river of God is full of water; you provide the people with grain, for so you have prepared it" (cf. also Pss 78:16; 105:41; Isa 43:20; Ezek 31:4).

Finally, water itself praises God. The mighty waters are a part of all creation that glorifies God. The Psalmist joins this hymn of all creation (Ps 93): "[3] The floods have lifted up, O LORD, the floods have lifted up their voice; the floods lift up their roaring;" or (Ps 98): "[8] Let the floods clap their hands; let the hills sing together for joy."

3. THE WILDERNESS

The wilderness, the desert, is obviously a special place, in the Bible a place for sacrifice (Exod 3:18), a place of God's epiphany (Exod 16:10), a place of temptation and preservation (Exod 16:32, Matt 4); yet the desert is a place of only temporary existence (Deut 11:1–15).

The Old Testament tells us that Israel's way from captivity through the water of the Red Sea first leads into the desert before the promised land of the fathers can be reached. The desert is the place where the people of God fall into temptation and are preserved, rebel and are guided, doubt and are saved (Ps 78). In the New Testament, the story of Israel's time in the desert again and again provides the imagery for God's mysterious revelation (Acts 7:30+38), for God's patience with his people's rebellion (Acts 13:18; Heb 3:8) and his punishments (1 Cor 10:5; Heb 3:17), and for the mystery of God's chosen people (Heb 11:38). The New Testament tells us how the Son of God, when being baptized in the Jordan River, heard the word of his Heavenly Father and received the Holy Spirit (Mark 1): "[12] And the Spirit immediately drove him out into the wilderness." Hence Christians receive the spirit of freedom in the water of baptism and are guided through the wilderness of their life's journey.

But the literal meaning of the word *wilderness* need not be abolished. We can understand the symbolic meaning of *desert* better when we expose ourselves to the experience of the wilderness literally. Perhaps with reference to the Old Testament prophets, who lived withdrawn from the world (1 Kgs 17f.), John the baptizer went into the wilderness to proclaim his message of repentance. In the wilderness he lived a lifestyle of simplicity (Matt 3:1ff.). Jesus repeatedly withdrew to desert places to pray (Mark 1:35; Luke 5:16 and 9:10; cf. also Matt 14:13; 15:33; Mark 6:31-35; 8:4; John 11:54). Throughout the history of the church, people followed Jesus' example and sought the wilderness to live a devotional life. In the early church, men like Pachomius (died AD 348) or Antonius of Alexandria (died AD 356) went literally into the Syrian or Egyptian desert; through the centuries eremites and monks withdrew to lonely places. Retreat homes and Bible camps are still built in remote areas, withdrawn from the noise of consumerism and distraction. Finding a place for prayer in the wilderness, a place without external stimulus, a place for being alone with God to experience more clearly dependency on God (Deut 32:10) can provide an extraordinary experience that will deeply affect our everyday life.

4. PRAYER TOWARDS THE RISING SUN

An African American spiritual has the line: "When I fall on my knees, With my face to the rising sun, O Lord have mercy on me."[1] The custom of praying with one's face to the east can be traced back to an old tradition.[2] Most churches have been built with the altar in the east, so that the congregation would face east when singing thanks and laud to Christ who comes in the Eucharist.

There are good biblical reasons for this custom. The Old Testament describes paradise as a garden in the east (Gen 2:8; 3:23); therefore the prayer facing east symbolizes the yearning for the lost home. God is light (1 John 1:5), and a prophetic promise calls the Messiah *Sun of righteousness* (Malachi 4:2), of course rising in the east. In the beginning of the Gospel of Luke (1:78), the prophet Zachariah describes the advent of the Christ with the metaphor *the dayspring from on high,* the meaning of *dayspring* of course being the *east.* The gospel of the resurrection begins (Matt 28):

---

1. *"Let Us Break Bread Together."*
2. John of Damascus (*675-†749), *An Exposition of the Orthodox Faith,* book 4, chap. 12.

"¹ In the end of the Sabbath, as it began to dawn . . . ." Therefore, awaiting the rising sun symbolizes hope for the resurrection. Jesus announced his second coming with the metaphor of lightning (Matt 24 KJV): "²⁷ For as the lightning cometh out of the east, and shineth even unto the west; so shall also the coming of the Son of man be."

Thus the imagery of light in the east is connected with the memory of paradise, with the mysteries of Christmas and Easter and with the hope for the second coming.

5. THE CLOSET

When we look for an appropriate place for prayer, Jesus' direct order in Matt 6 is of course most important. Here Jesus explicitly prohibits the abuse of prayer to show off with one's piety, and he advises going into a closet (see above 1.II). Jesus' disciples prayed together to *our* Father, so that the required privacy for prayer does not prohibit common prayer. Still, performing prayer in public to exhibit one's own piety or "to send a message" is clearly against Jesus' teaching. Prayer belongs behind closed doors. Jesus obviously advised so for individual prayer (Matt 6:6) and the meetings of the early church also took place behind closed doors, as Saint John writes about the first Sunday services (John 20): "¹⁹ Then the same day at evening, being the first day of the week, when the doors were shut where the disciples were assembled for fear of the Jews, came Jesus and stood in the midst" (cf. John 20:26). Likewise Saint Luke (Acts 12:12) reports—a little humorously—that, when Peter returned from prison, the door of the house where the congregation was praying for his release was locked. The young church had even a special office, the *ostiarius*, who was in charge of closing the doors of the church for worship.[3]

Jesus advises to pray in the *closet* (Matt 6 KJV): "⁶ . . . when thou prayest, enter into thy closet, and when thou hast shut thy door, pray to thy Father which is in secret." The meaning of the original Greek word for *closet* (τὸ ταμεῖον) is the inner room of a house, a room hidden from public view. In Gen 43:30 of the Greek version of Old Testament (LXX), for example, a closet in Joseph's house in Egypt is mentioned. Joseph, as yet unrecognized by his brothers, talked with his brother Benjamin, who unwittingly told him all about his own family, from which Joseph had been separated for years. Joseph planned to maintain the secrecy of his identity and plan for a while. Therefore he went into the closet to weep in hiding.

---

3. Eusebius, *Ecclesiastical History*, 1.6.43.

In 2 Kgs 9:2 (LXX) the word *closet* describes the chamber where God's prophet Elisha secretly anointed Jehu as the king-to-be, while the evil king Ahab was still in power. Likewise, in 2 Kgs 11:2, the same Greek word is used to describe a chamber where the legitimate heir of David's throne, Joash, was hidden from the henchmen of the usurper. In these two stories, the closet is actually the secret place where someone speaks to the ruler to be, chosen by God, i.e. to the legitimate heir and anointed king (*anointed* in Hebrew = *Messiah*, in Greek = *Christ*); accordingly we wait for the Messiah to seize power visibly while the outside world still obeys other powers.

The word *closet* can gain a mystic meaning used to describe the inward man (Prov 20, LXX): "²⁷ The human spirit is the lamp of the LORD, searching every inmost part" (= closet = τὸ ταμεῖον).

In prayer, we return to the familiarity and warmth of the Father's love, and this intimacy cannot bear to have spectators, and yet he or she who prays perhaps experiences the unhealthy desire to show off with this practice of piety. But ulterior motives will jeopardize the relationship of the heavenly Father with his beloved children. Therefore Jesus' advice to go into the closet is first of all meant to protect prayer from being perverted into a show for others. But we must not deceive ourselves; we could also turn our own mind into an audience to which we desire to exhibit our piety. Observing ourselves and our own state of mind, watching our own piety—all this distracts from God and turns prayer into a work that is done for our own glory rather than for God's praise. Therefore the closet protects our prayer from showing off for an audience, and it teaches also that we should give up all pride and self-centeredness and devote our prayer exclusively to God.

6. THE HOUSE OF GOD

The Old Testament knows the temple in Jerusalem as a place of God's special presence similar to the *House of God*, Beth-El (cf. above). King Solomon dedicated the temple and encouraged the people to pray toward this place in all kinds of individual and public issues (1 Kgs 8). In the time of the New Testament the (second) temple is obviously still a place for individual prayer, as the story of the Pharisee and the tax collector shows (Luke 18).

The prayer book of the Bible explicitly refers to the temple (Ps 135): "¹ Praise the LORD! Praise the name of the LORD; give praise, O servants of the LORD, ² you that stand in the house of the LORD, in the courts of the house of our God." A great number of pilgrimage Psalms (Pss 120–134) give witness to the pilgrimages of the faithful to the temple. Ps 84 sings: "How lovely is your dwelling place, O LORD of hosts! My soul longs, indeed it faints for the courts of the Lord; my heart and my flesh sing for joy to the living God. Even the sparrow finds a home, and the swallow a nest for herself, where she may lay her young, at your altars, O Lord of hosts, my King and my God." The Holy Family did such a pilgrimage to present Jesus in the temple (Luke 2:22ff.)

In the temple of the old covenant, the public service of God's people had been offered. But the prophet promised that the temple would be the house of prayer not only for Israel but for all nations (Isa 56): "⁶ Also the sons of the foreigner who join themselves to the LORD, to serve Him . . . ⁷ Even them I will bring to my holy mountain, And make them joyful in my house of prayer. Their burnt offerings and their sacrifices will be accepted on my altar; For My house shall be called a house of prayer for all nations." Jesus refers to these prophetic promises about the house of prayer (Mark 11) "¹⁷ He [Jesus] was teaching and saying, Is it not written, 'My house shall be called a house of prayer for all the nations'?" (cf. Matt 21:13; Luke 19:46; cf. Isa 56:7). The Evangelists' view is obviously that through Jesus Christ the prophetic promise is fulfilled. Therefore the term house of prayer is closely connected with the New Covenant, the gospel for all nations. Saint Luke emphasizes that the early Christians gathered in the temple for prayer, for example (Luke 24): "⁵³ they were continually in the temple blessing God," and in many other places in Acts. Saint Stephen's statement in Acts 7, "⁸ the Most High does not dwell in houses made with human hands" is actually consistent with Solomon's theology: God is in heaven and still his name is in the house (1 Kgs 8:29). Therefore, Saint Stephen's statement in Acts does not contradict the appreciation of the temple among the first Christians in other places of the same book.

Teachings about the appropriate place for prayer in the New Testament are perhaps different from the theology of the Old Testament, especially in regard to the temple.[4] How the practice of piety in the Old Testament is to be employed by Christians depends on their way of understanding the Old Testament. Some concepts emphasize the continuity and concurrence of the two parts of the Bible, which is after all word of the same God. Other concepts emphasize the newness of the New Testament. There are certainly variations in how Christians interpret symbols of the Old Testament. But whatever theory of symbols we presuppose, it is safe to say that the spiritual

---

4. In John 4 we read: "²³ *the true worshipers will worship the Father in spirit and truth, for the Father seeks such as these to worship him.* ²⁴ *God is spirit, and those who worship him must worship in spirit and truth.*" This verse has its place in the conflict between the two worship places: in Jerusalem and the Samaritan worship place. But there is no reason to assume that this verse would abolish special worship places altogether. The idea that the *Spirit* would be opposed to space and body is a pagan philosophical idea.

meaning of an Old Testament symbol does not necessarily abolish its literal use. Therefore the *house of prayer* may still be a *house*.

The New Testament already attaches to the symbol *temple* a variety of meanings. In the New Testament, the temple is the house of Jesus' Father (John 2:16), and yet Jesus' body now is called the temple (John 2:19-22). The New Testament employs the symbol *temple* to describe the new people of God (Eph 2:19f.; 1 Pet 2:5; 2 Cor 6:16), or the body of individuals (1 Cor 3:17-19). But again, these uses of the symbol *temple* do not necessarily abolish the literal meaning of the *temple* as a building where God's name and glory are present among his people. The worship services of the first Christians, after all, took place in a building (John 20; Acts 2).

Church buildings are indeed perceived as God's house by many people. My research on the guest books of churches that keep their doors open for visitors during the week shows that many visitors connect their prayers with the special place. The building is called *House of God;* people write that they feel near to God and can meet God in a church building. People pray that the house may be filled with God's word and Spirit. A beautiful building can be called a gift from God, and some people express that seeing the beauty of a church leads them to reflection and prayer. They profess that the building is able "to draw your eyes upward." Therefore the building is being visited to have a "quiet time." People often express their fellowship with other visitors. They also realize that the house is built through the sacrifices of God's people for God. The entries in those guest books show that people enter a church to pray, to give thanks, to confess their faith and to make intercession for loved ones. Especially in personal crisis or after its resolution, people visit a church to pray or to give thanks. Life's turning points are associated with the church building. People have come to pray after they have lived for decades abroad, or were cut off from their home by the Iron Curtain. Some entries show that young couples visit a church together. Often, people enter a church on special personal days like birthdays, anniversaries, or pay a last visit before they start off for a longer journey. Some people enter a church as a refuge from the worries of their life. Many visitors apply the story of Jesus' cleansing of the temple without hesitation to the church building, especially when it comes to entrance fees to historic buildings. Repeatedly I read entries in the guest books that identify the building with the community of the faithful which has built the sanctuary, and which both expresses and constitutes itself through this building. Hence it is safe to say: in popular piety the idea of *temple* is alive and well.

A church building seems to be indeed helpful for our prayer; keeping the church open for private prayer and reflection could be a service of the congregation to the community.

- ***Appendix: Frankincense***

Again and again, the Bible connects prayer and the offering of incense. The wording of Ps 141 suggests that private evening prayers are only a surrogate for the offering of incense in the temple (Ps 141): "²Let my prayer be set forth before thee as incense, and the lifting up of my hands as an evening sacrifice." In the time of the Old Testament, the meaning was probably: *May my prayer, that I offer here somewhere in the country or in exile, be as acceptable as the incense which is supposed to be offered at the same time in the temple in Jerusalem*. In the traditional *prayers of the hours* this Psalm is employed for evening prayer. (See below 3.III).

The background for this connection of prayer and the offering of incense is that, following God's commandment, frankincense was used for worship services in the tabernacle built according to God's law at Mount Sinai, the place of God's revelation (Exod 30): "³⁴ The LORD said to Moses: Take sweet spices, stacte, and onycha, and galbanum, sweet spices with pure frankincense . . ." Ever since, frankincense had been used in the Temple of Israel. Zechariah, father of John the Baptist, served as a priest in the temple (Luke 1): "⁹ He was chosen by lot, according to the custom of the priesthood, to enter the sanctuary of the Lord and offer incense."

The prophetic promises for the restoration of true worship can be understood from the context of Israel's sacrifices in the temple. These promises aim at the worship of all nations. The prophet Malachi chides Israel for having offered defiled food on God's altar (Mal 1): They had kindled fire on the altar in vain. The prophet proclaims God's word: "¹⁰ I will not accept an offering from your hands." After his stern reprimands against Israel, the prophet gives God's promise for the gentiles (Mal 1): "¹¹ For from the rising of the sun to its setting my name is great among the nations, and in every place incense is offered to my name, and a pure offering; for my name is great among the nations, says the LORD of hosts." Isaiah prophesied the good news for all nations: They will come as pilgrims to the Holy City and the sanctuary and (Isa 60) "⁶ They shall bring gold and frankincense, and shall proclaim the praise of the LORD."

In the New Testament, we read about the wise men who came as pilgrims from the east. They visited the divine child in Bethlehem—the meaning of this name is *house of Bread*—and (Matt 2): "¹¹ on entering the house, they saw the child with Mary his mother; and they knelt down and paid him homage. Then, opening their treasure chests, they offered him gifts of gold, frankincense, and myrrh." Adoration and incense are brought to Christ by the gentiles.

The book of Revelation tells us of the heavenly worship where the angels and the elders stand before God's throne and bring incense with the prayers of the saints to God and to the Lamb (Rev 8): "² And I saw the seven angels who stand before God, and seven trumpets were given to them. ³ Another angel with a golden censer came and stood at the altar; he was given a great quantity of incense to offer with the prayers of all the saints on the golden altar that is before the throne. ⁴ And the smoke of the incense, with the prayers of the saints, rose before God from the hand of the angel." We find the same picture in Rev 5:8.

Prayer and frankincense are therefore used, first, in the eternal worship in heaven; second, in the worship service of the Old Covenant; and third, after the prophets had promised that *all* the nations would come to offer incense, we read in the Christmas story of the New Testament that wise men from the East kneel before Christ and offer incense.

III.

Times of Prayer

When we want to meet with others, we obviously have to arrange a time and a place for our gathering. This is true for a nuclear family, a political convention, prayer group, concert, local church, or larger assembly. Gatherings may be organized as one-time events or on a regular basis, but they require that we agree on a place and a time. Small groups can try to find out which time is convenient for each individual. If, however, in a larger group all members expect the assembly to adjust to their individual preferences, no meeting will take place. So in larger groups, individuals must be ready to adapt to a given timetable. Regular schedules, like a calendar for major holidays, make it possible for larger communities to celebrate together. All countries, no matter what political systems they have, observe some public holidays. Those holidays are usually based either on regular events of the natural year, for example harvest celebrations, or they commemorate historic events like the foundation of a state. Festivals like Passover and Thanksgiving are actually based on both the natural year (harvest) and the commemoration of an important historic day.

Time flows like a stream, and Christians know about the end. But time has also its natural rhythms of hours, days, months and years, due to the rotation of the earth, the lunar orbit and the earth's revolution around the sun. The week of seven days is perhaps originally a quarter of the month, with the waxing, full, waning and new moon.

When during children's sermons in church I ask: "When do you pray?" I usually hear that it is in the morning and in the evening, at bedtime or before meals. The kids are certainly guided by their parents; still, a regular schedule seems to come naturally to them. Many Christians observe some daily routine for their prayers; most Christians observe some festivals of the ecclesiastical year, and all Christians gather regularly every seven days.

For centuries, daily prayer services were supposed to be held at certain fixed hours. In the Western church, those times of prayer were called just "hours," from the Latin word *hora* = hour. The whole set of these prayers of the hours is called the *office*, from the Latin word *officium*, which can be translated as *duty*. The *hours* can be traced back to the custom of regular prayer in the Jewish synagogues in the time of New Testament. These prayers, again, were probably organized according to the schedule of the sacrifices offered daily in the temple of Jerusalem. Thus the worldwide Jewish community remained connected with the temple worship on Mount Zion.

When we gather at the traditional hours for prayer, we are connected with the rhythm of creation, with one another in the present assembly, with the prayers of the worldwide church, and with the ancestors who prayed at these hours.

1. THE HOURS OF THE GOSPEL

The times of prayer—already customary in the Jewish community—received their specifically Christian meaning by the hours mentioned in the Gospel, more exactly by the hours mentioned in the passion story: the night of Jesus' Last Supper, his suffering and death on the cross and his resurrection. In biblical times, the day did not begin at midnight but at sunrise, roughly at 6 a.m., so that the third hour was 9 a.m., the sixth hour noon, and the ninth hour 3 p.m. The biblical places are:

Mark 14: "[17] When it was *evening*, he came with the twelve. [18] And when they had taken their places and were eating, Jesus said, 'Truly I tell you, one of you will betray me, one who is eating with me.'"

Mark 15:25: "And it was the *third hour*, and they crucified him." [9 a.m.].

Mark 15:33–34: "And when the *sixth hour* was come [noon], there was darkness over the whole land until the ninth hour. And at the *ninth hour* Jesus cried [3 p.m.] with a loud voice, saying, Eloi, Eloi, lama sabachthani? Which is, being interpreted, My God, my God, why hast thou forsaken me?"

Mark 16: "[1] When the sabbath was over, Mary Magdalene, and Mary the mother of James, and Salome bought spices, so that they might go and anoint him. [2] And *very early on the first day of the week, when the sun had risen*, they went to the tomb."

The Gospel gives us the hours of Jesus' last days; hence it is obvious that the hours of prayer can be understood from the core of the mystery of our salvation, Christ's passion, death and resurrection.

2. THE EARLY CHURCH

The Acts of the Apostles testify that the *hours* were observed by the first Christians. The hours of prayer were kept by individuals: Saint Luke writes (Acts 10): "⁹ On the morrow, as they went on their journey, and drew nigh unto the city, Peter went up upon the housetop to pray about the sixth hour" (noon). At another place, Luke writes (Acts 3): "¹ Now Peter and John went up together into the temple at the hour of prayer, being the ninth hour" (3 p.m.) The story about the praying community in Acts 4 shows that the church kept praying the Psalms.

In the story of Pentecost (Acts 2), when the Holy Spirit has been poured out on the assembly, Saint Peter in his sermon connects the hour (verse 15: "third hour of the day" = 9 a.m.) with a theory about the prayer of the Psalms: In Ps 16, Christ himself had spoken through the prophet King David about his resurrection; therefore the Psalms are Jesus Christ's own words. Hence, whenever we pray the Psalms Jesus leads us in prayer (see above Part 2.IV.1). Thus the usage of the Psalter as the prayer book of the Christian Church is based on faith in Jesus Christ.

Saint Luke describes how the early church prays the prayers of the hours. Once persecutions ceased at the beginning of the fourth century, the church was legalized and great numbers of people joined the church. Now most Christians celebrated the worship service of their parish mostly on Sundays. Hence monasteries became the refuge for preserving the old customs.

3. THE RULE OF SAINT BENEDICT OF NURSIA

Most influential for the Western churches was the monastic rule of Saint Benedict of Nursia (AD 480–543). He founded the monastery on Monte Cassino, organized monastic life, and thus confirmed the tradition of daily prayers (Rule of Benedict, chs. 8–20). The Rule of Saint Benedict provided a certain order to read and pray the Bible:

For the Year:	Monks were listening to scriptural readings in the morning, at the night Office and at Compline (Rule of Benedict chapter 8); also at meals in the refectory (Rule of Benedict chapter 38); they were studying and memorizing scripture; they would practise the *lectio divina,* the meditative reading, for which several hours were set aside daily and all day Sunday and feast days.	
For the Week:	The whole Psalter was to be prayed in the course of each week. (Rule of Benedict ch. 18).	
For the Day:	Ps 119: "[164] Seven times a day do I praise thee because of thy righteous judgments."	

From the cited verse of Ps 119, we have seven times of prayers. A midnight prayer was added, in keeping with Ps 119: "[62] At midnight I will rise to give thanks unto thee because of thy righteous judgments." Hence certain hours for the daily prayers were established and connected with the gospel narrative.

The hours are (Latin – English):

matutina hora	matins, also vigil or nocturne	midnight
laudes	lauds, dawn–prayer	3 a.m.
prima hora	first hour	6 a.m.
tertia hora	third hour	9 a.m.
sexta hora	sixth hour	noon
nona hora	ninth hour	3 p.m.
vespera hora	vespers	evening hour, 6 p.m.
completa hora	compline = night prayer	the last prayer, 9 p.m.

From this schedule it is obvious that those who are committed to religious life acquire a profound knowledge of the Bible. The term *liturgy of the hours* derives from the Latin word *hora* (= hour) meaning of *hours of prayer.* The day began with the morning hour, often called *lauds* (in Latin = *laudes*) at 3 a.m. Because monks were supposed to work and therefore should get enough sleep, the nocturnal prayer services were often combined.

In the Psalter itself, we find advice for the usage of some Psalms, which in turn gives us a glimpse into the prayer life of biblical times. We find a word about morning prayer in Ps 5: "[3] O LORD, in the morning you hear my voice; in the morning I plead my case to you, and watch." We read about evening prayer in Ps 141: "[2] Let my prayer be set forth before thee as incense; and the lifting up of my hands as the evening sacrifice." For the compline, the last prayer of the day, we read in Ps 4, "[8] I will both lie down and sleep in peace; for you alone, O LORD, make me lie down in safety." Saint Benedict assigned certain Psalms to the hours (Rule ch.18), but he also demanded flexibility: "we strongly recommend, however, that if this distribution of the Psalms is displeasing to anyone, he/she should arrange them otherwise, in whatever way she/he considers better."[1]

Over the centuries, in the life of the various denominations—Anglicans, Roman Catholics, Lutheran, Reformed, and others—customs varied, but a basic structure remains recognizable. The traditional order of the *hours* looks roughly like this:

- Ingressus (Beginning): e.g., "Lord, open my lips and my mouth will . . . proclaim your praise."
- Several Psalms or canticles.
- Lesson from the Bible, with a response sung by the assembly.
- Hymn.
- A sung verse.
- A canticle from the New Testament:

    "*Benedictus*" for the morning (cf. Luke 1:68ff.),

    "*Magnificat*" for the evening (cf. Luke 1:46ff.),

    "*Nunc Dimittis*" for the last hour in the night (cf. Luke 2:29ff.)

- Litany (Prayers).
- Lord's Prayer.
- Benediction.

The names of the canticles are simply the first words of the Latin version of the biblical text. The order of the Psalms and of the lessons followed that of the church year and also the idea of a continuous reading of the Bible.

In the *Liturgy of the Hours,* the Psalms were closed with "*Glory be to the Father and to the Son and to the Holy Spirit*" and thus turned into Christian prayers. A biblical reference for this Trinitarian conclusion of prayer is Gal 4: "[6] And because ye are sons, God hath sent forth the *Spirit* of his *Son* into your hearts, crying, Abba, *Father*." It is the spirit of Christ dwelling in our hearts who calls upon the Father (cf. also 1 John 5).

This is, of course, only a very rough introduction. Whoever is interested in the prayer of the hours can easily find more information about his or her tradition.

---

1. Benedict, *Rule for Monasteries.*

4. SINCE THE REFORMATION

The Reformation abolished the monasteries, but Lutheran schools and ministers mostly continued the traditional life of prayer. No new order of those prayer services had been laid down by the reformers. Usually the old order of the monasteries, sometimes in a somewhat simplified form, just continued in the reformed churches and schools for centuries to come. In order to improve the life of prayer, Luther recommended more deliberate prayer and more explanation in teaching and sermons; therefore he reduced the number of lessons and prayers.[2] The Lutheran reformers accepted the morning, noon and evening prayer as useful for their churches, according to the Psalm-verses mentioned above (5:3; 141:2; and 4:5). Luther did not expect the whole congregation to participate in those prayers, but assumed that a part of the congregation, especially pastors and students, who lived together in convents and the dorms of their schools, prayed on behalf of the congregation.[3] Luther reduced the number of Psalms to three, plus canticle, lessons and responses. The lessons were continuous readings of the Bible. Each of the services was supposed to take about an hour. It is noteworthy that this reduced *office* still required about three hours a day!

The English Reformation went different ways. The *Book of Common Prayer* of the Anglican Church still has an order for the reading of the whole Psalter in the course of each month and an "order how the rest of the Bible is appointed to be read," and orders for morning and evening prayer. With the metrical versification of the Psalms (Geneva Psalter), the Calvinist churches made it possible for the whole congregation to participate in the singing of the Psalms. Organized prayer life and the use of the biblical prayers were *not* questioned by the Reformation!

Only later, in the time of the pietistic movement, did the practice of praying written prayers come under criticism, with the allegation that those prayers would turn into a mechanical babbling of the words without much consideration. Matt 6 was used to support this criticism (but see above 1.II). Whoever has tried to live by a plan of prayers and readings will indeed experience this temptation. It is, however, still true that we owe God thanks and praise always. Moreover, it is certainly healthy for the soul to keep a certain order that protects our prayer from our whims and wants and from

---

2. Luther, "Order of Worship," 64 = WA 12,35–37.

3. This idea of vicarious prayer, i.e., prayer on behalf of others, can be taken from 1 Tim 5: "⁵ *The real widow, left alone, has set her hope on God and continues in supplications and prayers night and day.*" This Bible verse can be interpreted to be saying that the widows prayed on behalf of the church. Therefore a vicarious prayer can be offered by a group within the church on behalf of the whole church.

whatever "truths" happen to be trendy. Following the pattern of morning and evening prayer, we remain in communion with the church of all times and places.

After the pietist movement had its day, traditional concepts of prayer were not yet defunct. In the 1800s, the German pastor Wilhelm Löhe, who had some influence in America, especially in Missouri, reestablished a traditional form of prayer service that still has some influence on the hymnals of the Lutheran Church.

5. PROACTIVE PRAYER

In the time of pietism all *merely external* words became suspicious. Prayers allegedly said only out of obligation at a certain time, repeated words, or prayers said according to a given pattern were suspected of being disingenuous and therefore meaningless. Consequently, words spontaneously flowing from the heart of any individual became more important than those flowing from the Bible. But that still leaves the question of what, when and where to pray.

It is a well-known joke: The captain of a ship in distress moans, "Now we can do nothing but pray." Among the passengers is a pastor who replies, horror-stricken: Is it that bad!?" The underlying problem is whether we view prayer just as a reaction to external or internal distress, or as proactive action and as the shape of our Christian life. The concept of prayer as simply a reaction to a given situation could be based on a popular understanding of Ps 50: "[51] Call upon me in the day of trouble; I will deliver you, and you will honor me." We should, however, not forget that this divine promise is part of a Psalm and of the prayer book of the Bible.

If we view prayer mainly as a reaction to a situation, we pray when our will is weak, when our reason cannot understand, when our strength fails. If our prayer is only reaction to the challenges of this life, we pray to elude work, to avoid risk, to sustain illusions, to gloss over the fact that we are avoiding responsibility. It is hardly a prayer of righteousness (cf. Matt 6) when we turn to God only because we lack courage, will, or power. It is hardly the prayer of the king's men when terrified children mumble under the blankets in the night.[4]

The criticism of prayer as mere reaction is even more pointed when it comes to saying prayers of thanks and praise. Prayers motivated by feelings of thankfulness are fine. But it is hardly appropriate to God's never failing

---

4. Cf. Sölle, *Atheistisch an Gott glauben*. I agree with Sölle's criticism, outlined above, despite her very different intentions.

goodness if we give thanks only when, once in a while, we realize that a specific blessing cannot be taken for granted, when once in a while our sense of entitlement fails, and when once in a while God's beautiful works and majesty happen to catch our eye. We owe God thanks always, and always more than the limited thankfulness of our heart and our unrealistic ideas of merit and personal accomplishment might suggest.

The understanding of prayer as mere reaction is even more inappropriate to prayers of repentance. Should we say a prayer of repentance only when our otherwise reliable recklessness and dependable dullness fail, and when we are stunned by the realization that we committed a specific sin? We need to confess our sin more, much more than the limited sensitivity of our conscience is aware of. We need to pray for God's mercy always, and always more than our unrealistic pride wants to admit. This is why we have the penitential Psalms and the confessions of sin in church.

Prayers of intercession cannot be left to our ever-changing awareness and sensitivity. People in need, the homeless, those hit by disaster or war, those who have fallen ill, people in need both known and unknown, cannot wait for our prayers until we feel like it, but they need to be prayed for faithfully. And we cannot limit our intercessions to those with whom we have a personal relationship. A veteran of the confessing church—the part of the church in Germany that resisted the Nazi dictatorship—told me how they prayed in church for their brothers and sisters in prison every Sunday. Most of the parishioners had, of course, never heard their names before. However, he said, God knew the names, and the Gestapo officer lurking in the last pew knew them, too. A schedule of intercessions makes sure that those in need will not be forgotten. It is perhaps a good idea for each of us to keep a list of names and issues to pray about on a regular basis.

Finally, God's greatness is infinitely more to be praised than our heart can possibly feel or imagine. Therefore we need order and form for our prayers; we need a shepherd to remind us of real prayer. We need a shepherd to lead us, because our own heart cannot possibly guide us.

6. FAITHFUL PRAYER TO THE FAITHFUL GOD

On very few occasions we might experience a miracle, an extraordinary deed of God's power. But most of our life takes place in a world that is governed by God's ordinary providence. If our prayers, our petitions, intercessions, thanksgiving or repentance refer only to God's extraordinary deeds, we will lose sight of God's everyday doing. This attitude of expecting particular events for particular individuals will lead to disappointed prayers and thus a life of disappointment. Jesus' faith in God (Matt 5), who "[45] makes his sun rise on the evil and on the good, and sends rain on the righteous and on the unrighteous," calls us to perpetual prayer to the eternal God who is faithfully at work. Scheduled prayer challenges us to realize that God is at work always, in all things and for all.

Jesus calls himself (John 14:17) the "way, truth, and life," a phrase that suggests continuity. The Gospel of John calls Jesus the "Logos," meaning the internal logic of creation, so *Jesus* does not stand for *contingence*.

The eternal God deserves perpetual and well-organized responses to his perpetual care, free from our anxieties and wants in a given situation and free of what happens to be true at the moment.

Prayer is our response to the call of God, not the response to our inner moods or external situation. We are not slaves to fate or coincidence; prayer is the response to a God who is eternal and perpetually active, and to God's plans and promises. Such prayers, responses to the eternal God, can free those trapped in the moment. When we respond to God, all gains and losses, expectations and fears, promises and menaces, joy and sadness, hopes and fears fall into place. We gain perspective. Answering to God's word, I will turn away from myself, and so find myself in the right relation to God and to the world.

Saint Paul encourages (1 Thess 5): "[17] Pray without ceasing." It is worth discussing if and how this sentence refers to specific times and places for regular retreats for prayer. But whatever the answer to this question is, *without ceasing* cannot mean that prayer may be done merely on a whim or in reaction to a particular danger or expectation, to extraordinary distress or relief. The Bible itself, as we have seen, guides a well-ordered prayer life (Ps 119): "[164] Seven times a day I praise you for your righteous ordinances." This life doesn't just react to coincidental external or internal events. The Bible's guidance suggests that God, who has designed the seasons of this creation, shall be invoked always, in the rhythm of days, weeks and years.

The prayers of the Bible remind us of the mighty deeds of God. The fact that the faithful God has given us words to invoke him implies that we should not arbitrarily use scraps from the book but use the prayers of the Bible—and perhaps of the tradition of the church—faithfully and on a regular basis. Christian prayers may not always flow *from* the heart but will put God's word *into* our heart, as Moses says (Deut 11): "[18] Therefore shall ye lay up these my words in your heart and in your soul, and bind them for a sign upon your hand, that they may be as frontlets between your eyes." Regular use of the prayers of the Bible and of Church tradition remind us of needs of which we may not be aware. Daily use of the prayers of the Bible guides and encourages our petitions; the Bible actually urges us to say what we would not dare to say on our own. For example, Jesus in Gethsemane guides our prayer from petition to acceptance. Thus he encourages us where we, out of resignation or false piety, would give up on prayer, and guides us when we rebel against God's decree.

Daily use of the prayers of the Bible and of Church tradition encourages us to give thanks for all the goods we have and reminds us that nothing can be taken as a matter of course. The prayers of the Bible and liturgy based on the Bible remind us of God's majesty and his glory sung by the angels when our forgetful, negligent, and stubborn heart does not spontaneously wish to thank and praise. The Bible guides where our heart fails.

With the prayers of the Bible, we have words both given and faithfully heard by the eternal God, and we have these words in common with all Christians past, present, and future. Therefore the prayers of the Bible create and sustain a lasting community. Jesus has called us to abide in love (John 8), and Luke (Acts 2:42) describes the ideal community who would abide "in the teaching of the apostles, in fellowship, in the breaking of the bread, and in prayer." By abiding in the community of prayer, we abide in love for our brothers and sisters. If we pray the biblical words of lamentation and petitions *in due season* (Pss 104:27; 145:15) and continue to pray them when we are not in distress ourselves, we join the lamentation of our fellow Christians, of all people, and we join the mourning of all creation (Rom 8:22). The church prays the penitential Psalms and the lamentations together with all who suffer and mourn. Thus standing up for others before God, the Church reminds herself of God's continuous care and her own continuous responsibility beyond the news of the day.

When we pray the words of the Bible, which Jesus Christ prayed, we remind ourselves that the one who suffered for us stays with us; and in a sense we remind God of His promise to answer those lamentations (Ps 89): "[49] Lord, where is your steadfast love of old, which by your faithfulness you swore to David?" When we pray the words of the Bible, when we pray following Jesus' life and suffering, his death and resurrection, we are heirs of the Lord whose kingdom has no end.

IV.

Forms of Prayer

WHEN WE PRAY, WE use words. We use texts, which we produce spontaneously or have prepared beforehand, or we use texts from the Bible, from tradition or other sources. Since we use for our prayers texts, prayer is to some extent similar to enjoying and perhaps producing art and literature, which is more fruitful if we know the forms, rhetorical techniques and poetic devices we have inherited, and if we thus participate in a culture that nourishes our life. The old saying about music and arts is true for prayer as well: first learn the rules; then you may break them.

The prayers of the Bible and the prayers of the church tradition have their forms and patterns. Whenever we say a prayer, we participate, whether we are aware of it or not, in the language, forms, and metaphors we have inherited. Rhythms, sounds, and forms resonate with our souls. It is certainly an interesting question whether they resonate because they are part of our culture or because they are already woven into the fabric of creation.

Only very few of us will be inventive enough to establish a completely new literary form. On the other hand, a good look at the traditional forms will stimulate our own creativity. In the New Testament we find the Magnificat (Luke 1:46ff.) and the Benedictus (Luke 1:68ff.), two prayers that obviously employ forms of the Old Testament Psalms and thus show the creative force of the preceding biblical tradition. Spontaneous, shapeless prayers without relation to the forms and language of Bible and tradition must not be excluded from our prayer life. Knowing, however, and using the forms and metaphors supplied by our forefathers and mothers in faith, especially by the Bible, contributes to the wealth and beauty of our own prayer culture. Interconnectedness with other texts can be established by employing well-known forms. Deviation from, and rebellion against, traditional forms is interesting only in a community where traditions are established and well known.

1. PSALMS

In the history of the Church, the culture of prayer began with the custom of praying, on a regular basis, the biblical Psalms, which have their special forms; and based on biblical tradition the prayers of the Church have developed their own forms.

a. *The Poetic Form of the Psalms*

The poetic structure of the Psalms itself is an integral component of their testimony. In old manuscripts (cf. the community of Qumran, i.e., about the time of Jesus) the Psalms are laid out in verses. In some we find refrains (42, 43, 46, 56, 80), which suggests that these Psalms are composed in stanzas. Ps 104 is quite obviously composed in seven stanzas (cf. also the Pss 78, 105, and 106). We find rhymes and alliterations in the original Hebrew text of the Psalms. The most obvious characteristic of the Psalms is that they are composed in parallel half-verses, so-called parallelism: every idea, image or petition is repeated, in different words. This composition of the texts is contrary to our sense of efficiency, our tendency to rush through the words and our desire to finish our prayers hastily. The parallelisms encourage us to meditate, to immerse ourselves in these prayers, and to focus. A random example of this parallelism is from Ps 77:

"[5] I consider the days of old,* and remember the years of long ago.

[6] I commune with my heart in the night; * I meditate and search my spirit."

The form of the parallelism can vary: the second half-verse may lead to a contrasting idea (antithetic parallelism). In the Magnificat, for example, two verses juxtapose *help* and *punishment* with their half-verses (Luke 1):

> "[52] He has brought down the powerful from their thrones, * and lifted up the lowly;
> [53] he has filled the hungry with good things*, and sent the rich away empty."

The verses together present parallel thoughts, with the second verse presenting the contrasting ideas of the first verse in reverse order.

A third form of parallelism is synthetic parallelism: to the first idea a complementary thought is added (Ps 19): "⁷ The law of the LORD is perfect, reviving the soul; the decrees of the LORD are sure, making wise the simple."

In Ps 136, the second half-verse is always the same: "for his steadfast love endures forever." This Psalm was probably a kind of litany: a choir leader sang the text of the first half-verses, and the congregation responded, always with the same second half-verse.

Some Psalms are composed as acrostics, which means that the first letters of each verse or stanza follow the Hebrew alphabet, perhaps an aid to memorizing the Psalms (Pss 9, 10, 25, 34, 37, 111, 112, 119).

Some Psalms employ explicitly theological language. Ps 103, for example, uses theological terms: soul, blessing, Holy Name, vindication and justice, mercy, sin, compassion, righteousness, covenant etc. Other Psalms use metaphorical language: Pss 58 and 102, for example, employ animals as metaphors.

The Psalms are anonymous. The headings *of David* and others do not necessarily mean individual authorship. Only very few headings refer to some situation in the life of David. Therefore, the Psalms are not so much expressions of an individual but prayers meant to be reused by the faithful and by the faith community. Despite the fact that we find in the Psalms only very few hints to the author(s) or to concrete situations, exegesis since the 19th century has understood the Psalms often just as expressions of individuals in the distant past. This understanding is, however, very narrow. Jewish exegesis in the Middle Ages claimed that what David says in the Psalms is said in regard to himself, to the whole people of Israel and to all times (Midrash Tehillim, about Ps 18). Hence even the words *I* and *me* in the Psalms are not simply expressions of some unknown individual in the distant past, but are the *I* and *we* of all who pray the Psalm, at all times and in all places. Modern scholars speak of the *lyrical I*, i.e. the narrator within a poem, who is not necessarily identical with the author.

b. The Psalter as a Book

The book of Psalms is sometimes called the prayer book or the hymnal of the Jewish community. The Psalter is indeed not just a random collection of poems but designed as a whole. It starts with the double introduction about the law (Ps 1) and the Messiah (Ps 2). The Psalter ends with a number of Hallelujah Psalms, the Hallel (= Praise, Pss 145–150). The last Psalm concludes the Psalter by summarizing the praises in the *sanctuary*, in *heaven* (*the mighty firmaments*) and in *nature* (*all that breathes*). The Psalm-book is subdivided into five books, in analogy to the Mosaic Law (cf. again Ps 1). Each book concludes with a praise Psalm (Pss 41, 72, 89, 106, 149–150). Its composition suggests that the Psalter is meant to be used as a whole and not just as an accumulation from which we may pick and choose whatever seems to be convenient. The design suggests that this is not just a collection of examples from the past but is meant to be taken as a guide for the spiritual life today and in all generations. The tradition of the Benedictine monks, the Anglican *Book of Common Prayer*, the *Tagzeitenbuch* of the Evangelische Sankt Michaels Bruderschaft (Protestant Brotherhood of Saint Michael), and many other liturgical books, both Catholic and Protestant, have in different ways adopted the whole Psalter for their prayer life, as have the versified Psalms (metrical Psalter) of the Reformed traditions like Robert Crowley's *The Psalter of Dauid newely translated into Englysh metre* (1549) and the *Genevan Psalter* (^{1}1593).

The Hebrew name of the book is T^{e}hillim, meaning *Laud* or *Praise*. Hence the whole book is supposed to serve the purpose of praising God. The Greek version of the Bible, the Septuagint (abbreviated: LXX) calls the book *Psalmoi*, according to the most frequent heading in the book, and so does the New Testament (Acts 1:20, Luke 20:42). The word *psalmoi* originally referred to a stringed musical instrument and thus became the term for this collection of prayers. The English word *Psalter* derives from the Greek *psalmoi*. We know that instrumental music was added to the reciting of the Psalms; in Ps 150 a variety of musical instruments is mentioned. Because this Psalm is the last in the book, it is probably meant as advice for the use of the whole Psalter. Therefore it is appropriate to use the Psalms as lyrics for chanting and to accompany them with musical instruments.

Headings show that some Psalms were recited according to a specific method. Ps 22:1, for example, advises: "To the Chief Musician. Set to 'The Deer of the Dawn.' A Psalm of David." We do not know the exact meaning of those headings, but we can be sure that they refer to some way of musical performance.

Other poetic texts of the Bible are traditionally used in worship services, called the *Odes*, e.g. the First Ode of Moses (Exod 15:1–19), the second Ode of Moses (Deut 32:1–43), the Prayer of Anna (1 Sam 2:1–10), the Prayer of Habakkuk (Habakkuk 3), the Prayer of Isaiah (Isa 26:9–20), the Prayer of the Prayer of Jonah (Jonah 2:3–10), the Prayer of Azariah (the deuterocanonical Portion of Dan 3:26–45), Song of the Three Young Men (the deuterocanonical portion of Dan 3:52–88), the *Magnificat* (Luke 1:46–55) and the *Benedictus* (Luke 68–79), the Song of the Vineyard (Isa 5:1–9), the Prayer of Hezekiah in (Isa 38:10–20), the *Nunc Dimmittis* (Luke 2:29–32),

Gloria in Excelsis Deo i.e. a Canticle for the Early Morning (Luke 2:14 together with Pss 35:10–11; 118:12, and 144:2).

The Latin names are simply the first words of the passages in the Latin version; it is quite useful to know them if you look for music composed for these texts.

c. Some Forms of the Psalms

Research on the Psalms has revealed a lot about their various genres and how they relate to their historic use. Here are some very basic thoughts.

A common form of the Psalms is the **Petition**. This form usually starts with an imperative like: *Give ear to my words; Hear, O Lord; Hear my voice; Hear my supplication; or Let your mercy come*. After this invocation the petition follows, often against enemies; sometimes a reason for God's desired intervention is mentioned, especially *for thy name's sake* (Pss 25:11, 31:4, 79:9, 109:21, 143:11). Sometimes the petitions conclude with a vow to offer sacrifices of thanks: Pss 7:18, 22:26, 54:8, 56:13, etc.

Another frequent form is the **lament of the individual,** with often dramatic metaphors: Pss 3–7, 13, 17, 22, 25, 28, 31, 35, 38, 39, 40, 42,43, 51, 54–57, 59, 61, 63, 64, 69–71, 86, 88, 102, 109, 120, 130, 140–143. Especially important for Christians is of course Ps 22, the Psalm Jesus prayed on the cross, which provided the language Matthew used to tell his version of the passion story.

It is typical that in many Psalms, at a certain point the situation of the worshiper seems to change completely. The prayer turns from petition to thanksgiving, turns from lamentation to a profession of confidence (Ps 56:10: "This I know, God is for me"; Ps 140: "[12] I know that the LORD maintains the cause of the needy, and executes justice for the poor."

There are various explanations for this change in mood. Some theorize that between the two parts of these Psalms, an oracle of salvation, a word of consolation, a proclamation of forgiveness or something like that was given to the worshiper. But we have no such word in the extant Psalms; therefore, if this theory was right, the psalmist would not have mentioned the most important event of his/her prayer experience. There is no evidence for this theory.

Some scholars have tried to find the reason for the structure of these Psalms by assuming some change in the state of mind of the author, which means of an unknown person who prayed this Psalm centuries ago and who otherwise did not tell much about him- or herself or about the concrete situation that surrounded the praying of the Psalm. The problem with these explanations is that they treat the Psalm as a historical source, though not a very informative one, to discern the supposedly real historic event in the psyche of someone long dead and buried. But this interpretation turns our attention away from the actual text and towards some presumed historic reality that is actually just a construct of the reader.

Others speculate about the psychological possibility of how someone's state of mind can change during the prayers of lamentation or petition. Again, those speculations look for some kind of psychological reality behind the actual words, a presumed reality that would be only expressed or described by the Psalm. But what's certain is that, for the reader or the user of the Psalm, the only visible and audible, tangible and present reality is not the soul of David but his words.

If we take the Psalms seriously as what they claim to be, both prayers of the faithful and at the same time God's word revealed through the prophet, they do not describe someone's soul, but they guide our souls. When we understand the Psalms as God's word, they do not report on the state of anyone's soul, past or present, but rather guide our spiritual life today and allow us to participate in the community of all who have been guided by their words in the past, pray them today, and will pray them in future. Praying with the words of the Psalms, we are gifted with words of guidance that lead us from anxious petition to confidence in God's power, from lamentation to new praise. The Psalms will shape our petitions and lamentations, and lead us through the time of trial with the promise that we will come to thanksgiving and praise eventually. They allow us to participate in the prayers of all people in distress, praying together with them for salvation. When we are well off, these Psalms call us to participate in the laments and petitions of all people in need, known to us and unknown, and thus build a community. So we should not selfishly pick the Psalms that describe our own state of mind most accurately but rather pray *all* the Psalms on behalf of all people in need and mourn with those who mourn (cf. Rom 12:15).

The book of Psalms contains an abundance of **hymns of thanksgiving** (Pss 18, 30, 32, 34, 41, 66, 92, 116, 118, 138). The Hebrew word for giving thanks (ידי) is the same word that describes a sacrifice of thanksgiving (the noun from the same root is תודה). The Psalms were apparently used in the assembly of the faithful and were somehow connected with the fulfillment of a vow; for example Ps 22: "²⁵ From you comes my praise in the great congregation; my vows I will pay before those who fear him." The characteristics of *thanksgiving* are: the worshiper describes his or her distress, then invokes God, then tells about his/her salvation. For example, Ps 66: "¹⁶ Come and hear, all you who fear God, and I will tell what he has done for me."

Another important form of the Psalms is the **hymn of praise** (Pss 8, 19, 29, 33, 46–48, 65, 67, 68, 76, 84, 87, 93, 96–100, 103–105, 111, 113, 114, 117, 135, 136, 145–150). The basic form is found in the hymn of Miriam (Exod 15): "[1] I will sing to the LORD, for he has triumphed gloriously; horse and rider he has thrown into the sea." This form has an introduction that calls to praise God; various words can be used: *praise, extol, glorify, laud,* etc. This introduction may call a group of people, for example Ps 47: "[1] Clap your hands, all you peoples; shout to God with loud songs of joy," or the worshiper exhorts himself/herself, for example Ps 103: "[1] Bless the LORD my soul." Sometimes the call to praise is a passive clause: "Blessed be the Lord the God of Israel" (cf. Luke 1). This call to praise is followed by the main part of the hymn of praise. Here, God's qualities are praised, for example in Ps 103: "[8] The LORD is merciful and gracious, slow to anger and abounding in steadfast love," and God's deeds are retold, as for example in the Song of Miriam (cf. above). The deeds of God retold in the *hymns of praise* may be his actions in the past or his continuous doing. Some Psalms perhaps refer even to God's actions that are yet to come: Pss 68, 98, 149.

A special genre is the **Psalm for the king**, the anointed one of Israel (Pss 2, 21, 72, 101, 45). The Hebrew word for *anointed is Messiah*, the Greek translation is *Christ*. Hence Christians refer these Psalms to Christ, the King of the Jews: Matt 2:2, 27:29, 27:37.

Some Psalms (Pss 120–134) have the heading **Song of Ascents**, which refers to *ascending the mount of Zion*. They were probably used on pilgrimages to the Holy City and the temple.

2. THE COLLECTS

The *collect* is the short prayer of the day in traditional forms of worship service, said before the lessons. The meaning of the term *collect* is *summing up the preceding prayers* or *collecting the prayers of the whole congregation*. In contrast to our prayers in the closet (cf. Matt 6), where we may speak freely, this prayer in a public worship service has a strict form that prevents the individual minister from showing off and is usually designed by the church.

The collect begins with an invocation (*O God; Lord our God; heavenly Father*; etc.) then speaks of certain qualities of God which he has revealed to us and to which we want to appeal. For example: *God, almighty and merciful*. . . . Then we refer to a certain deed of God, often an act of God about which we read in the Holy Bible. According to Latin examples, this line used to be a subordinate clause: . . . *who hast given* . . . or . . . *from whom we have* . . . . Modern collects have usually transformed this part into a main clause, for example: *You have led your people out of captivity and away from the flesh pots in Egypt. . . .* Only then does a petition follow, one that refers to the mentioned quality and deed of God. This petition is always worded in the first person plural *we*. For example: *We pray, save us by Your power from the captivity of indolence and selfish desires. . . .* After the petition, the consequences of God's saving deed may follow. For example: *So that we may humbly praise Your glory and generously serve the community of Your faithful.*

Collects are usually prayed to God the Father *in the name of the Son Jesus Christ, in the community of the Holy Spirit,* or simply *through Jesus Christ.*

The collect speaks of God's qualities and deeds first and only then makes a petition. In a sense, God's revelation, God's response, precedes our petition. This form has a solid biblical basis: The prophet proclaims (Isa 65): "[24] And it shall come to pass, that before they call, I will answer; and while they are yet speaking, I will hear." And Jesus taught his disciples (Matt 6): "[8] your Father knows what you need before you ask him" (cf. Part 1. II). God's answer precedes our prayer; he has given us his eternal word in Jesus Christ, and he has spoken to us long before the idea of our speaking to God ever popped up in our sinful hearts. Therefore, all Christian prayer starts with listening—listening to God's word, to the answers already given.

Whenever we use the traditional form of the collect, the strict reference to God's qualities and deeds, to the already given answers, preserves us from focusing on ourselves and saves us from the risk of indulging in vain repetition of our wishes (cf. Matt 6:7), which would lock us up all the more in the prison of our own thoughts and feelings. A prayer that begins with God's revelation sets us free, opens our souls to "remember his marvelous works that he hath done" (Ps 105:5), opens our eyes to the beauty of creation, to the earth, "full of God's riches" (Ps 104:24), and to the needs of our neighbors, "For the LORD heareth the poor, and despiseth not his prisoners" (Ps 69:33).

The collect is a prayer meant for a specific time and situation (in Latin: *de tempore*); thus it is part of the *proper* (in Latin: *proprium*), which means the changing parts of the worship service that refer to particular Sundays or occasions. The terms *proprium* and *de tempore* describe the pieces of the worship service that change day by day, as opposed to those pieces that stay the same all the time, called the *order* (in Latin: *ordinarium*). The collects sometimes refer to the Gospel of the Sunday.

The collects may be chanted. The strict form of these prayers provides the opportunity to connect them with a certain chanting tone. Chanting allows the collect to be what it is supposed to be: the collection of the prayers of the church, and not just an arbitrary expression of an individual pastor.

3. THE LITANY

The *litany* (from the Greek word *litaneia* = *plea* or *supplication*) is a form of prayer that has its origins in the Old Testament and in antiquity, and has since been used in Christian worship. The petitions of the litany are used both in public services and in private devotions. The litany has been prayed in the calamities of the church or the community, to implore God's aid or to appease His righteous wrath.

The litany is a responsive prayer, meaning one prayed responsively between a leader and the assembly. The congregation answers with fixed phrases like "Lord have mercy" (Kyrie Eleison) or as in Ps 136: "For his steadfast love endures forever." Alliteration and rhythm, repetition and variations make up the special character and the meditative intensity of this form of prayer.

The repetition of the phrase *Kyrie eleison*, "Lord have mercy," was probably the original response of the litany. The Council of Vaison[1] in 529 passed the decree: "Let that beautiful custom of all the provinces of the East and of Italy be kept up, viz., that of singing with great effect and compunction the Kyrie Eleison at Mass, Matins, and Vespers, because so sweet and pleasing a chant, even though *continued day and night without interruption, could never produce disgust or weariness.*"

Litanies are a classical element of processions. Litanies flourished in the Roman Catholic Church of the Middle Ages. Martin Luther composed a litany in 1528, which is still kept in Lutheran hymnals.

4. COMMON PRAYER

In the first letter to Timothy we read: "[1] First of all, then, I urge that supplications, prayers, intercessions, and thanksgivings be made for everyone, [2] for kings and all who are in high positions, so that we may lead a quiet and peaceable life in all godliness and dignity. [3] This is right and is acceptable in the sight of God our Savior." (For a more detailed discussion of this passage, see below 3.V). With the prayers of intercession, we pray for the Church, for the world and for all in need. This prayer is perhaps the most informal prayer in Christian worship; it still follows certain patterns.

In the prayers of the Church we have two focuses: God, who listen to our prayers, and his works, for which we pray. In the early Church the prayers were called *common prayer* (*Oratio Communis*, Augustine, Ep.55,18). The meaning is *prayer of all*, which means of all who participate in the body of

---

1. Hefele and Leclercq, "Deuxième council de vaison en 529," 1114.

Christ. The essence of these prayers is that we pray for and on behalf of our community.

Since the early Church, a certain pattern of the petitions has been maintained, which by and large follows the petitions of the Lord's Prayer:

First we say prayers about the Kingdom of God: we pray for the unity of the church, for the spreading of the gospel, for firmness in temptation and persecution, for the blessings through the word of God and the sacraments, for the church and her leadership.

Then we say prayers that God's will be done: we pray for the nation(s) and for political leaders, for the law, for order and peace.

Thirdly we say prayers for our daily bread. According to Luther's explanation of this petition, *daily bread* pertains to all necessities of our temporal life. Therefore this part of the prayers includes marriage, family, education of youth, relationships between the generations, work, unemployment, weather, harvest, etc.

And now prayers follow about calamities of individuals: for those who are lonely or strangers, for those who are old and ill, for those who are about to die, for those who are in prison, for those who are persecuted, suffer from catastrophes, unemployment or famine.

Some traditions add thanks for the lives of the faithful departed, prayers about the consolation of the bereaved and a petition that God may remind us of our mortality (cf. The Sacramentary by Serapion of Thmuis, 330-360).

These prayers are deeply rooted in the New Testament itself, and therefore in the community of the Christian Church, as Saint Paul writes in Rom 12: "[15] Rejoice with those who rejoice, weep with those who weep" and in Gal 6: "[2] Bear one another's burdens, and in this way you will fulfill the law of Christ." We pray for one another following Saint Paul's teaching in 1 Cor 12: "[26] If one member suffers, all suffer together with it; if one member is honored, all rejoice together with it. Now you are the body of Christ and individually members of it."

We have examples of this common prayer from the early church; in the first letter by Clement of Rome (AD 95/96) we have actually a complete text of a prayer. The Greek church has preserved the *common prayer* until today. In the Roman Catholic Church it was temporarily lost. The churches of the Reformation reintroduced it; Luther writes about this *common prayer* in his *Treatise on Good Works*[2] (AD 1520): "This common prayer is precious and the most effective, and it is for the sake of this that we assemble ourselves together. The church is called a house of prayer (Matt 21:13) because we are

---

2. *Christian in Society I*, ed. James Atkinson, vol. 44, *Luther's Works*, 64ff.

all there as a congregation and with one accord to bring our own needs as well as those of all men before God and to call upon him for mercy. But this must be done from the heart and with sincerity; we must take to heart the need of all men, and pray for them in real sympathy and in true faith and trust. Where such prayer does not take place in the mass, it would be better to omit the mass. By assembling together in a house of prayer we show that we ought to make common prayer and petition for the entire fellowship. What sense does it make for us to scatter those prayers and divide them up so that everyone prays only for himself and nobody concerns himself with anybody else for another's need?" The Second Vatican Council of the Roman Catholic Church restored the common prayer.[3]

a. Three basic forms of the "common prayer"

The simplest form of this prayer is a plain text which the pastor or a lay person speaks alone; lay leaders usually stay in the pew or stand in the aisle, pastors usually face the altar. This form of the prayers is sometimes called a *prosphonesis*, a Greek word, the meaning of which is that the prayer is offered to God by a leader for and on behalf of the congregation. This is certainly the most convenient way to offer the prayers, but it is an issue to be considered that the congregation does not know what prayers will be said, has just to listen, and is not actively involved.

A second form of the *common prayer* is called *ektenia*, a Greek word that refers to the custom of extending the hands in prayer. The petitions are said by the leader and the assembly responds to each petition by repeating an invocation to God such as *hear our prayer*, or *have mercy on us* or something like that. This form is similar to a litany, which again is based on examples in the Psalms (cf. above). It is possible that the assembly chants the prayer response.

A third form is the *deacon's prayer*. The term *deacon's prayer* refers to the custom that a deacon or another person stands at the lectern and announces each petition: *Let us pray for . . . , who . . . .* The liturgist at the altar says each time a prayer corresponding with the announcement of the deacon, sometimes in the form of a collect. This form as well has its roots in the early Church. The congregation may say "amen" after each petition or

---

3. Vatican II Council, "Constitution on the Sacred Liturgy: *Sacrosanctum concilium*," chap. 2 (December 4, 1963), 53. "Especially on Sundays and feasts of obligation there is to be restored, after the Gospel and the homily, 'the common prayer' or 'the prayer of the faithful.' By this prayer, in which the people are to take part, intercession will be made for holy Church, for the civil authorities, for those oppressed by various needs, for all mankind, and for the salvation of the entire world."

another invocation. It is a beautiful and effective form to offer the prayers, but it requires careful preparation, and with at least two leaders involved it requires some organization.

The content of the prayers is usually petitions. Thanks and praise will be said in the Eucharistic prayer. There is nothing wrong with the fact that the prayers are not always original, but certain topics and phrases occur again and again. It actually makes sense: the members of the congregation thus receive a reminder and exercise to pray about the various needs of the church, the world and personal lives. Individual prayers *in the closet* hereby receive some guidance and structure. For the prayers in worship, Martin Luther suggested: "After the sermon shall follow a public paraphrase of the Lord's Prayer. . . ."[4]

As regards content, it is not necessary that the prayers refer to the sermon. It was a custom in the pietistic movement of the 1600s and 1700s to repeat the sermon in the form of a prayer. But the prayers should cover all kinds of issues of the church, of society and individuals; tying the prayers too closely to the sermon will necessarily result in neglecting what we need to pray about in any concrete situation of the church and of society. The sermon, however, may be concluded with a prayer from the pulpit.

At the end of the *common prayer*, a brief silence may give an opportunity for the petitions of individuals, prayed silently or aloud. It is the responsibility of the whole congregation to provide such an atmosphere in worship that nobody is prevented from praying, but also that nobody feels pushed to speak up, and everybody should restrain himself/herself from exploiting the opportunity for propaganda, or to correct others who said a prayer before, or to comment on the preacher. For the time of these prayers or silence, pastors need to decide where they want to stand; perhaps the best place is at the altar, where this prayer can be concluded with a word from the Bible.[5] The assembly confirms this word by saying *Amen*.

In traditional worship services, the prayers of intercession, the sharing of the peace, the offering with the offering prayer, and the Eucharistic prayers are closely connected (see below part 3, VI,1). The offering was, from the beginning, used for both the material requirements of the worship service, bread and wine, and for the support of the poor. Hence in traditional

---

4. Martin Luther, "The German Mass and Order of Service, 1526," in *Liturgy and Hymns*, ed. Ulrich S. Leupold, vol. 53, *Luther's Works*, 78.

5. Here are some examples (Matt 21): "[22] *Jesus answers: Whatever you ask for in prayer with faith, you will receive.*" (Ps 31) "[24] *Be strong, and let your heart take courage, all you who wait for the LORD.*" (Ps 55) "[22] *Cast your burden on the LORD, and he will sustain you; he will never permit the righteous to be moved.*" See also Matt 28; John 16; 2 Chr 7; Isa 66; Jer 29; Jer 33.

liturgies signs of reconciliation with one another and with God, prayers for those in need and material support for them, and the great thanksgiving for the works of the creator, i.e., the Eucharistic prayers, and for Christ's saving deed were closely connected.

Because of the understanding that prayers of intercession and the Eucharist belong together, some congregations have adopted the custom of collecting the offering and preparing the Eucharistic elements first, and then offering prayers. This way, the offering of gifts and the offering of prayers are visibly connected. The common prayer is then continued by the Eucharistic prayers.

It is certainly possible to sing the prayers, from which most pastors will probably shy away. A possibility easy to realize is the form of the *ektenia* (cf. above), with the congregation singing a response according to a certain tone, for example, *Lord have mercy*.

V

Prayer, Thanks and Praise
(1 Timothy 2:1–8)

CATECHETIC TRADITION HAS SUMMARIZED the biblical witness to prayer: Prayer, Thanks and Praise. This sequence of words perhaps describes a process from the more self-centered to the most self-less prayer. In the first letter to Timothy, we find an exhortation (1 Tim 2:1–8) to: "supplication, prayer, intercession and thanksgiving,"[1] a series of terms that can be taken as a kind of catechetical teaching.

1. CONTEXT

The letter begins as usual with the address and some conversation with the addressee. With the exhortation to prayer in 1 Tim 2:1–8, the main teaching of the letter begins. Its first part is summarized in 1 Tim 3: "[15] you may know how one ought to behave in the household of God, which is the church of the living God, the pillar and bulwark of the truth." Hence the life of Christians is to be consistent with the mystery of their salvation. The next verse concludes this first portion of the letter (1 Tim 3): "[16] the mystery of our religion (εὐσέβεια) is great: He was revealed in flesh, vindicated in spirit, seen by angels, proclaimed among Gentiles, believed in throughout the world, taken up in glory." This solemn proclamation is obviously quoted from Christian worship celebration. Therefore the exhortation to prayer in

---

1. To make δεήσεις, προσευχάς, ἐντεύξεις, εὐχαριστίας.

1 Tim 2:1–8 and the phrases in 1 Tim 3:16, taken from the prayers of the church, form a framework for the letter's teaching about the Christian life.

2. FOUR DIFFERENT TERMS FOR PRAYER (1. TIMOTHY 2:1)

Verse 2:1 says: "¹ I exhort therefore, that first of all supplications, prayers, intercessions and giving of thanks be made for all men." Saying *I exhort you*, the author speaks with the authority of an apostle (cf. Rom 12:1; 1 Cor 1:10; 2 Cor 10:1): *I exhort* or *I urge you*. The original text says *first of all* (dropped in some translations), which means that it is indeed most important for Christians to pray for *all people*.

The author employs four terms for prayer. These words have indeed different meanings and describe different forms of prayer, and their order in this sentence is probably not random. All of these forms of prayer have a universal perspective: Christians pray for *all people*.

Supplication (δέησις) is a petition, by which a person brings his or her concerns to God (Luke 1:13; Phil 1:4; 2 Tim 1:3; Jes 5:16). *Prayer* (προσευχή) is the common prayer in worship (cf. Acts 1:14; 2:42; 12:5; Rom 12:12; Rev 5:8, 8:3–4) and a frequent term in the Greek version of the Psalms. *Intercession* (ἐντεύξις) was in the secular world the plea to a king, so in church it is the prayer for and on behalf of others. *Thanksgiving* (in Greek: Εὐχαριστία transcribed as *Eucharistia*) is the thankful praise to God. Traditional material for this praise was first taken from the praise–Psalms, and later Christian hymns were added. If the term *Eucharistia* in this verse indeed refers to the Eucharist (see below), the sequence of the four terms in 1 Tim 2 would then perhaps follow the process of the worship service, from individual prayers to communal intercessions and supplications to the Eucharistic prayer.

4. THANKSGIVING

It is probably impossible to verify that here in verse 1 the term *thanksgiving* is the technical term for the *Eucharist*. It is, however, certain that this passage in 1 Tim 2 speaks about worship and prayer. It is also certain that the verbal form of the word *Eucharist*, i.e. *to give thanks*, is used in all the accounts of Jesus' Last Supper (Luke 22:17; Matt 26:27; 1 Cor 11:24). Moreover, the phrase *for all* in 1 Tim 2 (ὑπὲρ πάντων ἀνθρώπων) reminds us of the phrase *for all* in the account of the institution of the Eucharist (Mark 14:23

and Matt 26:27). So it's quite possible that the word E*ucharistia* in 1 Tim 2:1 reflects the worship service at the time.

In verses 5–6, again various hints to the Eucharist are found, which confirms the assumption that the word *Eucharistia* in verses 1–2 actually means *Eucharist*. The language of the verses 5–6 is quite solemn: "⁵ For there is one God and one Mediator between God and men, the Man Christ Jesus, ⁶ who gave Himself a ransom for all, to be testified in due time." These solemn verses are probably again a quotation from the worship service of the early Church, so that the author of the letter can prove to his addressee that his message is already present in the words the assembly uses on a regular basis.

Some scholars say the term *mediator* is a variation on the original acclamation of Jesus Christ as *Lord*. In Heb 8:5–6 Jesus Christ is the *mediator* of the better covenant and of a ministry more excellent than that of Moses in the tent of meeting, meaning the worship service of the old covenant; the Greek word in Heb 8 translated as *ministry* is actually *liturgy* (λειτουργία). Jesus is the one mediator between God and man by virtue of his sacrifice. Hence the term *mediator* in 1 Timothy also points to the role of Jesus' mediating between God and man in worship and prayer.

1 Tim 2:6 says that Jesus gave himself as a ransom *for all*. As it was in verse 1 this phrase *for all* perhaps refers here again to the chalice (Mark 14:23, cf. Matt 26:27) given *for all*. Hence all people, all nations may approach the table of the Lord. As already mentioned the verses 5–6 of 1 Tim 2 are perhaps a quotation of an older church tradition, which includes the *prayer for all*.

The *ransom* as well suggests that this phrase was used in the context of the Eucharistic celebration. The reason for this assumption is that according to some scholars Jesus' word in Mark 10: "⁴⁵ *For the Son of Man came not to be served but to serve, and to give his life a ransom for many*," was used in the context of Eucharistic prayers, and the author of 1 Timothy alludes to this practice. The *human Jesus Christ* in 1 Tim 2:5 is perhaps a translation of the ancient Semitic phrase *Son of Man*, here interpreted for a Greek-speaking Christian by the concept of the incarnation.

3. "FOR ALL" AND "FOR THE KING" (VERSES 1b+2a 5–6)

The verses 1 Tim 2:1–8 speak about the prayer *for all* and *for the king*. This short passage repeats four times that prayers are offered *for all*. In the prayer for *all people* the whole world is in view in contrast to certain Jewish prayers which were said on behalf of only the own nation, and for the government only if it could be useful for the Jewish community (they could refer to Jer 29). Christians are supposed to pray for all people.

Verse 5 gives the reason for the prayer *for all:* "⁵ For there is one God and one mediator between God and men, the man Christ Jesus." The argument of the letter is simple: God, the savior, is *one*; therefore salvation is offered to all. The monotheistic premise leads us to pray for all people. We read the emphatic expression *one God* as well in Eph 4: "⁵ one Lord, one faith, one baptism," and in 1 Cor 8: "⁶ But to us there is but one God, the Father, of whom are all things, and we in him; and one Lord Jesus Christ, by whom are all things, and we by him." The phrase in 1 Tim 2:5–6 reminds us of course of the *Shema Israel* (Deut 6:4), in the Jewish faith community the regular confession of faith in the one God.

Christians pray for all people, including the king. God's will to save is extended to all people; therefore, Christians pray for their rulers. The author, by the authority of an apostle, obliges the Church to pray for the king and all in authority (cf. as well Rom 13). In the eastern part of the Roman world, the term *king* (in Greek: βασιλεύς) was used for the Roman emperor, even though the official language in the West avoided the term *king* (in Latin: *rex*). Prayer for the government in times of persecution was certainly a challenge. Still, the letter to Timothy encourages a general trust in the organizational power and responsibility of government. The main reason is that government represents the universal community to which the good news is addressed, and for which the Church takes responsibility. The Church would pray that the government uses its power to maintain peace, law, and justice with clemency. Hence, the prayer for the king asks that he may govern irreproachably and provide acceptable living conditions.

Clement, bishop of Rome (martyred in 97 or 101) wrote in a similar way about prayer for the rulers and all people; he prays (1 Clement 60:4): "Give concord and peace to us and to all that dwell on the earth, as Thou gavest to our fathers, when they called on Thee in faith and truth with holiness, [. . .] while we render obedience to Thine almighty and most excellent Name, and to our rulers and governors upon the earth. (1 Clement 61:1) Thou, Lord and Master, hast given them the power of sovereignty through Thine excellent and unspeakable might, that we knowing the glory and honor which Thou hast given them may submit ourselves unto them, in nothing resisting Thy will."²

---

2. Transl. by J. B. Lightfoot.

5. A LIFE IN TRANQUILITY, VERSE 2b

The goal of Christian prayer is, according to the second part of 1 Tim 2:2, that we "may lead a quiet and peaceable life in all godliness and dignity (εὐσέβεια καὶ σεμνότητι)." This sentence describes the ideal of life that Christian prayer hopes to see realized. The term translated as *godliness* has been a fundamental term of ethics since the classical period of Greek culture. The meaning is: reverence for the deity and the divine order that makes life in a community possible. The fundamental assumption for this virtue among Christians is that the triune God is the creator and sustainer of all creation, and that he guarantees the good order of the universe and society. Contrary to gnostic beliefs (cf. 1 Tim 6:20), the material world is not a dark prison, but world, society, and government are still God's creation. Therefore Christian virtues and prayer are related to a life together with all people, in creation and community.[3]

The orientation towards the common good of all people is confirmed by the sentence that follows (v. 4): "God our Savior [. . .] desires everyone to be saved and to come to the knowledge of the truth." Prayer and salvation are obviously related to the *knowledge of the truth*.

6. CONCLUSION

1 Tim 2:8 says: "[8] I desire therefore that the men pray everywhere, lifting up holy hands, without wrath and doubting."

Prayer is described as *lifting up holy hands*. Christians would pray with open arms lifted up as a gesture of surrendering to God's will and imploring God's mercy. The internal attitude is mentioned only as an addition and only in a negative way: *without wrath and doubting*—vices mentioned because of their impact on others, both individuals and the community.

The author speaks about prayer *in every place*. This phrase reflects again God's universal will to save. The Christian hope is that people in all the world will gather in the name of Jesus for prayer.

---

3. The sources for our knowledge about the Gnosis are, however, from later times. So it remains an open question whether or not this term in 1.Tim. is related to that theology at all. Cf. Berger, Gnosis.

VI.

Prayer with Charity and Fasting

IN THE GOSPEL ACCORDING to Matthew, Jesus, after his baptism (Matt 3) and before he started his ministry, went to a lonely place and dedicated forty days to fasting and prayer (Matt 4). Only a little later in Matthew's Gospel (chapter 6), in the Sermon on the Mount, Jesus instructs his disciples about the threefold discipline of charity, fasting and prayer. Jesus teaches about taking responsibility for the poor: i.e., giving alms; Jesus teaches about prayer, specifically the Our Father, and about fasting, which presupposes that his disciples are to observe the fast.

Jesus bases this teaching on the Old Testament Bible, which in turn gives witness to him, Jesus Christ, and his fasting, prayer and sacrificial love. The Old Testament Law prescribes that God's people shall give alms for the poor (Deut 15), and the book of Psalms gives plenty of advice about what we need to pray. We find examples for fasting in the law and the prophets: Moses was fasting forty days when he met with God on Mount Sinai (Exod 34); the prophet Elijah ate bread and drank water and then went on a journey of forty days to the mount of God (1 Kgs 19); the people of Nineveh fasted forty days when Jonah brought a message of warning from God (Jonah 3).

In the time between the testaments, the Jewish community had already combined the three exercises of prayer, fasting, and giving alms (Tobit 12:8). In the parable about the tax collector and the Pharisee (Luke 18), the Pharisee mentions in his prayer that he regularly fasts and donates a tenth of his income. This story criticizes the attitude of the Pharisee but does not criticize the threefold discipline of fasting, prayer and almsgiving itself (cf. Part 1. I. 1).

Both Jewish customs and Church tradition have always set apart certain times (and places) for festivals and times for their preparation. In Church tradition, this piece of the Gospel in Matt 6 is read on Ash Wednesday, the beginning of the season of Lent. So prayer, fasting and giving alms are together called the discipline of Lent, three spiritual exercises Christians are encouraged to observe over those seven weeks. We find the number of the *forty days* of Jesus' fasting in Matt 4 prefigured in the Law and the Prophets: the stories about Moses, Elijah and Jonah.

Lent is the time when we prepare for the liturgy of the three days, the celebration of Jesus' death and resurrection. The seven weeks of preparation constitute a time when we want to follow more consciously the counsel Jesus gave in the Sermon on the Mount about prayer, charity and fasting. We are certainly supposed to pray, to take responsibility for the unfortunate, and to observe self-discipline all the days of our life. Martin Luther and the Reformers insisted that we should pray always and never neglect our neighbors in need, and that fasting means to maintain self-control. It is still helpful to have a time set apart with a special focus on these practices according to biblical models. Those special times provide a reminder and guidance for the whole of our lives. Martin Luther in his Small Catechism calls fasting *a fine external exercise,* and special times of prayer set aside in our daily, weekly and yearly routines call our attention to the idea that we should pray always. The season of Lent is an opportunity to refocus on these three disciplines, to make us aware of God's plan and order for us.

On Ash Wednesday, we are called to repentance, to turn away from our old ways, and turn to Christ. We confess our sins, and the imposition of ashes reminds us of the reality that our existence in this world is finite, that we will return to dust, that we will face our maker. With this Ash Wednesday liturgy of repentance in the beginning of Lent, the special season becomes an opportunity for the renewal of our whole life.

In Jesus' Sermon on the Mount, the three exercises are connected by Jesus' advice not to blow a trumpet but to pray, to fast, and to give *in secret.* Therefore, in Matt 6 Jesus doesn't merely give us a list of suggestions. These three exercises work together and reinterpret each other. What appears at first sight to be a random collection of practices is in fact a meaningful composition of spiritual exercises that would suffer damage if we took out any element. Prayer without charity and fasting could become self-centered and possibly foster an attitude of entitlement. Charity without prayer and fasting would be condescending and limited to our abundance (Mark 12:44). Fasting without charity and prayer would be aimless and possibly foster false pride.

1. PRAYER WITH CHARITY

Jesus has connected prayer with charity, *giving alms,* so that we don't focus our prayers on our own needs or wants. Prayer is, of course, first of all an appeal to God's love and power. Still, we understand the essence of prayer, especially of intercession, from its connection with fasting and giving alms: i.e., self-control and charity.

Whenever we do works of charity, we need to pray so that we understand our dependency on God, and so our work remains realistic, turns neither into a haughty attempt to solve all the world's problems, nor, in view of the gigantic challenges, suffers from the erosion of hope and love. Prayer protects our work of charity against both haughtiness and despair.

Whenever we pray, we need to do works of charity, so that we learn that the appeal to God's love and power is not a substitute for our love's hard work, and prayer remains sincerely and honestly concerned about those for whom we pray. Our works of charity protect our prayer from becoming uncharitable and disingenuous.

a. Pray and Work

Some might criticize prayer as an escape from reality, or suspect it of being a means to avoid the work of love. People who pray are sometimes reproached for closing their eyes to the work, burdens and challenges of the life in this world.

Then again, hands-on work for the unfortunate is sometimes suspected of being a substitute for the more necessary care for souls, of turning religion into ethics, of avoiding the work of prayer, or of avoiding the challenge of trusting in God's providence, even suspected of supporting the lazy.

In our personal lives, work and prayer often seem to compete for our time. We tend to spend on prayer only the hours or minutes left over when our work is done or even when our needs for leisure are met. At least we want to avoid the reproach of having prayed only where hands-on help was required.

The view that praying is a means of avoiding work and responsibility has had political consequences: In the late 1700s, the time of the Enlightenment movement, many monasteries in Europe that did not have an explicit purpose in terms of charitable work, or at least educational work, were closed. In the Napoleonic Era most monasteries in Europe were suppressed. People who lived a life of contemplation and prayer were considered useless. In Communist countries, prayer was considered a waste of time. In present-day Western societies, central days of the ecclesiastical year like Maundy Thursday or Good Friday are no longer guaranteed as holidays by governments or respected by society. The disregard for those festivals or even for Sunday in some Christian traditions is seemingly in accordance with the demands of modern economy.

At the same time, work not for profit, work to which we are called by God, called by the needs of our neighbors, called by a higher purpose, work beyond what is required is nowadays often viewed as *work nobody wants to pay for*. The fact that this loss of work ethics and the loss of regular prayer coincide suggests that work and prayer are not mutually exclusive but, on the contrary, mutually supportive. Martin Luther is credited with the saying: "I have so much to do that I shall spend the first three hours in prayer."[1] His opinion was obviously that prayer is not a luxury we can afford when our work is done, but rather that prayer is a necessary complement to all good work.

The appearance of a conflict between work and prayer, between our dedication to God and love for our neighbor, the appearance of a conflict between our own responsibility for our neighbor and prayerful trust in God's helping power, the appearance of a conflict between prayer for our own needs and intercession for the world, are themes that have permeated all Christian traditions from the beginning. The rule of Saint Benedict, the founding father of monasticism in the Western church, encouraged the monks: *Ora et Labora*, meaning *pray and work*. Next to prayer, *work* was held in high esteem. Saint Benedict designed his rule at the end of antiquity. When culture collapsed under the invasion of barbarians, Benedictine monks preserved civilization with this strict connection of work and prayer. The life of the monks was structured by the ecclesiastical year and the rhythm of the week. Every day was structured by the *hours* of prayer (see above). Hence a regulated and disciplined lifestyle evolved that shaped the Christian work ethic as well. Christians know about both prayer *and* responsible work. However, in the phrase *pray and work*, the word *and* requires some more reflection.

b. *The Beautiful Gate (Saint Peter and Saint John)*

Prayer and charity used to be visibly and physically connected: the doorsteps to houses of prayer and public worship were always preferred places

---

1. This quote is widely known, but I was not able to verify it. Perhaps someone can help for the next edition. This sentence is, however, consistent with what Luther writes in his tract on prayer for Peter Balbier, 1535. Luther, "A Simple Way to Pray."

for people in need to ask for charitable gifts. This is still a reality in many places of the world. Beggars sit at the entrance of a church and thus teach us the necessary connection between prayer and charity, and they remind us that social justice continues to be a challenge.

We read in Acts about two apostles meeting a beggar at the temple gate (Acts 3:1–10). Peter and John were walking up to the temple at the ninth hour, the hour of prayer, which is three o'clock in the afternoon. Many Jews kept the traditional hours of prayer and, if possible, went to the house of prayer; the ninth hour was in Jewish tradition the time for the Mincha prayer, and Christians would remember this as the hour of Jesus' suffering and death (Luke 23:44). It is perhaps not a coincidence that, according to Saint Luke, the apostles are confronted with the beggar's suffering and humiliation at the hour of Jesus' suffering. The apostles were going to pray in the temple at the hour of the suffering and death of him who prayed to the Father to forgive those who mocked him and made him suffer (Luke 23:34).

We read in Acts 3: "² And a man lame from birth was being carried in. People would lay him daily at the gate of the temple called the Beautiful Gate so that he could ask for alms from those entering the temple." The house of prayer appears to be the appropriate place to expect charity. In a sense, the apostles are kept from the place of God's glory by human poverty. He or she who wishes to enter the *Gate of Beauty* to glorify God needs to be confronted with the suffering and misery of humanity, lest the praise of God turns into an evasion from reality.

It is a common experience that people are prevented from praising God by the sight of suffering. Newspapers and news channels are full of messages about disaster and misery, which disturb our trust in God—and mostly fail to call us to responsibility. When beggars sit at the entrance of our churches, the embarrassment of those who want to enter the house of prayer might lead to compassion but might also cause anger and aggression if we claim the house of God as our own property and want to experience God's love while ignoring pain and the cross.

The paralyzed man in our story asks the apostles for a gift. The wording of the original Greek text indicates a persistent, perhaps even pushy begging. The apostles ask the beggar to look at them. They do not throw some coins at him and rush on into the temple, but instead ask him to look at them. We all know situations like this, when we are approached by a stranger, perhaps by someone filthy and smelly; we want to avoid contact, we want to ignore the challenge. But the apostles did not elude the encounter; on the contrary (Acts 3): "⁴ fixing his eyes on him, with John, Peter said, 'Look at us.'" The charity of Peter and John was not an attempt to get rid of an annoyance. They did not do a good deed to get over the obstacle that hindered them from entering the temple for prayer, and they did not help in order to feel good about themselves. They wanted to establish community; they wanted the beggar to look into their eyes.

The apostles had the power to perform miracles. They healed the beggar and thus empowered him. Their miracle was exactly not the kind of assistance that creates dependency, but they enabled self-reliance. The result of the story is that the healed man (Acts 3): "^{8} entered the temple with them, walking and leaping and praising God." The man praises God and joins the community of the apostles who had come to the temple to praise God in the first place. Praising God has become possible when God did his work of helping love through the hands of his servants. The disciples' intention to pray becomes an opportunity for charity, and charity in turn leads to praise and prayer in community. This community of prayer has an impact on the bystanders, who know that the man had been paralyzed. They are filled with *wonder and amazement*.

We pray with fasting and charity. Thus we pray selflessly and for the good of our neighbors. As we pray to the Father in heaven who is God, creator and Father of all creation, we cannot be selfish in our prayer. When we pray to the heavenly Father with charity, we seek the community of all the children of our Father in heaven, we seek to be in a community of all brothers and sisters in need who pray to the same Father. When we pray and give alms, we give up seeking our own personal comfort but rather seek the comfort of all creation. Christian prayer wants to be said together with the prayers of all people in need. Prayer means that we join the hymn of all creation and that we sing when the cherubim and all creation sing to God.

c. Come Ye Rich People (St. James)

Whenever we pray for our own needs, we must know that other people pray for their needs to the same God. Their neediness might be in some way connected with our opulent lifestyle. The fifth chapter of the Letter of James (5:1–6) gives a stern warning to rich people who expose the foolishness of their trust in their riches.

This passage is introduced with the same phrase as Jas 4:13–17, which offers advice for those who invoke the Lord ("you ought to say: if the Lord wishes . . . ."). Hence the warning in the Jas 5: "^{1} Come now ye rich people" continues the exhortations of the previous chapter, which are undoubtedly addressed to Saint James' fellow Christians. It would be foolish to interpret Saint James' warnings as if they were addressed to anyone but to us. The exhortation of this passage in James is based on the simple insight that the

Lord is mightier than we are, and that God has heard the prayers and cries of his suffering people.

In this passage Saint James explicitly speaks about employers cheating their employees. It is interesting that both the defrauded laborers and the withheld wages cry out to God (Jas 5:4). Saint James isn't speaking just about a personal relationship between employer and employee, but about the broader context of order and justice in God's creation, in which the treasures of the rich will rot and vanish (Jas 5:2–3), and withheld wages appeal to God. In this broader context of justice and prayer, the suffering laborers and harvesters appeal to God. As for the rich, Saint James gives us a quite graphic image: a man living in luxury is like a calf being fattened for slaughter. James warns those who, by their actions or negligence, make their workers suffer. James addresses his warning to us.

But Saint James goes a step further and turns the warning to rich people into an appeal to respect and honor those who suffer. The chain of argument is this: Saint James chides the rich (Jas 5): "⁶ Ye have condemned and killed the just; and he doth not resist you." The latter phrase refers to one of the *servant songs* in the book of the prophet Isaiah, which are viewed in the New Testament as prophetic witness to Christ (Isa 53): "⁷ He was oppressed, and he was afflicted, yet he opened not his mouth: he is brought as a lamb to the slaughter, and as a sheep before her shearers is dumb, so he openeth not his mouth" (cf. Acts 3:14, Matt 8:17). James wants his readers to view the suffering of the defrauded laborer as the suffering of Christ himself, *the just*. This thought is similar to Jesus' word in the parable of the Last Judgment, where he identifies himself with those who are naked, hungry, and thirsty, or imprisoned, the least of his brethren (Matt 25). Therefore we are first called to see Christ in the poor and suffering, and accordingly to honor them as *Christ in disguise* (Mother Teresa).

Secondly, we are called to be followers of Christ, the suffering Lord, or, to use the Pauline expression, to be *members of the body of Christ*. We take sides with the suffering Christ and with all of his sisters and brothers in pain. We participate in Jesus' prayers, we pray the petition for the daily bread, the Psalms of the poor, the servant-songs of the book of Isaiah, the Psalms that speak of persecution and enemies. We are called to take sides with those who are in pain and distress. Praying the prayers of lamentation, we lend our voice to the voiceless. As we pray, we get involved in the creator's plan of love and justice for all.

d. Charity, a Memorial before God (Cornelius)

In Acts 10 we read about another way to relate prayer and charity. The book of Acts tells us of a Roman soldier who is described as generous in his charitable giving, and as someone who prays. An angel of the Lord speaks to him about prayer and charity: "Your prayers and your alms have ascended as a memorial before God."

Cornelius is described as a Roman army officer. He has a traditional Latin name; we know his rank and unit. His observance of prayer shows that he had turned to Judaism, and he is described as a pious man who feared God. Cornelius is mentioned with *all his household*; as in Acts, faith is often not only a matter of individuals but of the *house*.[2] Saint Luke writes about Cornelius: "he gave alms generously to the people and prayed continually to God." That he prayed *continually* is the same expression that we find in the last sentence of Luke's Gospel about the apostles: "they stayed continually at the temple, praising God," which again perhaps refers to the observance of the hours of prayer. Cornelius connected prayer and alms as Jewish tradition and the Lord himself (Matt 6) had connected prayer and charity.

The story is this: Cornelius prayed at the ninth hour, i.e., 3 p.m., an hour for prayer according to Jewish custom.[3] This hour, when the vision came to him, was the hour of Jesus' death (cf. Luke 23:44), when the Lord bought our salvation through his blood. The traditional hour of prayer thus received a new meaning: we pray when Jesus suffers. Saint Peter prayed at the same ninth hour of the daily routine. Both men obviously observed the traditional Jewish order of prayer, and at this ninth hour both men received corresponding visions that would bring them together. Saint Peter—against his will—was sent to this Roman soldier to bring him the gospel. Here in the tenth chapter of Acts, the story begins of the gospel being spread in the Greek-Roman world while many Jews refused to turn to the Messiah. The two corresponding visions of Saint Peter and Cornelius brought the two men together to start the last chapter in the world's history, and they received their visions while both men were observing the hours of prayer.

Cornelius's practice of piety combined prayer with charity. Now an angel appeared to him, answering his prayer. This angelic message gives us another insight into how prayer and works of charity are tied together (Acts 10:4): "Your prayers and your alms have ascended as a memorial before God." Alms are obviously not just a legal obligation. Both spiritual exercises, prayer and charity, come to God as a *memorial* (μνημοσύνη). It

---

2. Cf. Acts 11:11; 16:15; 16:31; cf. also the final greetings at the end of the New Testament letters, for example 1 Cor 16:15; Phil 4:22; 2 Tim 4:19.

3. See above, chapter IV.2.b.

is not a stretch to say that alms and prayer are two forms of invocation to God. They belong together because both prayer and alms ascend to God as a memorial. God is not just a legislator imposing some law of charity, but the one who listens to invocations, in the form both of spoken words and of charitable gifts given for the poor.

In a sense, our charitable deeds are themselves prayers to the loving and sustaining creator, prayers that come as memorial before him. Therefore, with each dollar we give to the poor, to victims of poverty and disaster, we ask God to employ his sustaining power. Our charity is not the work we have to do because God would not do it, and God's deeds are not done to supplement our insufficient work. But with our charity, we bring the needs of the world to God in prayer, and God employs our hands to do his work.

Just as wages withheld by dishonest employers cry out to God, as Saint James writes (see above), so the works of charity come as a memorial to God. There is no conflict between work and prayer. Works of love are no basis for boasting, and prayer is no license for laziness. Our giving is actually an urgent prayer for God's giving, and God will remember it in his compassion and love. According to Jesus' words about the works of mercy in Matt 25, our good deeds done for the poor are done to him.

e. Washing of the Feet

Prayer and the offering of charitable gifts are connected in our traditional worship celebrations of the Eucharist. The offering is collected and brought to the altar, where the prayers of thanksgiving are said.

The Gospel of John connects the Eucharist with charity in a special way. At first sight, John's Gospel does not speak about Jesus' last meal. But the story about Jesus washing the feet of his disciples comes exactly at that point of the Gospel's narrative where we find in the other Gospels the story of Jesus celebrating his Last Supper.[4] In verse 4 we read (John 13) that Jesus: "[4] got up from the table, took off his outer robe, and tied a towel around

---

4. As is well known, the chronologies of the three Synoptic Gospels and the Gospel of John seem not to add up. The Synoptic Gospels present the Last Supper as a Passover meal (Matt 26:17; Mark 14:1-2; Luke 22:1-15). But the Gospel of John does not explicitly say that the Last Supper was a Passover meal. Rather, in the Gospel of John, John the Baptist calls Jesus the lamb of God (John 1:29), then remarks that not one of his bones was broken (John 19:31-34.36; cf. Exod 12:46 and Ps 34:20). This identifies Jesus with the Passover lamb; hence Jesus himself is the sacrificial Lamb of God. There have been various attempts to reconcile the chronologies, which is beyond the scope of this book. It is for us enough to understand that Jesus celebrated the Last Supper with his disciples, instituted the Eucharist, served and set an example for service, and was himself the sacrificial Passover Lamb, slain for our sins.

himself. ⁵ Then he poured water into a basin," etc. With this short remark about the getting up from the table (ἐκ τοῦ δείπνου), Saint John places the episode of the foot washing in the context of the Last Supper.

In paintings of the Middle Ages we find both scenes, the Last Supper and the foot washing, intertwined in the same picture: we see Jesus at table breaking the bread and Jesus washing his disciples' feet. Modern scholars agree with those painters of the Middle Ages: John presupposed that his readers knew the report of Jesus' Last Supper well already so that there was no need to tell this story again.⁵ The Evangelist John told the story of the foot washing to give another understanding of the Eucharist: Jesus gives himself as a servant to his disciples and thus sets an example for them. Therefore this pericope is a traditional reading on Maundy Thursday.

We must know that in antiquity this washing of feet was the work of slaves. It was a most humiliating work to wash the sweaty, dusty feet of their overlords. Jesus did this service for his disciples, and he told them to do the same for one another. Jesus wants to be a servant, and he served his disciples even to the point of giving his life for them.⁶ Jesus gave his life both as a sacrifice for sin and as a model for the godly life. We are his disciples, giving thanks for his loving sacrifice and learning from him to love and to serve. We celebrate both with the prayer of thanksgiving at the table and with charity for a world in need.

When we celebrate the Eucharist, we celebrate with prayer. We pray over the collected offering, we pray the intercessions for those in need, we pray the *Great Thanksgiving*, which is the very meaning of the word *Eucharist*. In all the biblical reports about Jesus' supper with his disciples, we read that they gave thanks to God (Mark 14:26; Matt 26:30; Luke 22:39; John 6:11,23; 1 Cor 11:24). Jesus has instituted the *Thanksgiving*, the *Eucharist*, on the eve of his death. On that Thursday night, he and his disciples celebrated, the day before he would sacrifice his life. At the table we give thanks for all that God through Jesus Christ in the Holy Spirit has done for us: our very creation, our redemption, and our sanctification.

---

5. Cf. Schlüter, "Selbstauslegung."

6. In the same Gospel of John, we read the famous line (John 3): "¹⁶ *for God so loved the world, that he gave his only begotten Son, that whosoever believeth in him should not perish, but have everlasting life.*" Jesus the Son of God is given because the heavenly Father loves the world.

f. Offering

Since the time of the early Church, the collection of goods for those in need was connected with the Eucharistic prayer over bread and wine, the *Great Thanksgiving*. The early Christian philosopher Justin, called the martyr, in a writing composed in about AD 150 (in Greek) writes:

"For all things wherewith we are supplied, we bless the Maker of all through His Son Jesus Christ, and through the Holy Ghost.... And they who are well to do, and willing, give what each thinks fit; and what is collected is deposited with the presider, who succours the orphans and widows and those who, through sickness or any other cause, are in want, and those who are in bonds and the strangers sojourning among us, and in a word takes care of all who are in need."[7]

When[8] the congregation gathered for worship, a member especially chosen for this task selected the most beautiful gifts, which then were designated for the Holy Meal of bread and wine and brought forward to the altar. The portion left over was then distributed to those in need, the widows and orphans of the congregation, or brought to prisoners. This was the task of the deacons.

It is safe to assume that the assembly understood how the portion of the gifts designated for the unfortunate relates to the portion of the gifts used for the Holy Meal: Christ present at the Holy Meal is also the hungry man to be fed when the congregation feeds the hungry; Christ present in the Holy Meal is also the naked man to be clothed when the congregation clothes the naked; Christ present in the Holy Meal is also the prisoner to be visited when the congregation visits those in jail, as the parable of the great judgment tells us in the Gospel according to Matt (25:3–45).

In the course of the centuries, for various reasons the meal was often omitted from Christian worship service. What remained of the Eucharist is the offering prayer and the prayers of intercession with the Lord's Prayer. Even though the connection between the offering and the Eucharist is no longer obvious, still every dollar on our offering plates contributes to revealing the presence of Christ, both in our thanksgiving to God and in our support for those in need.

The offering prayer and the great thanksgiving are connected, because those who are thankful for their lives will not keep pride, possession or position for themselves, but employ them happily to serve others. As we speak

---

7. From the *Apology* by Justin Martyr, chap. 67.
8. For the following thoughts, I thank Pastor Dr. Katharina Wiefel-Jenner.

about prayer and charity, we will not weigh our own welfare against the love for other people (2 Cor 9): "⁷ for God loves a cheerful giver."

g. Conclusion

We need prayer to remind ourselves of the work ahead of us. We still need to support the unfortunate, to cure the sick, and to comfort the mourning. We need prayer to keep us in communion with all who are in any need or distress, knowing that all who suffer stand together with us in the presence of the same heavenly Father. It is in prayer to God almighty, in prayer to the creator of heaven and earth, in prayer to the savior of the whole world that we understand reality, the reality that we are a portion of what God has created and wants to redeem and sanctify.

We need to pray so that we do not fall into despair when we realize how many of God's creatures are still in need. It would be arrogance if we believed that we could change the world alone, that we could fight to end all wars, hunger and disease. In prayer we remind ourselves of our limits. In all our efforts to help, we are heavy laden and need the rest only prayer can provide, surrendering ultimate responsibility to God.

With our prayers and our works of love, we actively participate in God's creative power. In prayer we adjust our souls to God's thoughts and merciful will for his creation. Our works, as self-centred or selfish they sometimes appear to be—or are even intended to be—are still always done within the framework of God's creation and providence. Willingly or not, we participate in God's work. Prayer is the way to call our attention to God's doing and to subordinate our work to God's work. In prayer we answer God's call and we report for duty. With our works of love we invoke God to support those in need.

2. PRAYER WITH FASTING

In the framework of the threefold discipline of charity, prayer and fasting according to Matt 6, prayer is done with fasting.

a. Nature

Fasting[9] does not necessarily express contempt for natural life but is a function of life itself. Often fasting happens involuntarily. In situations of stress,

9. For the following, cf. Josuttis, *Religion als Handwerk*.

the body refuses to sleep and to eat. Students preparing for examinations often have no appetite and no desire to sleep. With fasting, we are, for a period of time, in a state of heightened alertness and concentration. In those times, nature itself arranges a period of fasting. Fasting does not express somatophobia, i.e., hostility against the body, but actually employs natural processes of the body. Hence, fasting is a natural way to realize life's latent powers. Religious fasting employs potentials woven into the fabric of God's creation. Religious fasting is a method to cultivate this natural fasting.

b. Culture

All societies depend to a certain degree on abstinence and self-control. Personal integrity and honor depend on the ability to give up or at least to delay the fulfillment of personal wishes. The widespread misery of credit-card debt is a consequence of neglecting this rule. We need the ability to forgo the immediate satisfaction of our desires in order to live a decent life. Hence, fasting is a matter of personal integrity.

By prayer and fasting we cultivate our desires and hopes. In prayer we give words to our often confused and confusing wishes. By verbalizing our desires, we start coping with unfulfilled wishes. By articulating our needs and wants, we are able to put them in perspective. Having words for my desires, I can relate them to my self, both to my sinful self that I humbly submit to our merciful judge, and to the self that I am called to become. Once we have expressed our wishes in words, we can put them in the context of the whole of our life and in the context of the world in which we live; in prayer we can relate our wishes to the needs of other people. Thus, prayer helps us gain a better sense of reality. Prayer enables us to put our wishes in context, which again enables us to postpone, to limit or to give up the fulfillment of our wishes for a while, or for good. And this is the very meaning of fasting.

Our Western civilization has a specific culture of hope,[10] in which we do not just give in to the lures of the world around us or to the impulses of our own heart. On the other hand, we do not just kill our wishes and desires to become people without hope and future. But in our civilization, we have a culture of controlled wishing and hoping. This culture of hope has been shaped by a tradition of fasting and prayer. When praying, we do not give up our hopes, and yet we control our wishes so that we will not fall into despair. We look for a future and we are still realistic. The culture of prayer and fasting is a culture of controlled wishes. We are not driven by our animal instincts without a sense of context and perspective; we still sustain

10. For the following, see Barth, *Wohin—woher mein Ruf?*

hope and will to design a better future. Maintaining a culture of prayer and fasting means nothing less than maintaining Western civilization.

c. Repentance and Humility

In the Bible, repentance is done with fasting. David, after adultery and murder, repented with fasting to save the child of his adultery, though unsuccessfully (2 Sam 12:16). When Jonah preached to the people in the city of Nineveh, they repented with fasting (Jonah 3): "⁴ Jonah began to go into the city, going a day's walk. And he cried out, 'Forty days more, and Nineveh shall be overthrown!' ⁵ And the people of Nineveh believed God; they proclaimed a fast, and everyone, great and small, put on sackcloth."

Leaders in the Bible repented with fasting and prayer not only for their personal sins but also for their nation. Nehemiah, when he heard about the poor situation of those who had returned from captivity in Babylon to Jerusalem (Neh 1), "⁴ mourned for days, fasting and praying before the God of heaven." The prophet Daniel (Dan 1:4) and his friends, when they were provided by the Babylonian king with defiling food, would fast to demonstrate their independence. But later, in the first year of Darius, when the course of history was about to change, Daniel interceded for his people. He said (Dan 9): "³ Then I turned to the Lord God, to seek an answer by prayer and supplication with fasting and sackcloth and ashes. ⁴ I prayed to the LORD my God and made confession, saying, 'Ah, Lord, great and awesome God, keeping covenant and steadfast love with those who love you and keep your commandments, ⁵ we have sinned and done wrong, acted wickedly and rebelled, turning aside from your commandments and ordinances.'"

The Bible testifies to prayers of repentance combined with fasting, and the Bible testifies to both individual repentance and prayers in community.

d. Sacrifice and Commitment

If we do not understand our prayers as a tool to adjust God's plans to our wishes, we pray to correspond with the plan and order God the Father has given his creation. God has revealed his gracious will in Jesus Christ, who is among us, obedient to God and loving God, loving us and suffering together with us and for us. We are called to follow Jesus Christ, and by fasting and prayer we commit ourselves to follow him.

Whether God actually fulfills our wants and wishes or imposes suffering and challenge, by fasting we sacrifice the desires of the body and commit ourselves to God. With both the acceptance of hardship imposed by God and the voluntary spiritual exercise of fasting, we learn obedience to God. In prayer we surrender our life to Christ's leadership and protection and commit our life to praise God's glory and goodness.

Jesus calls us (Mark 8:34): "If any want to become my followers, let them deny themselves and take up their cross and follow me." Saint Paul writes (Gal 5): "[24] those who belong to Christ Jesus have crucified the flesh with its passions and desires." In our fasting, we follow Jesus' example and seek to join him on his way of the cross. In the forty days of Lent, especially, we remember Jesus' passion. With the threefold discipline of fasting, prayer and charity, we meditate on Jesus' love for the world, his fasting and suffering, and his intercession for the world. In fasting we seek to join Christ on his way of the cross with our thoughts and emotions and with our body. After having contemplated Jesus' passion with the exercises of both body and soul, we then celebrate that Jesus was raised for our justification (Rom 4:25).

For this Christian way of life we have beautiful promises (Rom 8): "[35] Who will separate us from the love of Christ? Will hardship, or distress, or persecution, or famine, or nakedness, or peril, or sword? [36] As it is written, 'For your sake we are being killed all day long; we are accounted as sheep to be slaughtered.' [37] No, in all these things we are more than conquerors through him who loved us."

e. Meeting the Holy One

In order to approach the majesty of God, we need to walk the way he has paved for us. He allows us to draw near to him, who is holy, almighty and righteous. According to Matthew's testimony, Jesus has given, together with the encouragement to pray, a warning (Matt 7): "[6] Do not give what is holy to dogs; and do not throw your pearls before swine, or they will trample them under foot and turn and maul you. [7] Ask, and it will be given you; search, and you will find; knock, and the door will be opened for you. [8] For everyone who asks receives, and everyone who searches finds, and for everyone who knocks, the door will be opened."

In the second portion of the quoted paragraph, Jesus encourages us to pray with three words: *ask, search,* and *knock.* Those verbs describe prayer as a quest that requires some effort, but all three verbs also indicate that the outcome is not measured by our efforts: more knocking will not gain more opening, etc.

We may draw near to the one who is holy and awesome. In whatever way we want to understand the warning of the first portion—*do not give to the dogs,* etc.—it is certain that in Matthew's Gospel the encouragement to prayer follows some kind of a rule for holiness. *That which is holy* must be kept from the profane.

Many scholars understand the *dogs* and the *swine* as people not belonging to the community of faith (non–Jews, apostates, heretics, pagans?) In prayer, however, we should perhaps not be too concerned with the alleged unholiness of other people. So what does this rule of holiness mean for us? It is certainly not so, that to see our prayers answered we need to be sufficiently holy or righteous (see Jas 5:16). If that were so, we could probably never hope for any answer to any prayer. After all, prayer means to submit to the almighty and righteous God. Still, if we want to approach the Holy One, the mentioned rule requires separation of what is holy from what is profane. Biblical guidance suggests to prepare: to set apart some space and time and get the body ready by fasting. Biblical examples of this are plentiful. In Exod 19, we read how God gave Moses rules for the people to prepare for the terrifying and indeed dangerous Epiphany of God's majesty: "[10] the LORD said to Moses: "Go to the people and consecrate them today and tomorrow. Have them wash their clothes [11] and prepare for the third day, because on the third day the LORD will come down upon Mount Sinai in the sight of all the people. . . . [15] And he said to the people, 'Prepare for the third day; do not go near a woman.' [16] On the morning of the third day, there was thunder and lightning, as well as a thick cloud on the mountain, and a blast of a trumpet so loud that all the people who were in the camp trembled."

Before God would reveal his terrifying glory, respectively before a man entered the holy place, even sexual abstinence was expected. In Exod 34, we read about Moses on Mount Sinai (Exod 34): "[28] He was there with the LORD forty days and forty nights; he neither ate bread nor drank water. And he wrote on the tablets the words of the covenant, the ten commandments." In the presence of God, Moses did not receive profane food but God's word. Moses' mountain tour and fasting show that we encounter God with our mind, soul, and also our body.

In the New Testament, Jesus himself leads us to meet God. God's Son took on human form, and as a human being of body, soul, and spirit he prayed and fasted. Thus Jesus leads us to meet his heavenly Father. It is true as well that in Jesus Christ God himself comes to us, to lead us to himself. Jesus Christ, his body and his blood, connects us with the Holy One (Col 2): "[9] For in him [Christ] the whole fullness of deity dwells bodily ($\sigma\omega\mu\alpha\tau\iota\kappa\tilde{\omega}\varsigma$)." The presence of the Holy One in the sacrament is healing and hallowing and wants us to be purged from profane burdens.

f. Discovering the Forces of Life

Meeting the divinity is a break from daily routine and its usual activities and its usual food. Through fasting in its basic, literal sense, we change the way we handle our own bodies. Fasting, we learn that (Matt 4): "⁴ Man shall not live by bread alone, but by every word that proceedeth out of the mouth of God." Fasting is a method that prepares the capacities of the body to interact with the divine.

We do not fast in order to weaken our vital force, which is a common misunderstanding, but on the contrary fasting opens us for life's latent powers.[11] Purging the body through fasting allows the influx of divine vital force. Through fasting the body is being cleansed from burdening stuff so that it can be filled with new power. By *fasting* we make room for the divine to come. With fasting we quite literally feel in our body the hunger for the divine. Through fasting, we empty our bodies and souls of the profane, and thus we can experience that God will enter not only our thoughts and emotions, but also our body. Fasting makes room for God's provision.

In the history of the Church, fasting before the Eucharist used to be common. The reason was not hostility towards food and body, but rather the alternative of the sacred meal over profane food. Receiving new food presupposes being empty of the old food. Christians who fast before receiving Holy Communion want to be literally an empty vessel ready to receive divine nutrition. Religious fasting is a conversion from eating profane food to receiving heavenly power. In the worship service, this change from profane eating to eating the bread from heaven is symbolized by the change of location. One leaves the space of the daily life and enters a sacred space to walk up to the altar. With the conversion from the profane to the Holy One, we then can return to our daily life as renewed people.

The practice of fasting follows the logic of breathing: breathing in is not possible without breathing out. According to the same rationale—the difference between the sacred and the profane, the old and the new—converts give up their previous life and hope to receive new life from God. By the same logic, receiving forgiveness presupposes the confession of sin. Before you go to the altar, you are required to reconcile with your neighbor (Matt 5:23), because the divine is not compatible with profane quarrels. According to Eph 5:18, wine and spirits are not compatible with the divine spirit. In Acts 14:19–23, we read that in the early church people prepared themselves with fasting and prayer to receive a blessing and the commission to ministry with the laying-on of hands.

---

11. Many of the following ideas I owe to Josuttis, *Religion als Handwerk*.

g. Regular Exercise

The biblical stories mentioned above often speak about fasting and prayer practiced on particular occasions, especially in the need of repentance. But fasting and prayer is also a regular exercise without particular cause. This exercise is again something that people do in community. According to an early Christian writing,[12] Christians would fast on Wednesdays and Fridays. Fasting used to be common during Lent, on Fridays, in the hours before the Eucharist. On Fridays, the day when on the cross Jesus' flesh was sacrificed, Christians would abstain from eating meat.

Fasting changes the way in which we handle ourselves, our time and our possessions. For a period of time, we give up certain things and thus we have the means to give. With our regular offerings in church, we return to God a little portion of all the good things the Creator has given us, and thus dedicate our whole life to God.

Saint Paul gives advice to married couples about temporary abstinence. Obviously the idea of fasting and even abstinence within marriage was so strong that Saint Paul needed to set a limit and recommended fasting and prayer for only a limited time of consent. He writes (1 Cor 7): "[5] Do not deprive one another except with consent for a time, that you may give yourselves to fasting and prayer; and come together again so that Satan does not tempt you because of your lack of self-control."

h. Coping with Disappointed Prayers

Fasting is a practical way to deal with disappointed prayers. In prayer the psalmist reminds himself of God's promise (Ps 50): "[15] Call on me in the day of trouble; I will deliver you, and you shall glorify me." However, we all have experienced that our prayers were not answered in the way we had expected, and our hopes can be disappointed.[13] We still cannot but acknowledge that many people who are forced to give up their hopes cling even more faithfully and trustingly to God's love and power. More than the fulfillment of our wishes, the surrender of our hopes and desires to God's plans brings us closer to God. The fact that we have answered to God's permission and command to invoke him has involved us in God's plans. Self-conquest and the sacrifice of time and attention make prayer meaningful even without the satisfaction of our desires.

---

12. Didache, chap. 8.

13. What this means in regard to our concept of God was discussed earlier: II God and prayer 3.3.

Prayer with fasting means to take control of our wishes. Giving up the wishes we bring before God can intensify our relationship with God. Fasting is a practical way to control our desires. We are not simply victimized by loss and disappointment, but rather give up things with intent and purpose. Prayer with fasting is about controlling and cultivating our hopes and wishes.

God has called us to call upon him with wonderful promises and encouragement. Jesus gives a promise for prayer in John 14: "[13] I will do whatever you ask in my name, so that the Father may be glorified in the Son." This is not a promise that every wish will come true. But Jesus speaks about prayers in his name, meaning consistent with a life as followers of Jesus, the suffering Lord (see above Part 2, I.3c and Part 2, I.4a).

Saint Peter encourages us (1 Pet 5): "[7] Cast all your anxiety (πάσαν τὴν μέριμναν) on him, because he cares for you." Saint Peter writes about *all* anxieties. Hence it is quite obvious that trust in God's care is not just a hope for the fulfillment of particular wishes. But we are promised that God cares for us always and in his way. Accordingly, Christian trust in God can endure that particular wishes are denied. With fasting and praying we adapt to God's ways.

Saint James encourages us (Jas 5): "[16] The prayer of the righteous is powerful and effective." It is indeed a great promise for the righteous.[14] We can, however, never call ourselves righteous based on our factual existence and conduct. But the context shows that Saint James is speaking about prayer, not about our own life but about intercession for one another, and in this context he speaks about confession and forgiveness. Walking the way of repentance, with fasting—abstaining from luxury and pleasure (Jas 5:5)—and prayer, with the confession of sins and the promise to be obedient again, we will be righteous. When we follow the way Jesus leads us, we can hope indeed that our prayers are powerful and effective. As we pray with fasting, we turn to God, giving up selfishness and comfort, our laziness and self-pity, and seek our God's love and glory alone.

i. Saint Anna's prayer and fasting

The Evangelist Luke tells the story of Saint Anna (Luke 2:37), "a widow to the age of eighty-four. She never left the temple but worshiped there with fasting and prayer night and day."

The latter phrase most certainly means that she participated in the regular prayer services at the traditional hours in the house of prayer. Together

---

14. We have discussed Jas 5 already in the context of prayer and charity: V.I.1.c.

with Simeon, she received Jesus when he was brought by his parents to the temple. We read in Luke's Gospel (Luke 2): "²⁷ Guided by the Spirit, Simeon came into the temple; and when the parents brought in the child Jesus, to do for him what was customary under the law, . . . ³⁶ There was also a prophet, Anna the daughter of Phanuel, of the tribe of Asher. She was of a great age, having lived with her husband seven years after her marriage, ³⁷ then as a widow to the age of eighty-four. She never left the temple but worshiped there with fasting and prayer night and day. ³⁸ At that moment she came, and began to praise God and to speak about the child to all who were looking for the redemption of Jerusalem."

The meaning of the term *to worship* (λατρεύω) is *to serve* or *to render homage*; so it is in Luke 1:74 (the *Benedictus*), or in the double commandment of love in Luke 4:8; in other parts of the New Testament, the meaning is *to offer sacrifices* (Heb 8:5 and 9:9). Here in Luke 2, the term *worship* is explained as *fasting and prayer*. After a long period of fasting and prayer, Anna received Jesus in God's house and was empowered to prophesy about Jesus.

Anna is actually the best-known character of early Christianity. About no other person in the New Testament do we know nearly as many biographical details. The name Anna is a Hebrew name: *Hanna* in the Old Testament. The meaning of this name is *Grace*. Hence her name reminds us of God's grace. Anna is what she is by the grace of God, a prophet, gifted with the Holy Spirit. She would receive Jesus, the Son of God, in the house of God after fasting and prayer.

Saint Luke writes: "She never left the temple but worshipped there with fasting and prayer night and day." Anna is presented by the Evangelist as a role model of religious life. Anna represents the ascetic ideal of dedicating one's life to God and receiving Jesus.

Prayer, fasting and charity are the cornerstones of a pious life in the Bible. A poor widow, Anna was probably not able to give any alms but was herself dependent on the goodwill of her relatives. But fasting and prayer was still her way of a religious life. She prayed in the temple, the house of prayer, the public place for the worship of God's people. We see her in the Temple, together with Simeon, and eventually she receives Jesus, the Christ. All she had waited for all of her life was now fulfilled.

This fulfillment was also a new beginning. Anna and Simeon gave their witness to the newborn Messiah. Anna had been waiting for the salvation at the end of the age. Now, "³⁸ at that moment she came, and began to praise God and to speak about the child to all who were looking for the redemption of Jerusalem." Anna praised God, and her chant of praise was heard. The Bible does not tell us about any personal wish expressed in prayer. On the contrary, Anna served God with fasting, meaning with denying her personal desires. Thus she is a role model for prayer, and thus she received Jesus. With the little child, Anna and Simeon held the future of God's people in their arms. Their life received its crown. They glorified God, because the hope for the redemption of Jerusalem, the hope of God's people, was fulfilled.

Simeon prays: "a light for revelation to the Gentiles and for glory to your people Israel." Simeon and Anna saw the salvation of Jerusalem, and they saw the salvation of all peoples. Simeon and Anna, who had served the one God and creator of the world, now saw the Messiah, the Christ, sent by their God for the salvation of all nations, all peoples of the world. Thus they gave glory to God in the highest and could depart in peace. Fasting, prayers of intercession, and receiving Jesus at the altar of God opens the future for the whole world.

3. CHARITY WITH FASTING

As we have seen, prayer can be understood from its relationship to fasting and to charity. Here are some additional thoughts about the relationship between fasting and charity.

That fasting and charity belong together is quite obvious. When we fast, we have things to spare for charity. I remember that a pastor in my hometown once suggested that for the season of Lent the parishioners should consider what amount of money they usually spend on candy, cigarettes, alcohol, eating out and movies; the same amount of money they should donate for charity. The congregation readily agreed. But after the first week, they were quite disturbed. Only then did they realize how much they spent on unnecessary—and unhealthy—pleasures, and how out of proportion their spending was with their charity.

When the Lord in the Sermon on the Mount speaks about prayer, fasting and charity, the command not to show off ties the three exercises together. When Christians fast in Lent, they follow Jesus Christ, who himself fasted and prayed. They understand fasting as an imitation of Christ and as a bodily exercise of freedom, obedience, and humility.

a. Freedom

Fasting is an exercise for special times. Of course, God expects self-control always, he wants us to pray always, and he has sent us to serve our neighbors all the days of our life. But special times set apart for God, Lent for example, are an opportunity to rethink our life.

During Lent, Christians consider what they can give up, and in this season they may consider what good they can do for their neighbors with those things they usually keep for themselves.

With fasting, with giving up pleasures, we experience how dependent we have made ourselves on unnecessary things; thus, fasting is an exercise of freedom. We often quite thoughtlessly speak about our possessions, but in reality we are often possessed by what we believe we possess. Do we really possess our TV set, or are we possessed by watching TV? It is not a coincidence that we read in the New Testament so much about people who are possessed by demons. We are actually not as free as we pretend to be. We are subdued by a lot of things, obsessed especially with things which we presume we are in control of. According to an old manuscript of the New Testament, Jesus casts out a foul spirit and then teaches his disciples that this kind of spirit can come out only through prayer and fasting (Mark 9:29).

By fasting, we may learn that we live by God's word and love. When we fast, we realize what freedom is: obedience to God. This means that we rule again over those things that have come to rule over us. Hence fasting is an exercise of freedom for our daily life. Fasting is an exercise of being free from our possessions, in the double meaning of the word: possessing and being possessed.

In the twelfth chapter of the Gospel of Luke, Jesus warns against greed (Luke 12:13-15), teaches the parable about the rich fool (Luke 12:16-21), then counsels against worries about food and drink (12:22-31), then speaks about fasting and charity (12:33). The sequence of these paragraphs proceeds from giving up avarice, to exposing the foolishness of riches, to renouncing legitimate desires, and finally even to denying basic needs. Some of the sayings in this chapter are written in poetic form (parallelism), which emphasizes that these sayings are universally valid rules for life. The rationale of this advice is: God is aware of our needs and we are supposed to seek the kingdom of God (12:30-31). The self-centredness of our anxiety is not necessary, and we may trust the heavenly Father that our worries about ourselves are taken care of so that we are free to work for the kingdom. *The little flock*, as Jesus calls us, shall not be afraid. The expression *little flock* alludes to Isa 41: "[14] Jacob smallest of Israel, I will help you." Jesus wants us not to worry because we need not worry. We are those to whom the kingdom of God is entrusted by the heavenly Father; we have a commission, and God will make sure that we are able to fulfill our task. The exercise of fasting is based on our trust in God, the creator who keeps caring for us. After the exhortations against greed and worry, the Gospel of Luke continues with Jesus encouraging us (Luke 12): "[33] Sell your possessions, and give alms. Make purses for yourselves that do not wear out, an unfailing treasure in heaven, where no thief comes near and no moth destroys. ³⁴ For where your treasure is, there your heart will be also." This counsel of Jesus contrasts possessions on earth with treasures in heaven. The goal is not necessarily to be poor, but the goal is to give to the poor. Religious exercise—fasting, prayer and charity—must never lose sight of those in need. Still, the same Evangelist Saint Luke who testifies to these sayings of Jesus also depicts the life of the early Christian community as a bucolic idyll (Act 5:1–10). The simple life of the shepherds in the field that we find depicted in Luke's Christmas story was indeed the longing and nostalgia of many of his contemporaries.[15] The main reason, however, for selling one's possessions is the prospect of a life beyond this world, the treasures in heaven. In sum, Jesus, in Saint Luke's Gospel, talks first about responsibility for the unfortunate, second about a lifestyle of simplicity, and third about the prospective new life in heaven.

The Bible encourages the practice of fasting, charity, and prayer. But the Bible also cautions us: Both fasting and prayer are religious practices that can be grossly self-centered. The Old Testament prophets were very much aware of the possibility that religious practice can be used to cover up lack of charitableness. In the third part of the book of Isaiah, the prophet quotes from the prayers of the people (Isa 58): "³ Why do we fast, but you do not see? Why humble ourselves, but you do not notice?" The people did pray and were obviously committed to fasting, but they were disappointed because the rewards for their religious efforts did not meet their expectations. The prophet responds to their complaints: "Look, you serve your own interest on your fast day, and oppress all your workers." Those who observed the fast day had, by their disregard for their dependent laborers, by their disrespect for the unfortunate, by their ulterior motives, revealed that their religious activities were in fact selfish. The prophet, however, does not demand abolishing religious fasting and prayer; neither does he demand replacing fasting and prayer by activities to promote social justice. The issue of this passage is not the alternative of either spiritual exercise and prayer on the one hand or on the other, commitment to the unfortunate and work for peace and justice. The prophecy aims at reforming the attitude of the fasting people. Their fasting and prayer is self-centered; they use fasting and prayer as a means to an end and thus try to use God as a tool to improve their own lives. They do not realize that their religious practice is inconsistent with their lack of social responsibility. Real fasting would liberate their attitude to themselves and to their unfortunate fellow citizens. They need a change of

---

15. See, for example, the *Eclogues* by the Latin poet Virgil, poems about the simple life of the shepherds.

heart and begin to focus on God and to care for those within their responsibility and thus for all in need.

b. Love

Whenever Christians fast, they give up things and do so for the sake of their neighbors. If we want to take responsibility for our neighbors, our works of charity have to make a real difference. Charity must not be merely a symbolic gesture, but has to aim at effectively supporting those in need. Success is, however, not the only standard. Telling the story of the two copper coins offered by a poor widow, Jesus says (Mark 12): "^{44}For all [the others] have contributed out of their abundance; but she out of her poverty has put in everything she had, all she had to live on." Public religion was not so different then from public religion today. Religion was established, and pious men able to say long and fine prayers and show their faith in public were as popular as nowadays pious men on television are admired. In contrast, Jesus reminds us of that poor widow. There are still such poor, seemingly unimportant people who do not attract much attention, who are not every day in the newspapers or on TV, who are not a target group for commercials. This poor widow is a heroine of faith who doesn't worry about even her last pennies, but offers her sacrifice in the temple. Sacrifice is the work of a priest, and in a sense the widow becomes a fellow priest with Jesus, the high priest (Heb 4) of the New Covenant. Jesus Christ, the high priest in the temple of God his Father, sees and knows who truly are the priests bringing their sacrifice to God.

The exercise of charity points out that Christians fast and pray as members of a community. King David prayed personally, but he did not forget that he prayed to the God of Israel, meaning of God's people (2 Sam 7): "^{27}For thou, O LORD of hosts, God of Israel, hast revealed to thy servant, saying, I will build thee a house...." The prophet Daniel said even a prayer of repentance on behalf of the people (Dan 9, see above part 3, VI.c). Psalms of lament are prayed on behalf of Israel to the shepherd of all Israel, for example in Ps 80. In Ps 102, the supplication of an individual (cf. Verse 1: "Hear my prayer, O LORD, and let my cry come unto thee...") is placed on the horizon of Zion, the city of God (verse 13: "Thou shalt arise, and have mercy upon Zion..."), on the horizon of future generations (verse 18: "This shall be written for the generation to come: and the people which shall be created shall praise the LORD..."), and finally on the horizon of the whole of creation (verse 25: "Of old hast thou laid the foundation of the earth: and the heavens are the work of thy hands.")

Christians pray as members of a community. We find actually very little confirmation in the New Testament for the theory that Christians primarily pray for themselves and for their own. The epistle to Timothy exhorts us *first of all* (!) to intercessions for all men and for the government (1 Tim 2): "¹ I exhort therefore, that, first of all, supplications, prayers, intercessions, and giving of thanks, be made for all men; For kings, and for all that are in authority". (For a more detailed discussion of this passage, see part 3.V). In Saint Luke's description of the early church, he puts prayer in the context of the faith community (κοινωνία) and of the breaking of bread (Acts 2:42). The Lord's Prayer starts with the words: *Our Father*—not *my* but *our*. The very prayer that Jesus Christ himself taught us incorporates us into a community. We pray to God (Ps 146), "⁶ the Maker of heaven and earth, the sea, and everything in them—the LORD, who remains faithful forever." Thus we pray as those who are but a portion of God's creation (Saint Augustine).

Prayer does not isolate the faithful from others; it binds them together with others in love. For this reason, Jesus himself warns us not to turn prayer into a substitute for social responsibility, when he speaks about those who (Mark 12) "⁴⁰ devour widows' houses, and for a pretense make long prayers: these shall receive greater damnation." Only those who in prayer focus on themselves, like the Pharisee in Luke 18:10–14, can feel superior to others. In prayer, Christians acknowledge the majesty and infinite superiority of God. Christians acknowledge the infinite difference between the almighty creator and his handiwork, and therefore in God's presence all differences among his creatures turn out to be very small. As creatures among other creatures, when confronted with the majesty of God, we are equals.

Ps 150, the end and goal of the Psalter, calls us to praise God in the sanctuary and in heaven and calls all living creatures to praise the Lord.

c. Giving and Forgiving

Fasting with charity means to give up things and to give, to give in and to forgive. Fasting may mean to give up gracefully what is taken from us, to forgive and intercede for others.

When I participated in a trip of our seminary class to South Africa in the 1990s, I had the opportunity to visit the German church in Johannesburg and to stroll through its neighborhood. Hillbrow used to be the cosmopolitan center of South African nightlife and entertainment. Within a few years, it had changed completely. It had become a slum with rundown buildings. The population had changed to predominantly black African, with a large Francophone contingent from the former Zaire and beyond.

I had company on this stroll, but even though we were careful, I was attacked in broad daylight. Someone choked me from behind and when I regained consciousness, my money was gone. I had been prudent enough to carry only some pocket money on me and only a photocopy of my passport, so I would not have major problems. Still, the shock was severe and my throat ached for days.

Worse than that was that I started to look at black Africans suspiciously, and all the statistics and horror stories that well-meaning people had told me were certainly not helpful to correct my corrupted attitude. Worst of all was a prayer in which someone included me. It was just about giving thanks that nothing worse had happened, about my quick recovery from pain, and that our trip would continue safely. I listened, and I thought to myself about the situation of Hillbrow, about those who remained without education, job, or decent housing.

A few days prior to this assault, we had participated in an activity of a soup kitchen, distributing food to the squatter camps around the central railroad station. An icy wind had blown through our far too thin clothes; when we had packed for the trip, we had thought we would be in Africa, after all. We helped to distribute leftovers provided by the hotels of the rich. At the central railroad station, people wrapped themselves in newspapers and literally lived in cardboard boxes illuminated by the red light of a huge, obscenely glittering neon sign advertising real estate insurance.

Those were the images still on my mind when we sat down for prayer, after some poor guys had robbed me of a few dollars. The few stolen dollars did not hurt me too much, but for the attackers it was a fortune. It was a day of conversion for me. When I pray, I must never forget in which context I am to pray: namely as a member of a rich white society that protects its wealth, has the power to make the laws and to define crime. Whenever I come across the Psalms of lament or the Psalms against enemies, I know that these are the prayers of the only righteous one, of the poor, and of my enemies. Praying those Psalms, I will, whether I am aware of it or not, pray the prayers of the unfortunate, including my poor robbers.

Having returned home, I am forgotten and invisible to them, and they are invisible to me. The creed's assertion that God made both the visible and the invisible world has taken on an additional, haunting meaning for me. As we pray, we cannot pray isolated from the world God has made and humanity has ruined. We are a portion of God's creation, visible to us or not. Our petitions must not omit all the others who remain beyond our immediate experience and who pray to the same God for help. Our thanksgiving must not forget that other people want to give thanks as well. When we give thanks, we must not forget from whom we withhold that for which they want to give thanks. In prayer, we must not forget that those who hurt us and those whom we hurt pray to the same God.

PART 4

A Call to Common Prayer

AFTER ALL THESE CONSIDERATIONS about prayer, the question remains to be answered: who shall pray, where, and when?

Prayers are commonly said on Sundays in the assembly of the church, in prayer meetings, and by many people individually at home. On Sundays, the prayers of the church are said: biblical prayers, liturgical prayers and the prayers of intercession. In many congregations, individual members are given opportunity to contribute their petitions; in some churches the prayers of intercession are regularly said by lay people. The worship service on Sunday is the core of Christian life, and yet many people have the desire to do more. The hymnals of many church bodies provide forms for daily prayer for groups and individuals

It can be a great help for the congregation if a group of members commit themselves to daily prayer. Twelve faithful and committed men and women who make this commitment to regular prayer, praying the Psalms, the prayers found in the Old and New Testament, and intercessions for the congregation and for the needs of all, a group of people who promise to partake in Holy Communion and to give thanks as often as possible will make a difference in any congregation of any denomination. Twelve men and women who take upon themselves the responsibility of daily prayer in the morning, in the evening and in the night can revive the church and the whole world. There are, however, some obstacles in our hearts that need to be addressed.

CHALLENGES: WORK AND LEISURE, WORK AND CONSUMERISM

In our society, life is somehow divided into work and leisure time. Since our specific religious activities, such as prayer, do not take place during our work hours —with the exception perhaps of a few spontaneous arrow prayers—we tend to view religious life as a form of leisure, a luxury that we allow ourselves when our duties in this world, work and family, are fulfilled. As a consequence, our spiritual life competes with other opportunities of spending our leisure time and might not be first on our priority list.

Moreover we perhaps unconsciously or even consciously think in terms of economic base and religious superstructure: Religion seems to be an addition to what we call *real life* or *daily life*, an addition in the sense of a stimulant or as *opium of the people*. Many people accordingly demand that religion needs to be relevant and useful for this *real life*.

But this way of thinking profoundly misunderstands reality. The basic reality is that this temporal world is made through God's eternal word. God, the creator, was in the beginning of this world and of each individual life, and he will put an end to this life, which therefore is just a transitory phase. Christ says (Rev 22:13): "I am Alpha and Omega, the beginning and the end, the first and the last." If we take seriously that our life on earth comes from God and will be ended by God, we cannot but make God our life's first priority and the ultimate goal of our life.

If we realize that God gives our daily bread and the air we breathe, actually creates our breathing itself, then petition and thanksgiving will be our priority. If we take seriously that our lives will be judged by God, we cannot judge religion by its relevance for our daily life, which is after all not *our* life but God's. It is God's to give and to take (Job 1:21). If we realize that what we call *our life* is not really our life but a loan, that one day we have to hand back to God, we will not ask whether God is relevant. The challenge is not whether God is relevant for our life, but if our life is relevant for God and for life eternal. Saint Paul writes: "yet not I, but Christ liveth in me." God is not just an addition to life or some nice company on our way. We are called to follow Jesus on *his* way (Matt 16:24).

An old spiritual goes, "I want Jesus to walk with me." The song speaks about life's pilgrimage in trials and sorrows. It might have done a lot of good in the original context of slavery, giving dignity and hope amid an existence of pain and exploitation. But can I, a relatively well-to-do white male, more than a hundred years later, appropriate this song[1] for my own purposes?

---

1. For all I know, the origin of the song is still undetermined. But however it is, this cultural appropriation possibly inflates our sense of self-importance and tends to justify self-pity.

Should we expect Jesus to walk with us on our dubious ways? Or aren't we rather called to follow Jesus as he calls us to walk with him, who is the "way, the truth and the life" (John 14:16)?

*

An additional problem is that the work–leisure dichotomy often coincides with the division of productive work and consumption. With hard work, we seem to earn the right to consume.

If this thinking in terms of work and consumption supersedes the distinction between works and faith, church turns into a consumer good, a commodity, or even an expendable luxury. In church we want to consume, e.g., sermons or music. Misunderstood, *grace* seems to confirm this concept of the religious life as an opportunity to consume and to have fun.

Consumerism is certainly a problem in all areas of life. We "go to the pictures" but we no longer paint, carve, or draw. Most people no longer write, not even a journal. When I was a student, many students, especially the girls, had autograph books and would ask friends and relatives to write some lines for them. Some copied a favorite poem or the lyrics of a favorite song, many tried to compose some original lines, and a few actually wrote poems. Nowadays you can no longer even buy those books. Many gadgets allow us to listen to music of any kind, any time, anywhere, but the custom of singing or playing an instrument is on the decline; choirs often have a hard time recruiting male voices. Many people love to eat out but rarely cook. Most people fail to exercise, but the absurdity of watching sports on TV is big business. We watch talk shows and sitcoms on TV, but many families do not even have a dinner table around which they can entertain and enjoy conversation. The culture of doing things ourselves is almost lost. We have given up on caring for our souls even in this life.

Accordingly, worship is too often viewed as something to consume as entertainment by preachers and professional musicians. If our concept of worship is narrowed down to the *proclamation of the word*, worship can easily be misunderstood as entertainment that needs to sell, needs to be more attractive, needs to be tailored to the demand of the consumer. Endless disputes about worship style are based on this underlying concept.

It is true that most people in our congregations need not accept any reproach for being lazy. A wealth of activities takes place in our churches. We donate time and work for our church; we serve on committees and write postcards; we engage in many kinds of fundraising activities, we do car washes, plant-, bake- and rummage sales, we take care of the building and the parking lot, we fold bulletins and recycle the paper. Indeed, we have a lot of busy and committed people in church whose work is unreservedly commendable.

But the logic of production and consumption puts enormous pressure on our congregations, because work needs to be gratifying and to pay; consumer goods need to be in demand, and, well, cheap. So congregations permanently feel the need to prove to all actual or potential workers in church and to all consumers of the church's ministries that they will get something out of it. The burnout of the most dedicated members of our churches stands in stark contrast to the message of grace versus the demand of good works.

And yet, despite all their hard work, many Christians live in spiritual poverty. The reason is that we shy away from taking responsibility for our spiritual life. Spiritual life is often viewed as a part of the consumer's life. We listen to a preacher or to the radio, listen to church music, perhaps listen to the liturgy or enjoy some easy reading. In our congregations we find, paradoxically, both a lot of activity and yet the desire to be entertained by the pastor or other professionals.

But we need to recognize, first, that spiritual life does not fit the labor–leisure model. Prayer for the sustenance of our life, for health and career, for the health and welfare of neighbors, for the sustenance of the planet, for good government, justice and peace, prayers for God's mercy in this life and the life to come—those prayers can hardly be called leisure activities.

Secondly, spiritual life does not fit the logic of production and consumption. Prayer and sacrifice, celebration and confession, meditation and adoration will fit neither in the category of work nor of consumption. Fasting and sacrifice are actually the exact opposite of consumption. The *word* needs to be meditated, *liturgy* is a contribution to the common good, and therefore worship needs to be prayed, not consumed.

Moreover the logic of workdays and weekend, of earning and shopping, is hardly consistent with the images of the church in the New Testament.

PRAYER OF THE CHURCH

It is far beyond the scope of this conclusion to develop a teaching about the Church, and the amount of tradition is quite overwhelming. But some hints might be helpful to determine what role prayer plays in the life of a Christian community.

In the New Testament, the Church is described by various complementary images. The word for *church* in the original Greek of the New Testament is *ekklesia* (cf. French *église*, Spanish *iglesia*), and the literal meaning of the underlying verb is: *to call out of*. The word described the meeting of those who are called out of their private homes to the meeting place, the decision-making assembly of all free citizens, in a city state. This term *ekklesia* is employed by the Greek translation of the Old Testament as the word for *the people of God* (הָעָם). Consistent with this origin of *ekklesia* is 1 Pet 2: "⁹But you are a chosen race, a royal priesthood, a holy nation, God's own people." Both contexts of the word *ekklesia*, the Old Testament nation and the Greek city state, suggest that the assembly is not so much a freewill association of individuals, but a body in which the individual members participate and which existed long before they were joined to it, often originating from some ancient, mythical, perhaps fictional forefather. The Greek city or the Jewish nation would by far outlast the life of any individual member. According to both backgrounds of the word, *ekklesia* is mainly a public affair, something that calls people to step out of their private life and to take on public responsibility. The Church is both the suffering and fighting Church on earth and the Church triumphant in heaven—according to Roman Catholic teaching, also the suffering Church in purgatory. With worship and prayer, we join the whole people of God on earth and in heaven.

Consistent with the image of the church as a city is the imagery of the *building*. In the Gospel of Matthew, Jesus says (Matt 16): "¹⁸And I tell you, you are Peter, and on this rock I will build my church, and the gates of Hades will not prevail against it." The imagery is indeed taken from the building of a house (cf. 1 Pet 2:4–9 *house [οἶκος] of living stones*). In the world back then, heaven was thought to be above and hell below. The idea of *building on a rock* is that the building will not sink down through the gates of hell into the pit. This imagery of the building suggests durability: the church is something that is supposed to last for generations, actually forever, and of which we are but a portion. Hence prayer is not just a spontaneous response to a random situation but refers to a lasting building. The apostolic letters of the New Testament adopt the imagery of a building. In Eph 2, images of the *city* and *building* are connected. The keywords in this passage are: *building, foundation, cornerstone, structure, joined together, holy temple.*

The latter phrase points to another concept. The imagery of the Old Testament temple is adopted by Saint Paul in 2 Cor 6. First, the church is described as the true temple, as opposed to the temples of idols. The alternative is obviously not temple or no temple, but the temple of the one living God, versus the temples of false gods. Second, being part of the temple community means belonging to the people of God. Third, being part of the temple community requires separation from what is unclean. Fourth, God is present in the temple.

Another passage comparing the church to a temple is found in 1 Cor 9:13–14. Here, Saint Paul speaks about the role of ministers in the church, in analogy to the Old Testament priests. He also speaks about the builders of the temple (1 Cor 3), pointing out that the standard for the final judgment is the durability of what is built.

Another image of the Church in the Pauline letters is the famous image of the *body of Christ,* of which we are the members (Rom 12, 1 Cor 12, Eph 1, 3, 4, Col 1). The idea of a body had been, in pre-Christian times, already applied to the state (e.g., Cicero's book *On the Republic*). Eph 4 is obviously some kind of liturgical text that reveals the importance of this topic. Various consequences are drawn from this concept. The one body is alive through one Spirit, and the Spirit is manifested in different gifts to different people. The image of the body shows that the various gifts are supposed to work together for the common good.

None of these metaphors for the church in the New Testament is really consistent with the image of an audience entertained by a preacher. The image of an entertained audience, in turn, is hardly consistent with the imagery of the people of God participating in common prayer. To revive our spiritual life, especially the life of prayer, we need to regain the biblical understanding of the church: the house, the body of Christ, the public assembly of citizens, a temple in the center of the city. Prayer means, accordingly, participation in something that transcends individual wants, and building something that is meant to last, e.g. a schedule for prayer services, an order for the readings, form, style, and beauty.

The church is not an audience for a professional speaker who is supposed to do everything—to stir up, convert, make people believe, motivate, etc.—and who is accordingly tempted to avoid unpopular topics like preaching Christ crucified (1 Cor 1:23), or, if necessary to call the assembly *a brood of vipers* (Matt 3:7; 12:34; 23:33; cf. also Gal 1:10). The church is instead the assembly of citizens who are called to step out of their private homes, to go to the marketplace, to get involved in the business of the city.

Among the various complementary concepts of the church in the New Testament, we find the already mentioned idea of the faithful as priests. In 1 Peter we read about the church as the *royal priesthood.* From here the concept of *the priesthood of all believers* has been developed, for example in the Catechism of the Catholic Church (CCC para. 1268). The letter in the Bible reads (1 Pet 2:9): "But you are a chosen race, a royal priesthood, a holy nation, God's own people, in order that you may proclaim the mighty acts of him who called you out of darkness into his marvelous light." Therefore the term *priesthood of all believers* does not mean that we do not have priests, as it is often misunderstood, but challenges us to accept the duties of biblical *priesthood*, which mainly are about proclaiming God's acts, prayer and sacrifice.[2]

According to Matt 18—the chapter in Matthew's Gospel that discusses the order of the church—prayer is central in the church, and community is central to prayer. A prayer group in church could be an exemplary network supporting the whole church. If a group of parishioners take on responsibility for prayer and intercession, they can rebuild the church.

PRAYER IN COMMUNITY

It is essential for the church that we, the people of God, the royal priesthood, take on responsibility for praying the biblical prayers, for faithfully meditating on the Bible, and for praying on behalf of and for all people. This way we rebuild a Christian culture.

Traditional devotions of individuals and groups often begin with the verse (Ps 51:15): "O Lord open thou my lips, and my mouth shall show forth thy praise." We prepare for prayer with prayer, knowing that not our wishes but God's grace and work alone make us pray. This prayer for God to make us pray is answered when the Holy Spirit gives us words to pray, namely the Lord's Prayer, the Psalms, and canticles of the Old and New Testaments. It is by God's grace alone that we have received those beautiful biblical prayers, and we pray for the Holy Spirit to lead the people of God so that they engage in those prayers of the Son to the Father.

It is true that we say prayers all the time; we address a lot of petitions to God. We hear long prayers, often of aesthetically and theologically good quality, and they are not altogether selfish. But often our prayers remain incarcerated in the small world of our immediate experience and personal relationships, hardly connected with the joys and sorrows of God's people, and often out of touch with the issues God wants us to pray about. Then the prayers the Holy Spirit has given us in the Holy Bible are helpful to guide us to new experiences and to new responsibilities. We may pray that the Holy Spirit, who has inspired the prayers of the Bible, may inspire us to pray these words. The inspiration of the Holy Spirit gives us these prayers; the grace of the Holy Spirit makes us pray them.

---

2. Speaking about the *royal priesthood*, Saint Peter refers to Exod 19, which tells the story of God's awe-inspiring revelation on Mount Sinai and the gift of God's law. In this context, the whole *house of Jacob*, i.e., the people, is called a *royal priesthood*. God's law, however—given in this very pericope!—has also instituted a ministerial priesthood. Why would the term *royal priesthood* in Saint Peter's letter now have the meaning that there is no ministerial priesthood?

God's Spirit makes us pray, and so we take on the responsibility of the priesthood of all believers. We pray for one another, together with one another, and on behalf of one another. Prayer in community allows us to participate in the church both in heaven and on earth.

Saint Luke tells us the story of the visitation (Luke 1), about two women praying together. Mary, the mother of the Lord (Luke 1:43), leads in prayer, in the prayer that we know as the Magnificat (Luke 1:46ff.) The actual content of the Magnificat reminds us that we are members of a community with ancestors and future generations, and that we are cared for by the prayers of our fellow Christians, and that they in turn are in need of our prayers. The image of Saint Mary and Saint Elisabeth praying the Magnificat together can be a great encouragement for us. Mary was neither a professional priest in the temple, nor was she a professional prophet, but a lay person who led her cousin in praying the words which were handed down to us in Luke's Gospel and have led Christians in prayer ever since.

Elisabeth and Mary prayed together for, together with, and on behalf of each other. Many Christians today cannot pray, cannot because they are too busy with the necessities of life, because they have lost heart (cf. Luke 18:1), because they are too sick to pray. All of them need our prayers. As long as we are able to do it, we are called to take over some of the prayers for them. The standard is not if we like it or what our heart tells us, but God's holy Name, the needs of the people in his kingdom, and God's will. Mary's prayer and all prayers of the Bible allow us and guide us to participate in the great communion of all who have prayed these prayers over the centuries, pray them now, and will pray them forever. These prayers allow participation and give guidance.

It can save the church from ruin if we don't expect everything to come from a few good people, especially from pastors, but take on the responsibility of prayer. If we realize that it is the task and priestly dignity of all Christians to meditate on the Bible, to pray the biblical prayers, to pray for and on behalf of our fellow Christians, to pray for the church, for the government, and for all of God's creation, this will save the church from ruin.

It will make a difference when we find twelve faithful men and women in each congregation who commit themselves to morning and evening prayer at home, and who meet once a month in church for praying together, for mutual consolation, for exchanging experiences with their prayers, and to celebrate

Holy Communion. In the hymnals of most church bodies, forms for daily prayer are available in which the experience of centuries is collected.

*

Each of us, however, is responsible for his or her own prayer life. A community of prayer is not a soft pillow to support tired heads. But each member must have the self–discipline to pray in spite of personal wants and inclinations and not to give in to weakness.

Responsible prayer means precisely not following our own hearts, which is most obvious when considering that we are called to pray for our enemies. To pray for the enemy, we need the leadership of Jesus, which he granted us when he was suffering on the cross. This is certainly not a prayer that would pop up in our minds naturally, but by the grace of God we have been given this prayer through the gospel. We need not work out this prayer on our own, but only need to follow the words of our Lord, the crucified Christ. Thus we conquer ourselves. Prayer requires that we pray in spite of our feelings, in spite of our weakness, actually in spite of our will. Prayer requires self–discipline.

The first three petitions of the Lord's Prayer give us a threefold standard and guide for all our prayers: the holiness of God's name, the needs of the people in God's kingdom, God's sacred will. Our own heart, in contrast, is hardly a good leader for prayer and should not replace Jesus' teaching and encouragement.

Prayer requires discipline, because its meaning does not necessarily reveal itself immediately. The meaning of many Psalms seems hard to grasp; the internal logic of traditional prayer services seems strange; and at first, perhaps we do not find any sense in it. Praying the prayers of the Bible is like the adventure of an explorer in a strange country. If you go into a foreign realm, you do not know what you will discover; but this is exactly why you go! It is a great learning opportunity when we cross the border of our comfort zone and find a way up along the flowing waters to the source and to the tree of life, and when thus the prayers of the Bible open themselves up to us. It is a great piece of self–education, not only in the knowledge of the Bible, but for our whole life.

We should not deceive ourselves. It is difficult to keep the promise of daily devotion. When we experience our own failure to keep the promise—and it is almost certain that we fail, especially in the beginning—we are probably tempted to give up. But in this situation, when we want to give up, when we lose heart, when we get angry with ourselves, or when we get angry with these promises because we fail to keep them, then it is especially important to be persistent. Then we need the consolation of our brothers and sisters who share in this experience and encourage us. Once we have recovered from the temptation to fall asleep, we will be stronger than ever. In the hour of Jesus' fear and his disciples' failure, Jesus says (Matt 26): "stay with me, watch and pray."

*

Being faithful in praying the biblical prayers, we will make our home in the prayer book of the Bible and sing (Ps 84):

> "Even the sparrow finds a home,
>   and the swallow a nest for herself,
>   where she may lay her young,
> at your altars, O Lord of hosts,
>   my King and my God."

Bibliography

The Apostolic Fathers [...]. Revised texts with introductions and translations by J. B. Lightfoot. Edited and completed by J. R. Harmer. London: Macmillan, 1891.

Aquinas, Thomas. *The Summa Theologica of St. Thomas Aquinas*. Translated by the Fathers of the English Dominican Province. Rev. ed. London: Burns, Oates, and Washbourne, 1920. 1st complete American ed. 3 vols. New York: Benziger Bros., 1947. Online ed., New Advent. https://www.sacred-texts.com/chr/aquinas/summa/index.htm.

Aristotle. *Poetics*. Edited and translated by Stephen Halliwell. In *Aristotle: Poetics; Longinus: On the Sublime; Demetrius: On Style*, edited and translated by Stephen Halliwell, W. Hamilton Fyfe, and Doreen C. Innes. Vol. 23 of *Aristotle*. Loeb Classical Library 199. Cambridge, MA: Harvard University Press, 1995.

———. Vol. 1, book 2, chap. 12 in *Physics*, translated by P. H. Wicksteed and F. M. Cornford. Loeb Classical Library 228. Cambridge, MA: Harvard University Press, 1957.

Augustine. Letter 130 (to Proba). Translated by J. G. Cunningham. In vol. 1 of *The Nicene and Post-Nicene Fathers*, Series 1. Edited by Philip Schaff. 1886–1889. 14 vols. Revised and edited for New Advent by Kevin Knight. http://wpww.newadvent.org/fathers/1102130.htm.

———. *The Augustine Catechism: The Enchiridion on Faith, Hope and Charity*. Translated by Bruce Harbert. Edited by Boniface Ramsey. Hyde Park, NY: New City Press, 2008.

———. *Augustine: Confessions*. Commentary by James J. O'Donnell. 3 vols. Oxford: Clarendon 1992. Reprinted online as *The "Confessions" of Augustine: An Electronic Edition*. https://faculty.georgetown.edu/jod/conf/index.html.

———. *Commentary on the Lord's Sermon on the Mount with Seventeen Related Sermons*. Translated by Denis J. Kavanagh. Washington, DC: Catholic University of America Press, 1951.

———. "Psalm LXXVII: Exposition." In vol. 4 of *Expositions on the Book of Psalms*. A Library of Fathers of the Holy Catholic Church 32. Oxford: Parker; London: Rivington, 1850.

Babylonian Talmud, Taanit. Translated by Adin Even-Israel Steinsaltz. William Davidson edition. https://www.sefaria.org/Taanit.

Barth, Hans-Martin. *Wohin—woher mein Ruf? Zur Theologie des Bittgebets* [Whence—wither my call? On the theology of supplication]. Munich: Kaiser, 1981.

Basdevant, Brigitte, and Jean Gaudemet, eds. and trans. *Les Canons des Conciles Mérovingiens (VIe–VIIe siècles)*, vol. 1. Sources Chrétiennes 353. Paris: Cerf, 1989.

Basil the Great. *On the Holy Spirit*. Translated by David Anderson. Crestwood, NY: St. Vladimir's Seminary Press, 1980.

Benedict of Nursia. *Saint Benedict's Rule for Monasteries*. Translated by Leonard J. Doyle. Collegeville, MN: Liturgical Press, 1948. Reprint, Collegeville, MN: CrossReach Publications, 2001.

———. *Oratio Sancti Benedicti*. In Alcuin, *Officio per ferias*. Patrologia Latina, edited by J.-P. Migne, vol. 101, col. 0553C. Paris, 1844–1864.

Berger, Klaus. "Gnosis / Gnostizismus I." 1984.*TRE* 13:519–35.

Bernet, Walter. *Gebet* [On Prayer]. Stuttgart: Kreuz-Verlag, 1970.

Boethius, Anicius Manlius Severinus. *The Consolation of Philosophy*. Translated by P. G. Walsh, Oxford: Oxford University Press, 1999.

———. *The Theological Tractates and the Consolation of Philosophy*. Translated by H. F. Stewart and E. K. Rand. Loeb Classical Library 74. 1918. Reprint, London: Heinemann, 1968.

Bonhoeffer, Dietrich. *Temptation*. In *Creation and Fall / Temptation: Two Biblical Studies*. Translated by John C. Fletcher and Kathleen Downham. New York: Touchstone, 1997. Originally published as *Versuchung* (Munich: Kaiser, 1953).

Brueggemann, Walter. *The Message of the Psalms: A Theological Commentary*. Edited by Terrence E. Fretheim. Augsburg Old Testament Studies. Minneapolis: Augsburg, 1984.

Brümmer, Vincent. *What Are We Doing When We Pray? A Philosophical Inquiry*. London: SCM, 1984.

Cassian, John. *John Cassian: The Conferences*. Translated by Boniface Ramsey. Ancient Christian Writers 57. New York: Paulist, 1997.

Catechism of the Catholic Church. 2nd ed. Washington, DC: United States Catholic Conference–Libreria Editrice Vaticana, 2000.

Catena Aurea: Commentary on the Four Gospels, Collected out of the Works of the Fathers by Saint Thomas Aquinas. Vol. 1, translated by John Henry Newman. Oxford: Parker, 1845. New York: Cosimo Classics, 2007. tps://www.chicagomanualofstyle.org/book/ed17/part3/ch14/psec119.htmlr

Chrysostom, Dio. *Discourses 1–11*. Translated by J. W. Cohoon. Vol. 1 of *Dio Chrysostom*. Loeb Classical Library 257. Cambridge, MA: Harvard University Press, 1932.

Cleanthes. *Cleanthes' "Hymn to Zeus": Text, Translation, and Commentary*. Edited and translated by Johan C. Thom. Studies and Texts in Antiquity and Christianity 33. Tübingen: Mohr Siebeck, 2005.

S. Clement of Rome. Part 1, vol. 1–2 of *The Apostolic Fathers* [...]. Revised texts with introductions and translations by J. B. Lightfoot. Edited and completed by J. R. Harmer. London: Macmillan, 1891. Prepared for katapi by Paul Ingram, 2014. http://www.katapi.org.uk/ApostolicFathers/ApFathers-Contents.html.

Cyprian. *Treatise 4: On the Lord's Prayer* 3. In *The Treatises of Cyprian*. Translated by Robert Ernest Wallis. In vol. 5 of *The Ante-Nicene Fathers: Translations of the Writings of the Fathers Down to A.D. 325*. Edited by Alexander Roberts, James Donaldson, and A. Cleveland Coxe. Buffalo, NY: Christian Literature, 1886. Revised and edited for New Advent by Kevin Knight. http://www.newadvent.org/fathers/050704.htm.

Daube, David. "A Prayer Pattern in Judaism." In *Studia Evangelica: Papers Presented to the International Congress on "The Four Gospels in 1957" Held at Christ Church, Oxford, 1957*, edited by Kurt Aland, F. L. Cross, Jean Danielou, Harald Riesenfeld, and W. C. van Unnik, 539–45. TUGAL 73. Berlin: Akademie-Verlag, 1959.

The Didache. In *The Apostolic Fathers: Greek Texts and English Translations*, translated and edited by Michael W. Holmes, 334–69. 3rd ed. Grand Rapids, MI: Baker Academic, 2007.

Ebeling, Gerhard. *Dogmatik des Christlichen Glaubens* [Dogmatics of the Christian Faith]. 3rd ed. Tübingen: Mohr, 1987.

Epictetus. *The Encheiridion* [Manual]. Pages 479–537 in *Discourses, Books 3–4: Fragments; The Encheiridion*. Translated by W. A. Oldfather. Loeb Classical Library 218. Cambridge, MA: Harvard University Press, 1928.

Eusebius. *Ecclesiastical History*. Translated by Kirsopp Lake and J. E. L. Oulton. 2 vols. Loeb Classical Library 153, 265. Cambridge, MA: Harvard University Press; London: Heinemann, 1926–1932.

Evangelical Lutheran Church in America. *Evangelical Lutheran Worship*. Minneapolis: Augsburg Fortress, 2006.

Fichte, Johan Gottlieb. *Appellation an das Publikum: Dokumente zum Atheismusstreit um Fichte, Forberg, Niethammer; Jena 1798/99* [Appeal to the Public: Documents on the Atheism Dispute . . .]. Edited by Werner Röhr. Leipzig: Reclam, 1987.

Fitzmyer, Joseph A. *The Gospel according to Luke X–XXIV: A New Translation with Introduction and Commentary by Joseph A. Fitzmyer*. The Anchor Bible 28A. Garden City, NY: Doubleday, 1985.

Foster, Kenelm, ed. and trans. *The Life of Saint Thomas Aquinas: Biographical Documents*. London: Longmans, Green; Baltimore: Helicon, 1959.

Hefele, Karl Joseph, and Henri Leclercq. "Deuxième council de vaison en 529." In vol. 2, part 2 of *Histoire des conciles d'après les documents originaux*, 1110–14. Paris: Letouzey et Ané, 1908.

Jacobi, Friedrich Heinrich. "Jacobi to Fichte (1799)." In *The Main Philosophical Writings and the Novel "Allwill,"* edited and translated by George Di Giovanni, 497–536. McGill-Queen's Studies in the History of Ideas 18. Montréal: McGill-Queen's University Press, 1994.

John of Damascus. *An Exposition of the Orthodox Faith*. Edited by D. P. Curtin. Translated by E. W. Watson. New York: Barnes and Noble Press, 2019.

Josephus, Flavius. *The Antiquities of the Jews*. In *The Works of Flavius Josephus*. Translated by William Whiston. Auburn, NY: John E. Beardsley, 1895. https://www.perseus.tufts.edu/hopper/text?doc=Perseus:text:1999.01.0146.

Josuttis, Manfred. *Religion als Handwerk: Zur Handlungslogik spiritueller Methoden* [Religion as a craft: On the rationale of spiritual methods]. Gütersloh: Gütersloher Verlagshaus, 2002.

Jungmann, Josef A. *The Place of Christ in Liturgical Prayer*. Translated by A. Peeler. Collegeville, MN: Liturgical Press, 1989.

Justin Martyr. *Apology*. Translated by Marcus Dods and George Reith. In vol. 1 of *The Ante-Nicene Fathers: Translations of the Writings of the Fathers Down to A.D. 325*. Edited by Alexander Roberts, James Donaldson, and A. Cleveland Coxe. Buffalo, NY: Christian Literature, 1885. Revised and edited for New Advent by Kevin Knight. https://www.newadvent.org/fathers/0126.htm.

BIBLIOGRAPHY

Kelly, J. N. D. *The Athanasian Creed*. Paddock Lectures, 1962–1963. London: Black, 1964.

Luther, Martin. *Luther's Works*. Edited by Jaroslav Pelikan and Helmut T. Lehman. 55 vols. Philadelphia: Fortress, 1958–1986.

———. *D. Martin Luthers Werke: Kritische Gesamtausgabe [Schriften]*. 73 vols. Weimar: H. Böhlau, 1883–2009, hereafter WA.

———. "Concerning the Order of Public Worship" (1523). In *Liturgy and Hymns*, edited by Ulrich S. Leupold, 64ff. Vol. 53 of *Luther's Works*. (WA 12 / 31 – 37).

———. "An Exposition of the Lord's Prayer for Simple Laymen." In *Devotional Writings I*, edited by Martin O. Dietrich, 20. Vol. 42 of *Luther's Works*. (WA 2/ 80 – 130).

———. "The German Mass and Order of Service." In *Liturgy and Hymns*, edited by Ulrich S. Leupold, 78. Vol. 53 of *Luther's Works*. (WA 19 / 44 – 113).

———. *"The Magnificat."* Translated by A. T. W. Steinhaeuser. In *The Sermon on the Mount and the Magnificat*, 311. Vol. 21 of *Luther's Works*. (WA 7 / 538 – 604).

———. "A Simple Way to Pray" (1535). In *Devotional Writings II*, edited by Gustav K. Wiencke, 194. Vol. 43 of *Luther's Works*. (WA 38 / 351 – 375).

———. "Treatise on Good Works" (1520). In *Christian in Society I*, edited by James Atkinson, 64ff. Vol. 44 of *Luther's Works (WA 6 / 196 – 276)*.

Stjerna, Kirsi I. *The Large Catechism of Dr. Martin Luther, 1529: The Annotated Luther Study Edition*. Minneapolis: Fortress, 2016. Excerpted from *Word and Faith*, edited by Kirsi I. Stjerna. The Annotated Luther 2. Minneapolis: Fortress, 2015.

Luz, Ulrich. *Das Evangelium nach Matthäus* [The Gospel of Matthew: A Commentary]. EKK I/1–4. Zürich: Benziger; Neukirchen-Vluyn: Neukirchener, 1985ff.

Maier, Paul L. *Eusebius: The Church History; A New Translation with Commentary*. Grand Rapids, MI: Kregel, 1999.

Mershman, Francis. "Litany." In vol. 9 of *The Catholic Encyclopedia*. New York: Appleton, 1910.

Munier, Charles, and Charles de Clercq, eds. *Concilia Galliae*. 2 vols. Corpus Christianorum: Series Latina 148, 148A. Turnhout: Brepols, 1963. https://codecs.vanhamel.nl/Munier_1963a.

Origen. *Sacred Invocation: Origen on Prayer*. Translated by William A. Curtis. Introduction by Theodore J. Nottingham. Self-published, Theodore J. Nottingham, CreateSpace, 2014.

Pascal, Blaise. *Pensées*. Edited by Léon Brunschvicg. Éditions Hachette, 1897. Paris: Garnier-Flammarion, 1976.

Pennington, M. Basil. *Lectio Divina: Renewing the Ancient Practice of Praying the Scriptures*. New York: Crossroad, 1998.

Philo. *On the Embassy to Gaius: General Indexes*. Translated by F. H. Colson. Index by J. W. Earp. Loeb Classical Library 379. Cambridge, MA: Harvard University Press, 1962.

Rosenau, Hartmut. "Gott höchst persönlich: Zur Rehabilitierung der Rede von der Personalität Gottes im Durchgang durch den Pantheismus und Atheismusstreit." In *Personalität Gottes* [God in Person], 47–76. Marburger Jahrbuch Theologie 19. Edited by Wilfried Härle and Reiner Preul. Marlburger Theologische Studien 101. Leipzig: Evangelische Verlagsanstalt, 2007.

Schlüter, Astrid. "Die Selbstauslegung des Wortes, Selbstreferenz und Fremdreferenzen in der Textwelt des Johannesevangeliums." PhD diss., Ruprecht-Karls-Universität,

1996. Heidelburg: Heidelberg Universitätsbibliothek, 2012. http://d-nb. info/1179785851/34.

Seeley, David. "The Background of the Philippians Hymn (2:6–11)." *Journal of Higher Criticism* 1 (Fall 1994) 49–72.

Slenczka, Notger. "Einleitung." In *Personalität Gottes* [God in Person]. Marburger Jahrbuch Theologie 19. Edited by Wilfried Härle and Reiner Preul. Marlburger Theologische Studien 101. Leipzig: Evangelische Verlagsanstalt, 2007.

Sölle, Dorothee. *Atheistisch an Gott glauben* [Believing in God in an atheistic way]: *Beiträge zur Theologie*. Olten and Freiburg: Walter, 1968.

Tanner, Beth. "King Yahweh as the Good Shepherd: Taking Another Look at the Image of God in Psalm 23." In *David and Zion: Biblical Studies in Honor of J. J. M. Roberts*, edited by Bernard F. Batto and Kathryn L. Roberts, 267–84. Winona Lake, IN: Eisenbrauns, 2004. University Park: Pennsylvania State University Press, 2021. https://doi.org/10.1515/9781575065519-016.

Tertullian. *Adversus Praxean. Gegen Praxeas*. Translated by Hermann-Josef Sieben. Freiburg im Breisgau: Herder, 2001. Fontes Christiani, Series 2, vol. 34.

———. *Against Praxeas*. Vol. 15 of *Ante-Nicene Christian Library: Translations of the Writings of the Fathers Down to A.D. 325*, translated by Peter Holmes, 333–409. Edinburgh: Clark, 1870. Reprinted in vol. 3 of *The Ante-Nicene Fathers: Translations of the Writings of the Fathers Down to A.D. 325*, edited by Alexander Roberts, James Donaldson, and A. Cleveland Coxe, 597–627. Buffalo, NY: Christian Literature, 1885.

———. *De oratione* [On prayer] 1. In vol. 1 of *Quinti Septimi Florentis Tertulliani opera ex recensione Augusti Reifferscheid et Georgii Wissowa*, 180–200. Prague: Tempsky; Vienna; Tempsky; Leipzig: Freytag, 1890.

Theologia Deutsch—Theologia Germanica: The Book of the Perfect Life. Translated by David Blamires. Sacred Literature Series. Walnut Creek: AltaMira, 2003.

Thomas à Kempis. *The Imitation of Christ*. Translated by Leo Sherley-Price. Penguin Classics L27. Harmondsworth: Penguin Books, 1959. *De imitatione Christi libri quatuor*. Edited by Tiburzio Lupo. Storia e attualità 6. Vatican City: Libreria Editrice Vaticana, 1982. http://www.thelatinlibrary.com/kempis.html.

Vatican II Council. "Constitution on the Sacred Liturgy: *Sacrosanctum concilium*." Solemnly Promulgated by His Holiness Pope Paul VI on December 4, 1963. https://www.vatican.va/archive/hist_councils/ii_vatican_council/documents/vat-ii_const_19631204_sacrosanctum-concilium_en.html.

Virgil. *Eclogues*. In *Bucolics, Aeneid, and Georgics of Vergil*. Edited by J. B. Greenough. Boston: Ginn, 1900. http://www.thelatinlibrary.com/verg.html.

———. *Eclogues, Georgics, Aeneid: Books 1–6*. Translated by H. Rushton Fairclough. Revised by G. P. Goold. Loeb Classical Library 63. Cambridge, MA: Harvard University Press, 1916. Reprint 1999.

Wilckens, Ulrich. *Der Brief an die Römer* [The Letter to the Romans, a commentary]. EKK VI/3. Zürich: Benziger; Neukirchen-Vluyn: Neukirchener, 1982.

www.ingramcontent.com/pod-product-compliance
Lightning Source LLC
Chambersburg PA
CBHW050843230426
43667CB00012B/2118